Drew Provan

Mac Basics

3rd Edition

Covers OS X Yosemite

In easy steps is an imprint of In Easy Steps Limited
16 Hamilton Terrace · Holly Walk · Leamington Spa
Warwickshire · United Kingdom · CV32 4LY
www.ineasysteps.com

Third Edition

In Easy Steps Limited supports The Forest Stewardship Council (FSC), the leading international forest certification organisation. All our titles that are printed on Greenpeace approved FSC certified paper carry the FSC logo.

MIX
Paper from
responsible sources
FSC® C020837

Printed and bound in the United Kingdom

ISBN 978-1-84078-603-3

Contents

1 Welcome to the Mac! 9

The Mac Desktop	10
Launchpad	11
Set up a User Account	12
System Preferences	13
Mission Control	14
Security	15
The Mouse and Trackpad	16
Keyboard Options	17
Keyboard Settings	18
Mail, Contacts and Calendars	19
Networking the Mac	20
Setting up Sharing	21
Date and Time	22
Setting up Time Machine	23
Power Management	24
Spotlight	25
Notifications and Reminders	26
Facebook and Twitter	27
About This Mac	28

2 Dealing with Documents 29

The Finder	30
Finder Views	31
Folders	32
Move Files into Folders	34
Deleting Files from Folders	35
Where's My User Library?	36
Tags	37
Opening Documents	38
Quick Look at Documents	39
Dictation	40
Notes App	41
Mac and PC Compatibility	42

3 Working with PDF Files 43

What is a PDF? 44
Programs to Read PDF files 45
Opening PDF in Preview 46
Add Text to PDF 47
Creating a PDF 48
Making PDFs Secure 49
Emailing PDF files 50
Acrobat Reader 51
Skitch 51
Handoff 52

4 Mastering Email 53

The Mail Window 54
Add an Email Account 55
Create an Email Message 56
Send an Attachment 57
Receive Email Attachments 58
Reading Emails 59
Mailbox Folders 60
Smart Mailboxes 61
Searching Mail 62
Change Fonts and Colors 63
VIP List 64

5 Surf with Safari 65

Go on Safari 66
Full-Screen Browsing 67
Reading List 68
Search the Internet 69
Bookmarks 70
Organizing Bookmarks 71
Importing Bookmarks 72
Browsing Using Tabs 73
Making Browsing Secure 74

6 Calendars and Contacts 75

Calendar 76
Calendar Views 77
Add an Event 78
Edit an Event 79

Create Quick Event 80
Multiple Calendars 81
Sending Invites 82
Searching Calendar 83
Contacts 84
Add a New Contact 85
Add a Contact From Email 86

7 Photos and Videos 87

Programs for Viewing Photos 88
iPhoto 89
Opening iPhoto 90
Importing Photos 91
Create a New Album 92
Editing Photos 93
Videos on the Mac 94
DVD Player 95
Editing Your Own Movies 96
Sharing Your Movie 98

8 The World of iTunes 99

What is iTunes? 100
Importing Audio CDs 101
iTunes Preferences 102
Playing Audio 103
Buying Music from iTunes 104
Pause and Skip 105
Playlists 106
Smart Playlists 107
Changing iTunes Views 108
Genius 109
Sharing Your Music 110

9 Networking the Mac 111

Networking is Easy! 112
Getting Online 113
Sharing Internet Connection 114
Connecting to Other Macs 116
Screen Sharing 118
Share Files Using AirDrop 119
Wireless Printing 120

10 Video Chat 121

FaceTime Video Chat 122
Messages 124
Skype 126
Google Voice and Video Chat 128
Other Video Chat Options 130

11 Personalizing Your Mac 131

Name Your Hard Drive 132
Using Wallpapers 133
Screen Savers 134
Wake and Sleep Options 135
Change the Clock Display 136
Set Your Time Zone 137
Change Your Icon Sizes 138
The Dock Options 139
Add Folders to the Sidebar 140
Set the Screen Corners 141
Mouse and Trackpad Settings 142
Empty Trash Without Warning 143
Pimp Your Windows! 144
Customize Keyboard Shortcuts 145
Change the Alert Sounds 146

12 Installing Software 147

Installing Apps is Easy! 148
Installing From a .dmg File 149
Put an App onto the Dock 150
Removing Preference Files 151
How to Uninstall Apps 152

13 Switch from PC to Mac 153

Mac Desktop and Windows 154
Single-Click Mouse? 155
Where's Windows Explorer? 156
The Start Menu 157
Keyboard Shortcuts 158
Control Panel 159

Network Settings 160
Printers & Scanners 161
User Accounts 162
Migrate Your PC Files to Mac 163
Run Windows on the Mac 164

14 **Burn CDs and DVDs** 165

Burning Music to CD 166
Burn Photos onto CD/DVD 168
Copy Files and Folders onto CD/DVD 169
Burn CD/DVD with Disk Utility 170

15 **App Store & iBooks** 171

What is the App Store? 172
Top Charts 173
Categories 174
Purchased 175
Updates 176
How to Buy an App 177
Tell a Friend 178
iBooks 179
Searching for Apps 180

16 **Keep Things in Sync** 181

Keeping Email in Sync 182
Calendar Syncing 184
Google Calendar 185
Syncing Contacts 186
Keep Your Notes in Sync 187
Keeping Safari in Sync 188

17 **Back up Your Files!** 189

Simple Copy Methods 190
Keep Files on the Cloud 191
Time Machine Backups 192
Restore Files with Time Machine 194
Scheduled Backups 195
Cloning Your Drive 196
SuperDuper 198

18 Tips & Tricks 199

Keyboard Tricks	200
Organizing System Preferences	201
Compare Documents Quickly	202
How Much Disk Space is Left?	203
Extract Pictures from PDFs	204
Where are the Scroll Bars?	205
Application Switcher	206
Select the Default Browser	207
Sharing Map Locations	208
Access Someone's Drop Box	209
Change the Login Picture	210
Undo Mistakes with Versions	211
Make Mac Always Open With	212

19 Mac Maintenance 213

Repair Permissions	214
Maintenance Programs	215
Clear Your Desktop!	216
Reset Safari	217
Rebuild Spotlight Index	218
Rebuild Mail's Database	219
Defragmenting Drives	220
Remove Unneeded Login Items	221
Don't Ignore Software Updates	222
Remove User Accounts	223
Scan for Viruses	224

20 Troubleshooting 225

My Mac Won't Start!	226
This Disk is Unreadable	227
App Crashes	228
Duplicate Fonts	229
Spinning Beachball	230
Folder Moved to Wrong Place	231
Can't Find Network Printer	232
Safe Boot	233
Deleted File or Folder in Error	234
Can't Eject a Disk	235
Yosemite Recovery Disk	236

Index 237

1 Welcome to the Mac!

Macs running OS X Yosemite are easy to use, making even the most complex task appear simple. In this introductory chapter we will look at the basic features of the Mac so you can get started exploring the inbuilt apps.

The Mac Desktop

The New icon pictured above indicates a new or enhanced feature introduced with the latest version OS X Yosemite.

If you're used to a Windows PC then you'll pick up the Mac operating system (OS) pretty quickly. The interface of the desktop is made up of icons representing disk drives, folders, files and programs. Most actions can be carried out using click, double-click, triple-click or gestures. With the Mac OS X (X stands for number 10, not the letter "X") Yosemite, gestures feature heavily. You can swipe the trackpad or Magic Mouse with one, two or three fingers to achieve different things.

On a Mac, the desktop looks like this

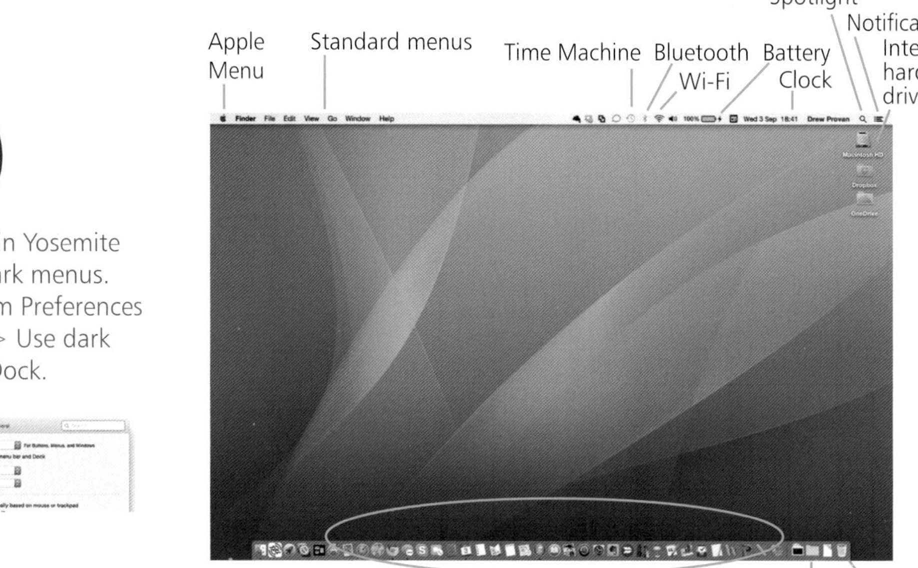

Dark Mode in Yosemite gives you dark menus. Go to System Preferences > General > Use dark menu and Dock.

All programs have similar menus.Once you master the menus for one program, you will find they are all pretty similar (e.g. File, Edit, View, etc.). To see the menu, click on the name and the menu options will drop down. Scroll down to the one you want and click to select.

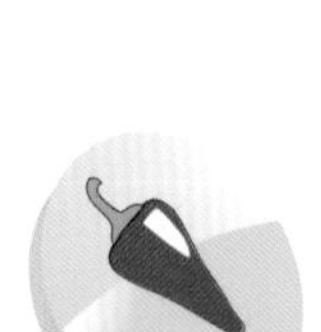

Once you get the hang of the menus in one program you will find they are all pretty similar, e.g. File, Edit, etc.

Here we have clicked on the Apple Menu and its options are shown.

Most menus will drop down (hence they are called *dropdown* menus) to show the menu options.

Launchpad

Launchpad is designed to resemble iOS devices such as the iPhone, iPad, and iPod Touch. Launchpad provides ready access to your apps and saves you having to navigate to the Applications folder to find an app.

Create a folder for your apps

Drag an app onto a related app, e.g. web-based apps. This will create a folder which you can rename to suit your needs. In the example shown, all the Microsoft Office apps are contained within one folder called Microsoft Office 2011.

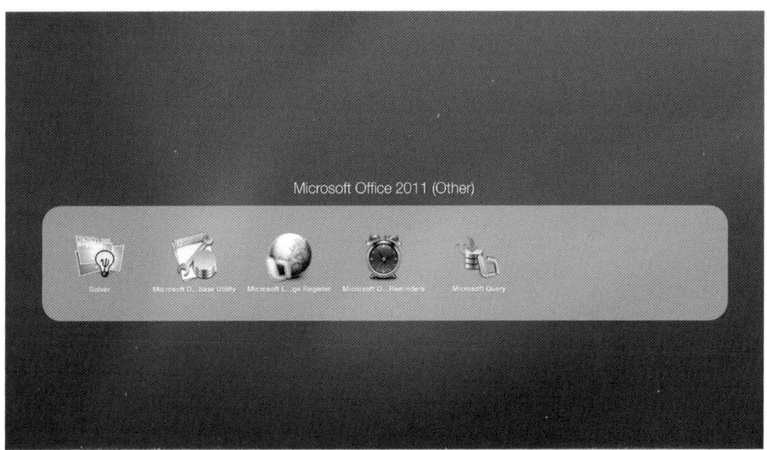

Set up a User Account

The Mac OS uses a Unix-based system and requires accounts for each user. You will need to set up an account and choose your name and password (which you *must* remember or you will not be able to install software or make changes to your Mac!).

Setting up an account

1. Click on **Apple Menu** (see page 10)
2. Choose **System Preferences > Users & Groups**
3. Click the **padlock** to unlock, type in **password**
4. Click the **+** to add account
5. **Enter Full Name** and press the **Tab key**

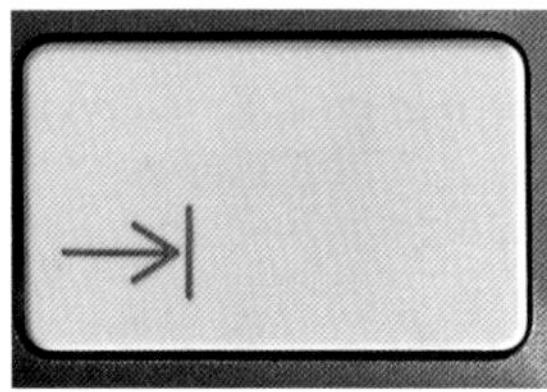

6. Enter **password** and repeat then click **Create User**

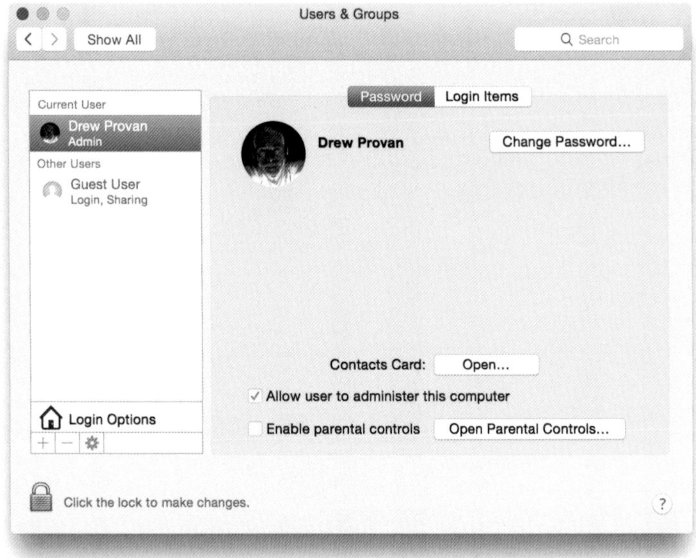

To change the account name the Mac creates for you, right-click your name in the left pane and select **Advanced Options**. You can then change the username to the one you want.

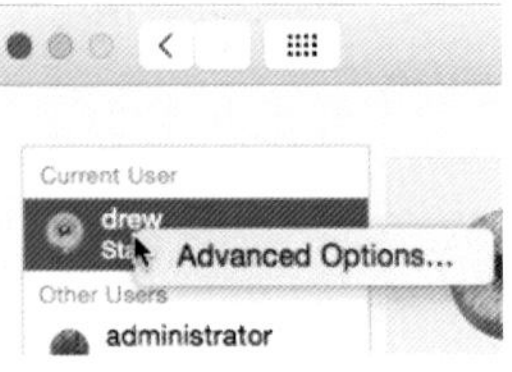

System Preferences

You can control the look and feel of your Mac by adjusting the settings in the System Preferences (similar to Control Panel on the PC).

What are the colored buttons at the top of the windows?

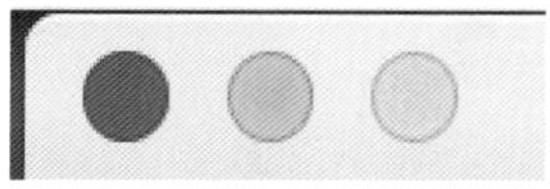

Red: close window
Orange: minimize
Green: full screen

Change the Desktop

You may not like the background picture (called the desktop picture) Apple has chosen but you are free to choose any of the other options or even use one of your own photos instead. You will find this under **System Preferences > Desktop & Screen Saver**.

Play around with various desktop wallpapers until you find the one you want. They are easy to change if you get bored with them.

Mission Control

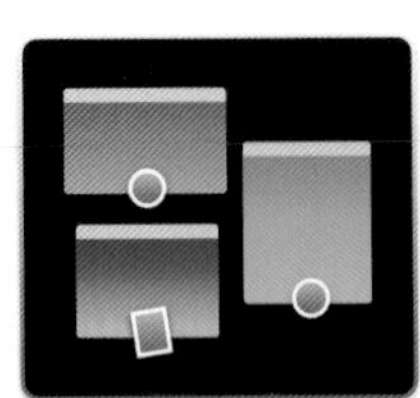

This feature allows you to see all your open windows, which makes life easier if you have several programs open at once and the window you want to see is obscured by another window.

1. Start **Mission Control**
2. Click the Mission Control icon in the dock
3. Or Swipe upwards with three fingers on the trackpad

Mission Control lets you keep different activities separated, e.g. you can keep Safari on one desktop, Mail on another, and a third program on yet another distinct desktop. This saves you having loads of windows on top of each other!

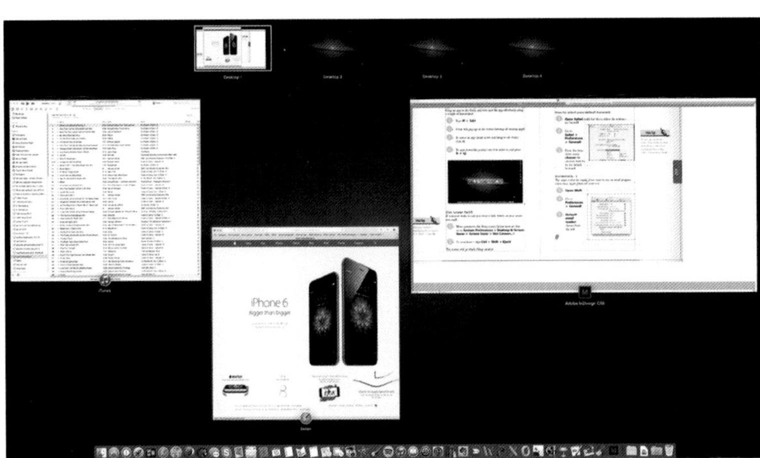

In the example shown there are three apps running (iTunes, Safari, and InDesign. You can allocate each app its own desktop to prevent having windows stacked on top of each other. Click Mission Control, go to the top right of your screen and click + to create a new desktop. Drag each app onto a separate desktop. You can toggle between desktops and apps by clickling Control + arrow left or right.

To leave Mission Control click on any window or desktop.

Security

Macs are safe and secure, with few viruses around that target the Mac OS but basic common sense tells us that setting up basic security is sensible. Essentially you can make your Mac secure by:

Setting up initial security features

1. Go to **Apple Menu > System Preferences**
2. Select **Security & Privacy**
3. Work through the options as required (if you have a wireless router the chances are it will have a firewall anyway so there is no need to set up two firewalls)

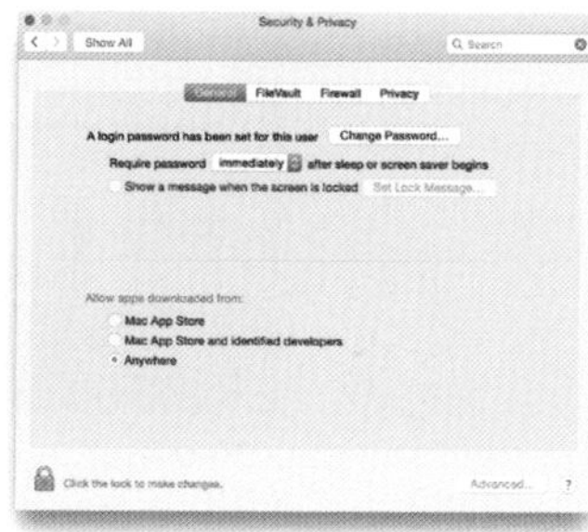

Gatekeeper

Gatekeeper prevents you installing software that may cause harm to your Mac. You can by-pass Gatekeeper's warnings by selecting **Allow applications downloaded from: Anywhere** in the Security & Privacy System Preference.

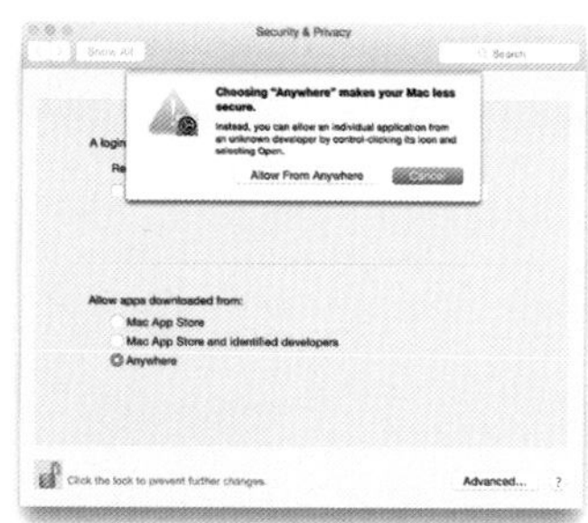

Take computer security seriously and protect your Mac from hackers. The Security System Preference can be used to: set up your Mac to require a password when you wake it from sleep, encrypt all your files using FileVault (you must never forget this password or you will not be able to view any files) and set up a Firewall. The Privacy tab lets you decide which apps have access to your data. See page 224 for information on viruses, and page 217 on resetting Safari.

The Mouse and Trackpad

In general, desktop Macs use mice and MacBooks use trackpads, although separate trackpads can be purchased for use with desktop machines. The default settings are usually fine for most people but you may find the tracking speed (the speed at which the pointer moves over the screen) to be too slow, or the double-click speed too fast. You can adjust all these features by going to **Apple Menu > System Preferences > Mouse or Trackpad** (see also page 155).

The Natural Scrolling feels a bit odd at first. Natural scrolling was introduced with OS X Lion. When this option is selected, if you slide your finger down the mouse or trackpad, the page (e.g. Safari) will scroll down. This is opposite to the scrolling method used by PCs and Macs prior to OS X Lion. If you want to switch it off, uncheck the button.

Mouse options

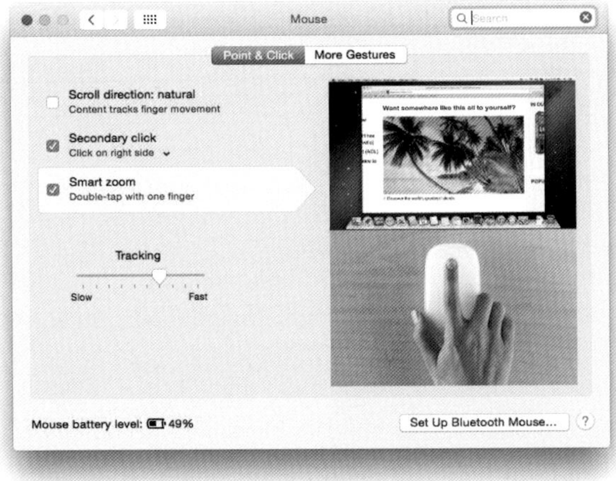

Trackpad options

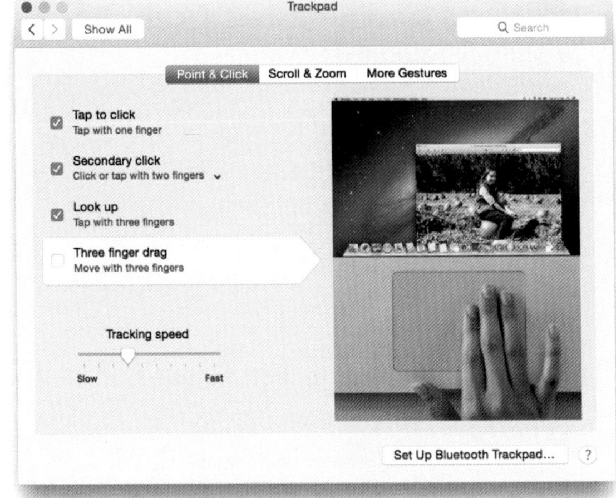

Keyboard Options

The keyboard has many settings including Repeat rate, Delay until Repeat, Modifier keys (e.g. Caps Lock key and others). Using the Keyboard System Preferences you can also modify all the keyboard shortcuts if you want to assign shortcuts to other functions.

Key Repeat and Delay until Repeat

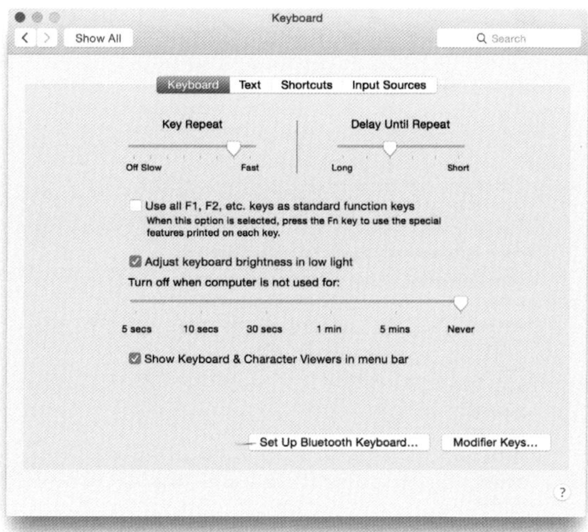

Keyboard Shortcut options

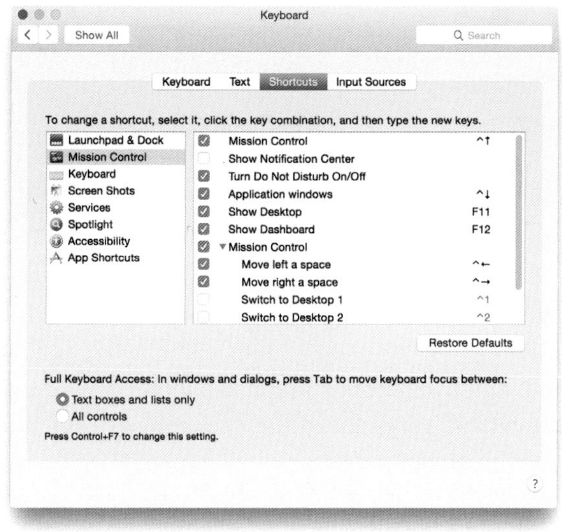

Keyboard shortcuts can save you time. Try to learn a few basic shortcuts like Copy, Paste, Cut, and Undo (see pages 145 and 158).

Keyboard Settings

You can add other languages and keyboards such as Arabic, Chinese, Dutch and many others.

Changing the keyboard input

1. Go to **Apple Menu > System Preferences > Keyboard**

2. Choose **Language** or **Input Sources** to change to, for example, the Arabic keyboard

Changing the language

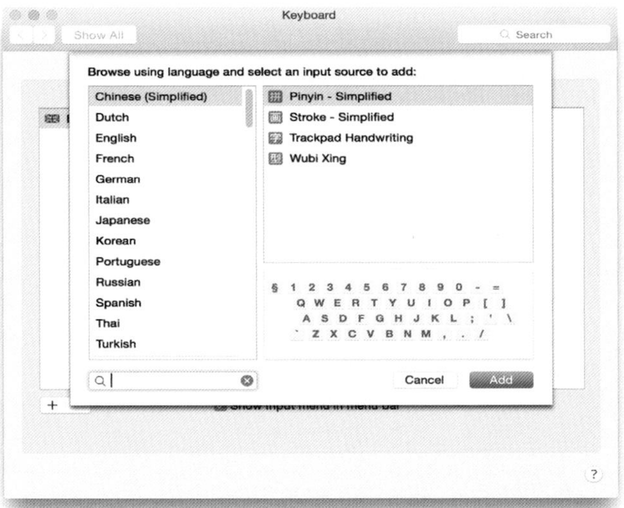

Text shortcuts

1. Go to **System Preferences > Keyboard > Text**

2. Click **+** and enter the shortcut in "Replace" and the full expanded text in "With"

3. Each time you want to type the word or sentence use the abbreviated version and the Mac will expand it for you

Mail, Contacts and Calendars

You can set up email, contacts and calendars within the individual programs (Mail, Contacts and Calendar) or you can use the Internet Accounts System Preference to add new mail accounts, contact lists and calendars.

Apple Mail makes it very easy to set up accounts and will walk you through the whole process. Where possible try to choose IMAP rather than POP3 (see pages 55 and 182).

Set up a Mail account

1. Go to **Apple Menu > System Preferences > Internet Accounts**

2. Click **Add Account** to add a new account or click the **–** to remove an account

3. You can choose Microsoft Exchange server, iCloud, Gmail, Yahoo!, AOL, Twitter, Facebook or other

See page 55 for further help with adding email accounts.

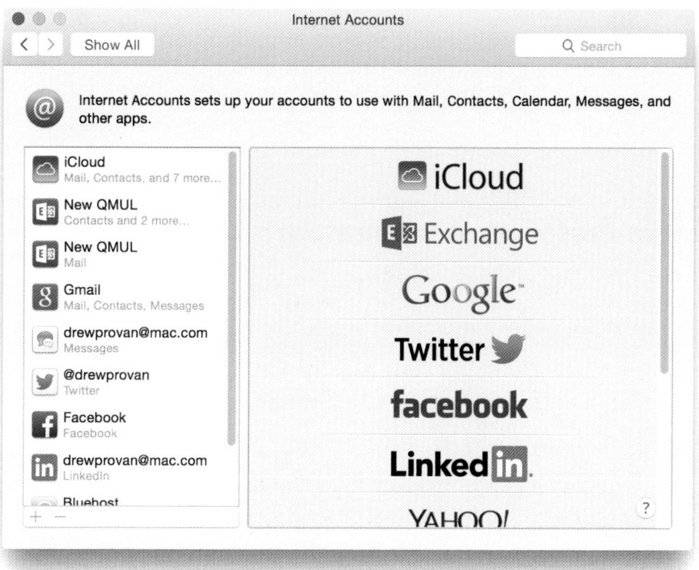

Networking the Mac

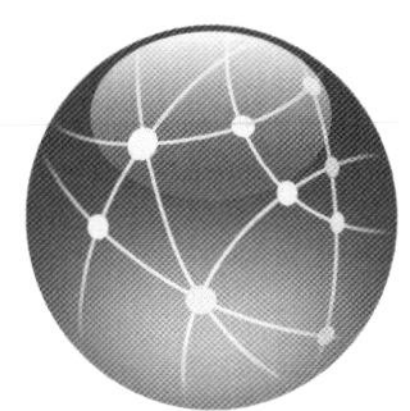

You can connect your Mac to a wired or wireless network, which will allow you to see other hard drives and printers, share files and many other items.

Your Mac can connect to other Macs, printers and other wireless devices easily.

To access network settings

1. Go to **Apple Menu > System Preferences > Network**

2. Adjust settings depending on network type (Ethernet, Wi-Fi, etc.)

This is discussed more fully in Chapter Nine.

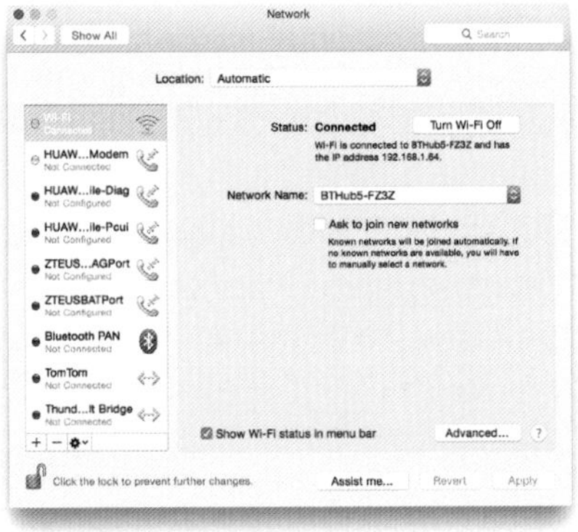

You can also add Bluetooth devices by going to **Apple Menu > System Preferences > Bluetooth**

Setting up Sharing

To share files, folders and other content you have to allow the sharing of these items using the Sharing System Preference.

You cannot let other people share your files unless you have set up File Sharing using the Sharing System Preference.

Extending the Mac desktop using AirPlay

With OS X Yosemite Apple has introduced a way of extending your Mac's desktop using AirPlay and Apple TV. The settings are found within **System Preferences > Displays.**

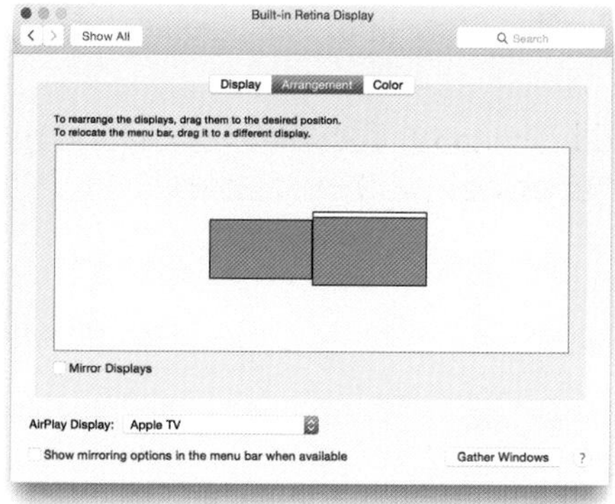

Full details can be found at the Apple Support site (**support.apple.com/kb/PH19037**).

Date and Time

Your computer needs to be set to the correct date and time otherwise your files will be incorrectly dated, and keeping a diary using Calendar will be impossible.

1. Go to **Apple menu > System Preferences > Date & Time**

2. Choose location, server (e.g. *Apple Europe time.euro.apple.com*), type of clock (12 hour, 24 hour etc.)

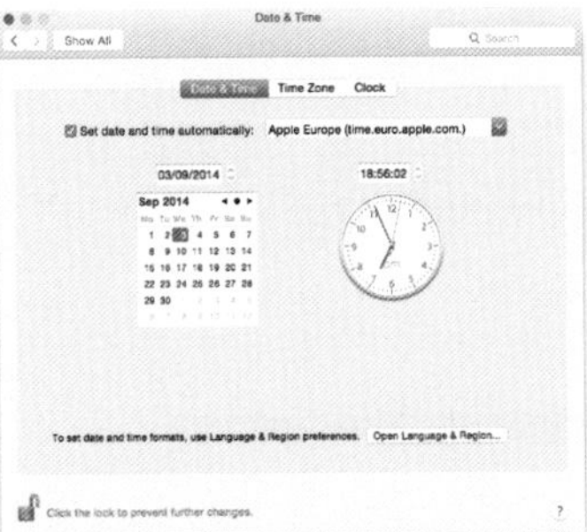

Choosing the server.

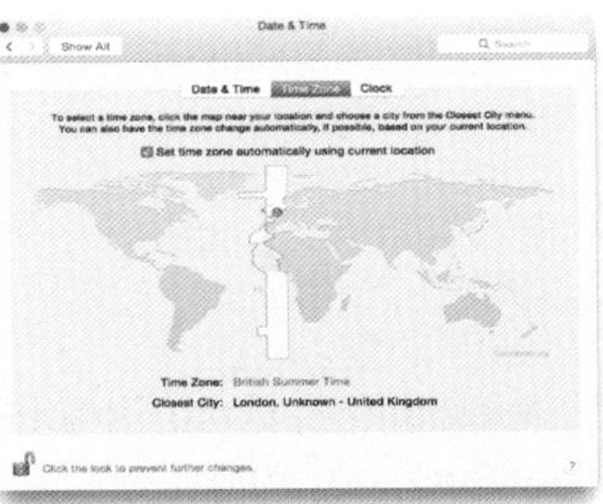

Make sure the time zone is correct. You may need to enter this manually if Wi-Fi fails to identify your time zone.

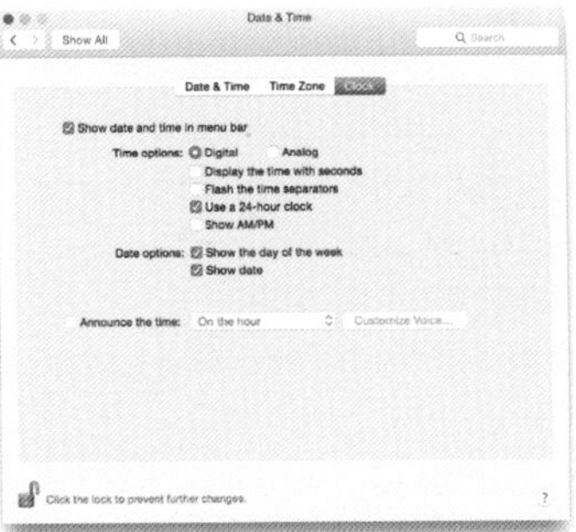

Choose the style and location of your clock.

Setting up Time Machine

Computers sometimes go wrong, and files are lost. People generally forget to back up their work until it is too late and a problem has occurred.

Backing up your files and folders can be done manually (dragging files around to separate drives) or you can allow Time Machine to do all the hard work for you.

Time Machine will back up your entire computer then do an incremental backup every hour. This means that if a file becomes lost or corrupt you can go back in time and retrieve a previous saved version.

Time Machine is a great app which will help you if you ever delete a file by accident or a file becomes corrupted.

To use Time Machine

1. Go to **Apple menu > System Preferences > Time Machine**
2. Choose the drive to use, and that's it!

Open Time Machine preferences, select the disk you wish to use (not your main hard drive – needs to be a distinct drive). If you don't want to back up certain files, e.g. applications, go to Options and exclude these.

Buy yourself a decent-sized external hard drive for Time Machine (e.g. 1-2 TB).

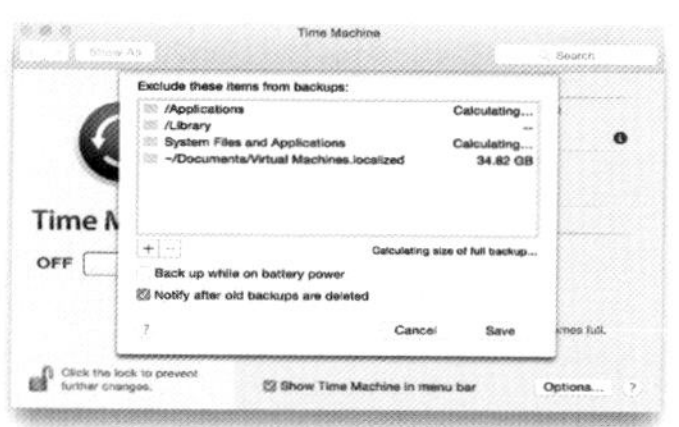

This picture shows the available drives that can be used with Time Machine.

Power Management

The Energy Saver setting is useful if you have a laptop, but can also be useful with desktop Macs. For example, if you want to use the printer attached to the computer you may not want the Mac to go to sleep, otherwise if you try to print remotely the printer may not be seen.

You can also use this panel to make your Mac wake up and sleep at specific times.

Setting up sleep and wake options

1. Go to **Apple menu > System Preferences > Energy Saver**

2. Choose options which suit you

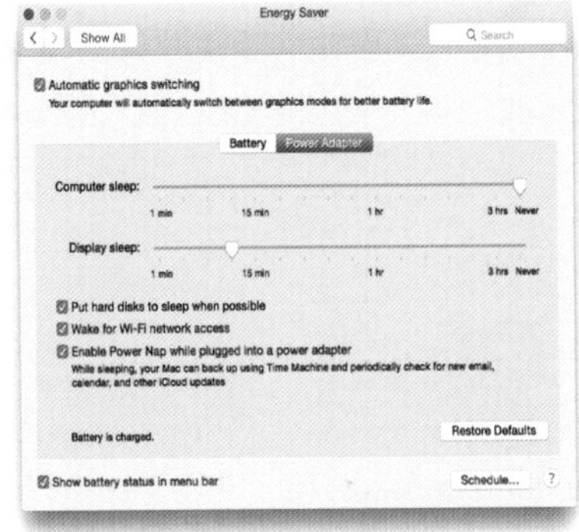

Choose when to make the drive and screen sleep. There is an option to wake for network access (this would include remote printing).

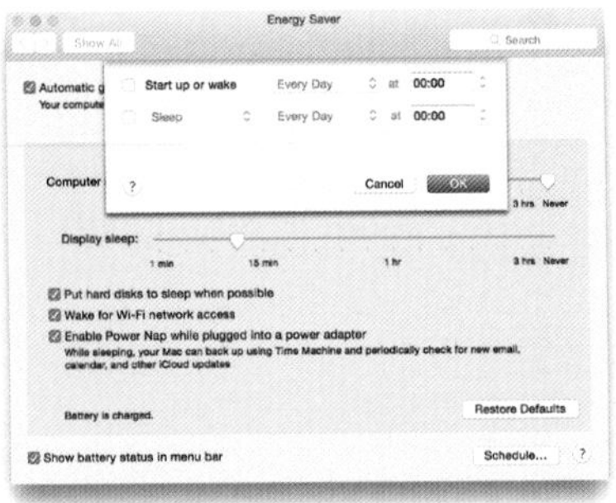

Set up your wake up and sleep options here.

Spotlight

Spotlight in Yosemite has become more powerful than ever. As well as finding files on your Mac it will also look on the Web, search Wikipedia, show where films are showing, and other features. Spotlight can even do calculations!

Activate Spotlight

1. Type ⌘ + **Spacebar**
2. The Spotlight window will open
3. Type in your search term

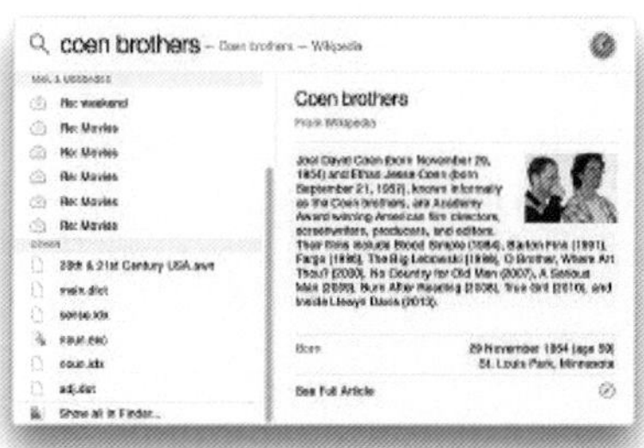

Calculations using Spotlight

1. Type ⌘ + **Spacebar**
2. The Spotlight window will open
3. Type in your calculation

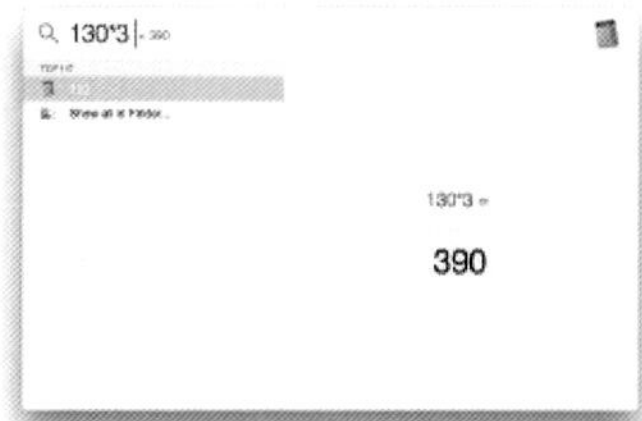

Notifications and Reminders

Hot tip

You can reply to Tweets or emails directly from the Notification pop-up.

Yosemite adds Notifications, similar to Apple's iOS devices (iPhone, iPad, and iPod touch). Notifications will show you what's in your diary, messages you may have received, software updates, and notifications from many of your apps.

Show Notifications

Click the Notifications icon at the top right of your screen or swipe left to right on the trackpad with two fingers.

You can adjust how you see Notifications (banners, etc.) using **System Preferences > Notifications**

Reminders

This app provides a place for you to store reminders. It is simple to use but the great thing is you can make the reminders location-based (on arrival or leaving).

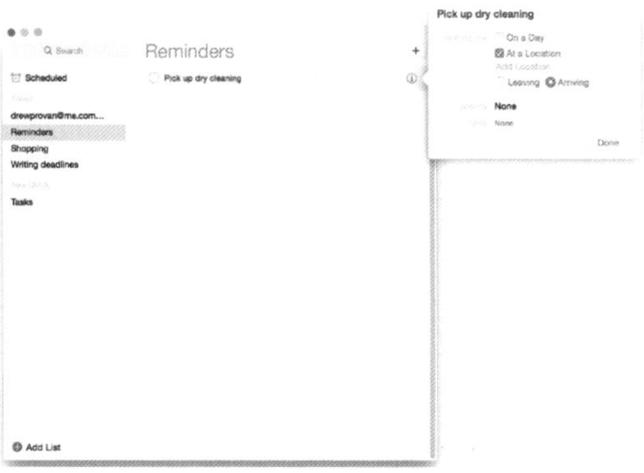

Facebook and Twitter

Mac OS X has integration with Facebook, Twitter, LinkedIn and other social networking sites, which means you can easily update your Facebook page and send Tweets from within many applications. You can do all this with a single sign-on for each app.

1. Open **System Preferences**
2. Go to **Internet Accounts**
3. Click on Twitter or Facebook and enter your credentials

The image below shows how you can send a Facebook update directly from Safari (click the Share icon for options) – see page 66 for details on Safari.

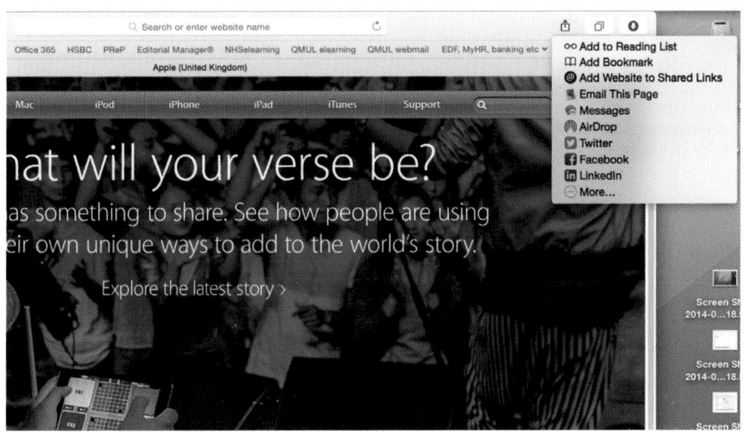

About This Mac

Want to know more about your Mac?

1. Go to **Apple Menu**

2. Select **About This Mac**

3. Select the tabs to learn about display, storage, and memory slots

Apple introduced OS X, following on from OS 9, as a Unix-based Operating Syestem (OS). The "X" is a Roman 10 and signifies the link between the OS and Unix. OS X was the first really major change in appearance of the user interface since Apple designed it's GUI (graphical user interface) in the 1980s. OS X Yosemite (10.10) is the latest version and is built to closely resemble iOS, the current mobile OS used on the iPhone, iPad, and iPod Touch.

4. Click on **More info** to see the tabs below

Display information

Attached drives

Memory slots

Support

Hot tip

About This Mac tells you everything you need to know about your Mac including serial number, RAM, drives, installed software and much more. Familiarize yourself with the various panes by clicking on them in turn.

Hot tip

People get confused about "memory", confusing RAM memory with hard drive capacity. The hard drive is where you store files and apps. As you add files the disk will fill. RAM (Random Access Memory) is usually around 2-4 GB and is the space used to hold running apps and documents temporarily while the apps are running. It's like a workspace for the apps. If RAM is low, your Mac may slow down until you quit some apps or close windows to free up some RAM for the apps to use.

2 Dealing with Documents

Many apps allow you to create documents. Here we will look at how documents are best filed, copied, edited and handled by the Mac.

The Finder

You use the Finder to open Finder windows, move files, and many other functions.

Open the Finder

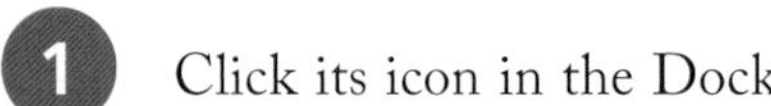

1 Click its icon in the Dock

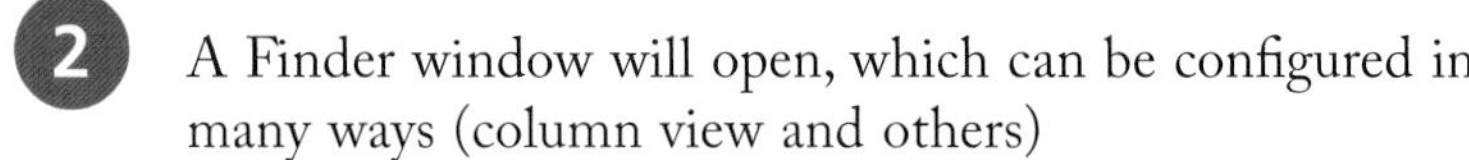

2 A Finder window will open, which can be configured in many ways (column view and others)

The Finder is the Mac's equivalent of Windows Explorer.

Click on the Finder (bottom left)

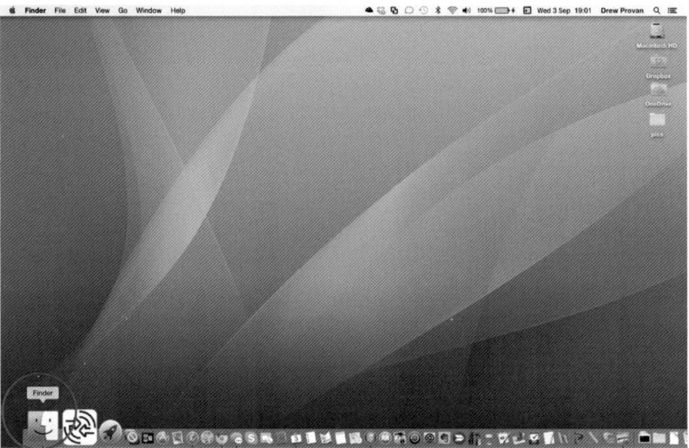

Many apps work in full screen mode (click the green button on the Finder window).

New Finder window opens in column mode

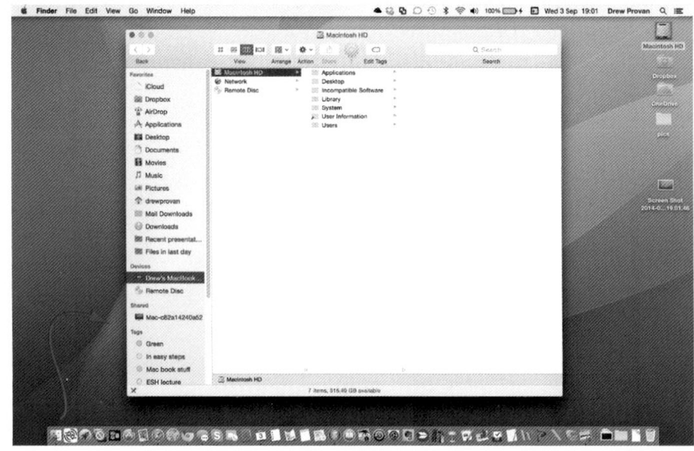

Finder Views

Apple has provided a number of different ways to look at Finder windows. For basic documents, List or Column view is useful. For pictures, the icon view is better. To preview documents (without actually opening them), choose the Cover Flow option.

Change Finder window view options

1. Open a new window and select from the icons at the top of the window

2. Or go to View at the top of the screen and select option

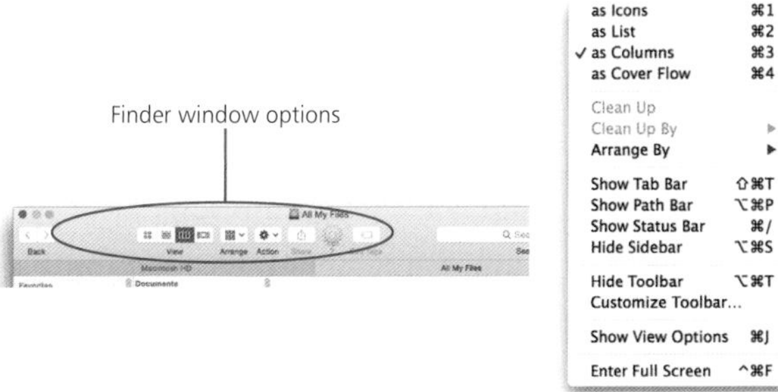

Choose from icons in Finder window or

Select View from Finder window

Using the tabbed Finder

Instead of having cluttered Finder windows on your desktop you can group them together in a tabbed view. Open a Finder window then use **Cmd (⌘) + T** to generate a new tab. You can even merge open windows by going to the Window menu and selecting **Merge All Windows**.

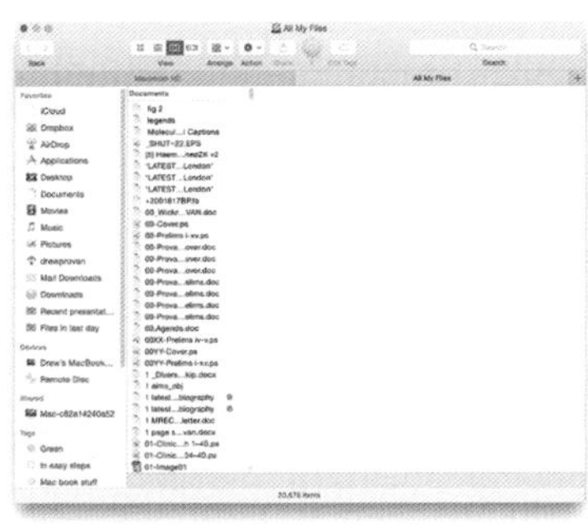

⌘ is the Apple Command Key and is used for most shortcut combinations for Macs (similar to the Windows Key for PCs).

Folders

You need folders to contain your files, text documents, photos, music, and many other items. It's worth learning how to make folders, name them, move and copy them.

Make a folder

1. Go to **File > New Folder**
2. Or tap ⌘ **+ Shift + N**

Rename a folder

1. Click on the name of the folder, you will see the box turn blue, simply start typing and the name will be replaced by the new name

Move a folder

1. Click and drag folder to wherever you want

To duplicate a file or folder you need to Option-Drag them (unless you are copying to a different disk in which case you can simply Drag).

Duplicate a folder

1. Click on folder, and drag while holding down the Option (Alt) key

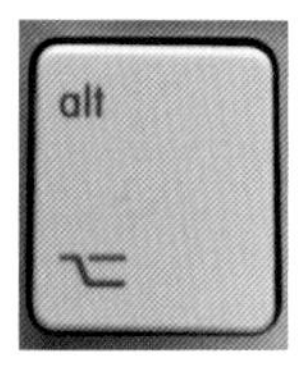

Make an alias of a folder

An alias is like a dummy folder that points you to where the real folder is, and acts a bit like the real folder. For example, you may want easy access to your Mail downloads folder but it's a real pain having to navigate to your Home Folder > Library > Mail Downloads so you can click on the Mail Downloads folder, then right-click and choose Make Alias. Drag the alias (you know it's an alias because it has a black curved arrow on the folder) to the desktop. When you double-click the alias folder you can see all the Mail Downloads as if it were in that folder (it is actually still in its original location).

The same can be done with documents. You can move them around, rename them, make copies by Option-dragging them and make aliases to them.

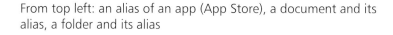

From top left: an alias of an app (App Store), a document and its alias, a folder and its alias

Create aliases (shortcuts) to your most commonly accessed folders and apps so you can find them quickly.

TextEdit is a simple text editor provided with Yosemite. You can use pinch to zoom text easily. It is found in the Applications folder.

TextEdit also supports the cloud (e.g. iCloud).

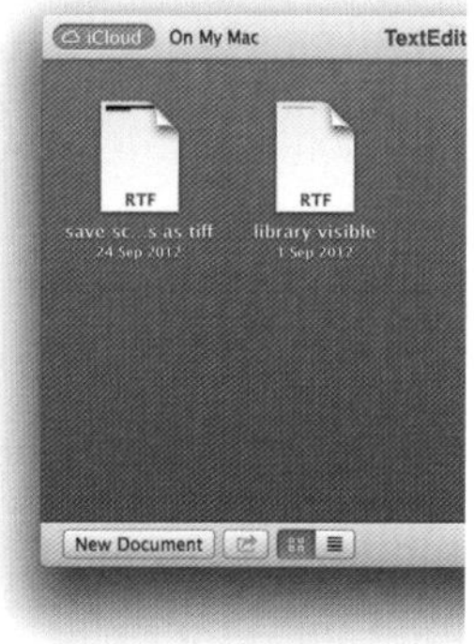

Move Files into Folders

This is very straightforward.

Adding a file to a folder

1. Click and hold the file you want to add to the folder
2. Drag the file to the folder
3. The folder will turn darker and may spring open (depending on your settings)
4. Unclick the mouse (take your finger off)
5. The file will drop into the folder

To move the document out of the folder

1. If you add the wrong document to the folder immediately hit **⌘ + Z** (this is the Undo command – works with most programs, and will reverse your last action)
2. Or you can double-click the folder to open it and drag the file out

Copy (rather than move) a file to a folder

This leaves the original file (or folder) where it is but makes a copy.

1. Press **Option** and click the file you want to copy
2. **Drag the copy of the file** to the folder (you should see a green **+**)

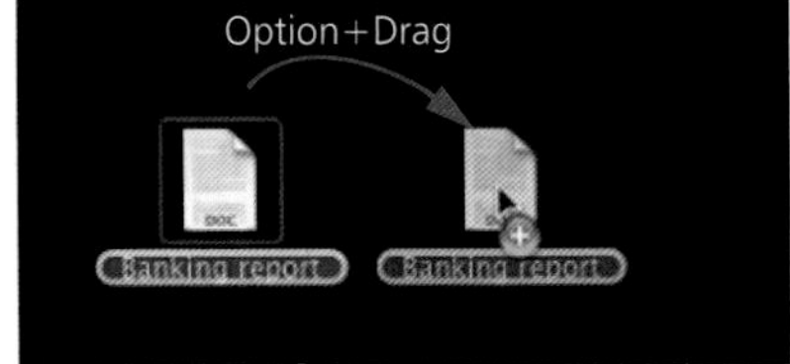

3. Your original file should remain in its position and the copy should be where you dropped it

Deleting Files from Folders

This is easy.

1. **Find the folder**
2. **Double-click** to open
3. **Locate file** and **drag to Trash**
4. Or **click once on the file** to select it then type ⌘ + **Backspace**
5. Or click once to select then right-click and choose **Move to Trash**
6. To **undo** (retrieve a file or folder from the Trash) type ⌘ **+ Z**

Delete files fast by clicking once then typing ⌘ **+ Backspace**.

Delete multiple files/folders

1. Click the pointer on the screen and **lasso the documents** you want to delete
2. Or hold down **Option** key and **click the files** you want to delete
3. **Drag the files to the Trash** or type ⌘ **+ Backspace** or right-click and select **Move to Trash**

Where's My User Library?

There are at least two libraries on your Mac – the main Library for the Mac Hard Disk that you shouldn't touch, and your own Library (**~/Library**) in your Home Folder (again, you shouldn't really touch this but many of us do look in the Library folder and delete and add items).

Apple has chosen to hide the User Library from us, probably to stop people deleting crucial files that keep your Mac working properly. *Note*: take care when tinkering with files in the Library – you could cause your Mac to crash!

Your User Library (~/Library) is hidden by default. You can access it temporarily by holding down Option then choosing Go > Library or use the permanent option using the Terminal app.

To make your own Library visible

1. Go to the **Go** menu (top of Finder window)
2. Then hold down **Option**, and the Library folder will appear (take your finger off Option and Library vanishes)

To make your Library folder permanently visible

1. **Open Terminal** (one of your Utility programs)
2. Type in **chflags nohidden ~/Library**
3. Hit **Return**
4. Your own Library will be visible permanently

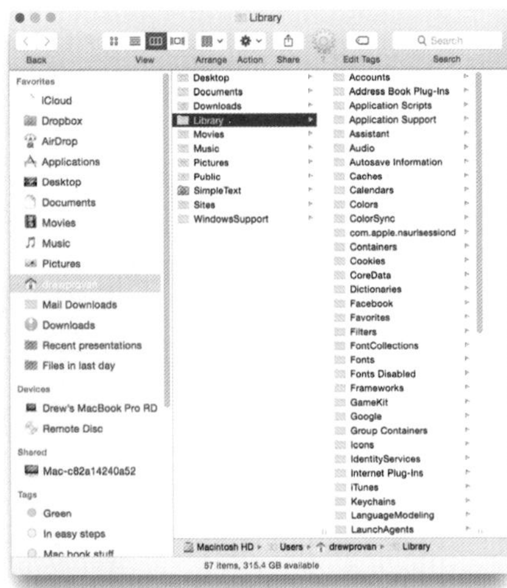

Tags

If you go to **Finder > File** you will see Tags at the bottom. These are color-coded. You can use these codes for specific items – for example, very important files and folders could be red, and personal items green. You can also name the tags.

Take Tags even further

1. Instead of color-coding, you can actually name the labels
2. Go to **Finder Menu** (top of screen) and select **Preferences > Tags**
3. Rename the color to anything you want, e.g. Important, Personal, Banking, etc.
4. This makes it easier to sort and find your files

Tags can be given any names – just amend the ones provided by Apple.

Find files using label tag

If you want to find a file which you know has, for example, a Banking tag assigned by you:

1. Type ⌘ **+ F**
2. Type the name of the file if you know it
3. Select **Kind** and use the dropdown menu to get **Other...**
4. Select **Tag > Banking**
5. You should find your labeled files easily

Is your work saved?

As you work on documents the red button at the top left will have a small black dot in the center if you have not saved the document.

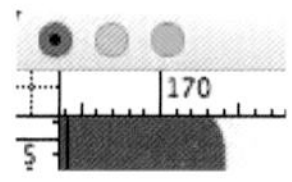

Unsaved (*note the black dot*)

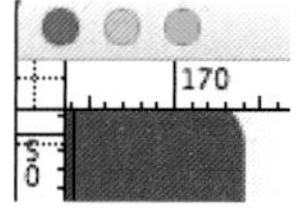

Saved (*black dot gone!*)

Opening Documents

Usually when you click a document it will be opened by the program that was used to create it. But if you take pictures using a camera then transfer them to the Mac, you might find that when you double-click the photo it gets opened by Preview when you really wanted to open it in Photoshop.

Specifying a program to open a document

1. Locate the document
2. Right-click on the document and select **Open With**
3. Choose the program you want to open the file
4. If not shown, choose **Other...** or **App Store...** (to look for a program that will open the file)

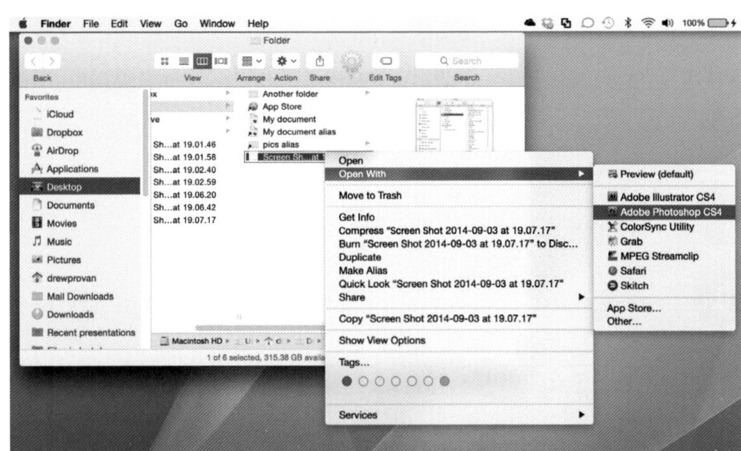

To force the Mac to always open photos using a specific program use Right-Click then press Option on the file and choose "Always Open With...".

Saving documents

For most apps you can go to **File > Save** or **File > Save As...** But with OS X Yosemite, Apple now uses **Versions** with many of its own apps (e.g. Pages). Now there is no Save As... so to open a document and save under a new name you need to choose **Duplicate**. Once the document has been duplicated you can rename it.

Quick Look at Documents

Often you want to find a document but you don't want the hassle of opening each one until you find the one you want. There are ways of viewing documents (Word or Pages files, PowerPoint, Keynote, MP3s, videos and many others) without opening any programs at all using Quick Look.

Using Quick Look

1. Find the document(s)
2. **Select** the document by **clicking once**
3. Go to **Quick Look** in the Finder menu
4. Or tap **⌘ + Y**
5. Or simply select the file and tap the **spacebar**
6. You can then preview the contents. If it's the document you need, double-click to make it open in its respective program

Click on a document and hit the spacebar for a Quick Look at its contents.

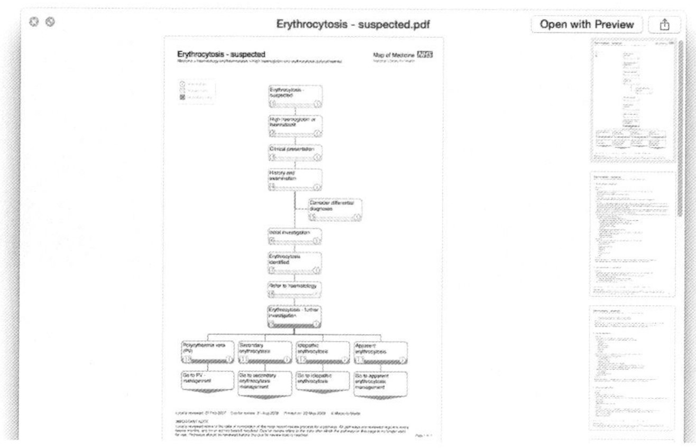

The above shows a PDF file which was viewed by selecting the PDF file then tapping Spacebar. After doing a Quick Look the document can be opened properly using Preview (see top right for Preview button).

Dictation

Rather than type documents you can use the internal microphone on the Mac to dictate text.

Activate Dictation

1. Go to **System Preferences > Dictation**
2. Click the radio button to switch it on
3. Within any app **tap the Function (fn) key twice**

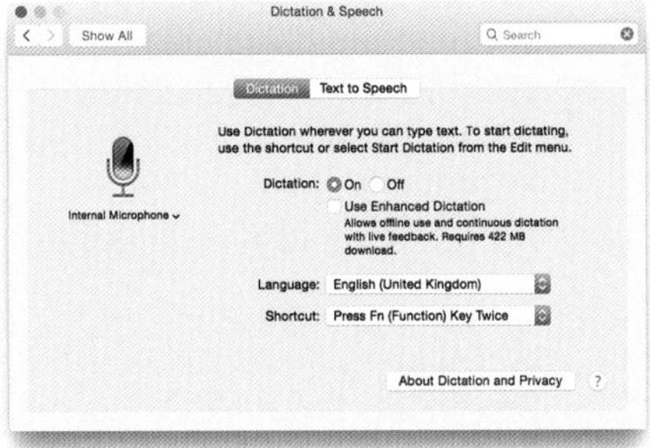

Dictation can even be used offline. Go to System Preferences > Dictation & Speech and select Enhanced Dictation.

With no training at all the accuracy is extremely high (unlike most conventional voice recognition apps). Below shows some dictation in TextEdit (see page 33). All text and punctuation are correct.

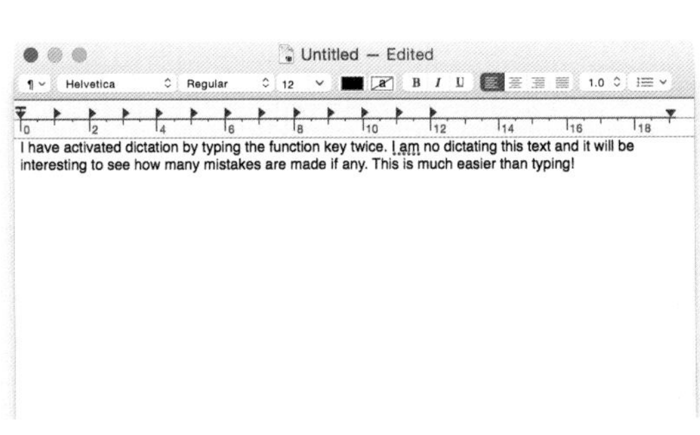

Notes App

The Notes app has been ported over from iOS devices, having gained popularity on the iPhone and other iOS devices. The concept is simple: Notes is a straightforward note-taking app that syncs to your iPhone or other iOS device (if you select this in the iCloud System Preference).

As well as text, you can drop in images.

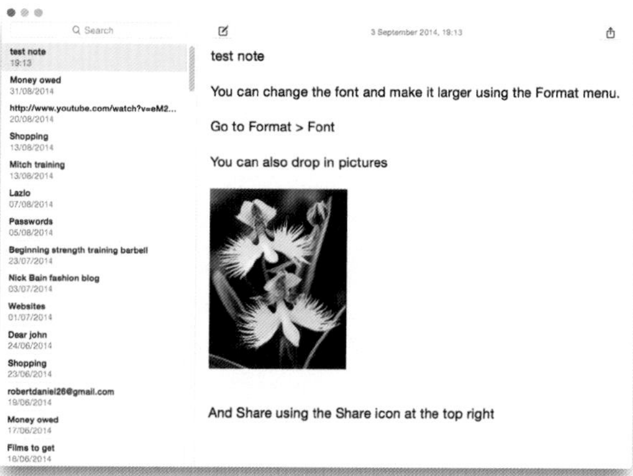

Sharing notes

Click the Share icon (bottom right) to send the note using Mail, Messages, Twitter, Facebook, LinkedIn or others.

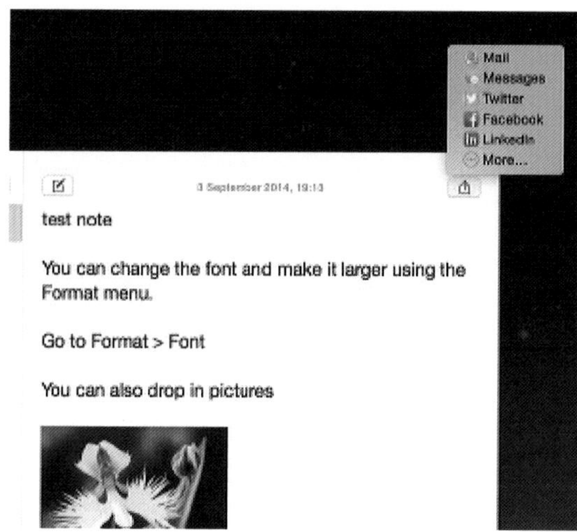

Mac and PC Compatibility

If you regularly work with documents on both Mac and PC (e.g. if you use Word for Windows on the PC at work and Word for Mac at home) you can copy your files onto a USB drive.

However, you cannot use PC-formatted (NTFS) disks with a Mac, or Mac-formatted disks with a PC.

Instead, use FAT32 which can be read by both Mac and PC.

Format a drive as FAT32

1. Open **Go > Utilities > Disk Utility**
2. Select your USB drive
3. Click **Erase** and give the drive a **name**
4. From the drop-down menu select **MS-DOS (FAT)**
5. The drive will be formatted and will be readable on PC and Mac!

PCs can't read Mac-formatted drives and vice versa. Use FAT32 as the format type if you intend to use a USB drive on both PCs and Macs.

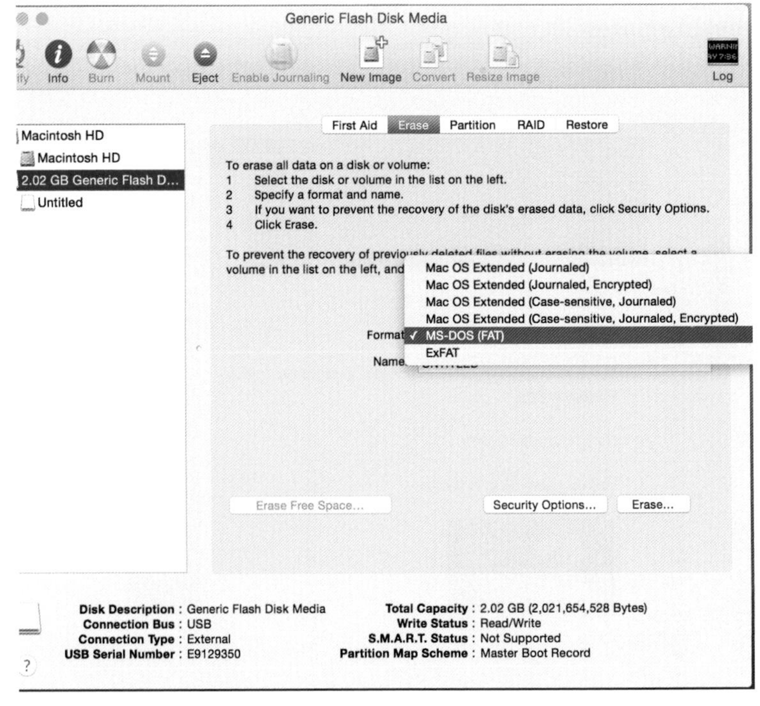

3 Working with PDF Files

Using Preview *on the Mac makes generating PDF files incredibly easy. For collaborative work or sharing of documents, PDFs make the whole process painless.*

What is a PDF?

PDF stands for *Portable Document Format*. Basically it means you can create a document in any program, with graphics and fonts and save it in a format that anyone can open (Mac or PC), even if they don't have the program you used to generate the document. For example, you may use Adobe Illustrator to generate a newsletter but there's no point sending this file to your colleague since he does not have Adobe Illustrator. Instead, save it as a PDF which he can open on his Mac or PC and see the document in all its detail.

PDFs are great for sending someone a document which was created using a program they don't have on their Mac.

Upsides

- Anyone can open and read a PDF even if they don't have the specific program used to create a document
- Small file size
- Quick and easy way to share documents

Downsides

- May not look 100% like the original document, e.g. the fonts may change
- Can be tricky to edit

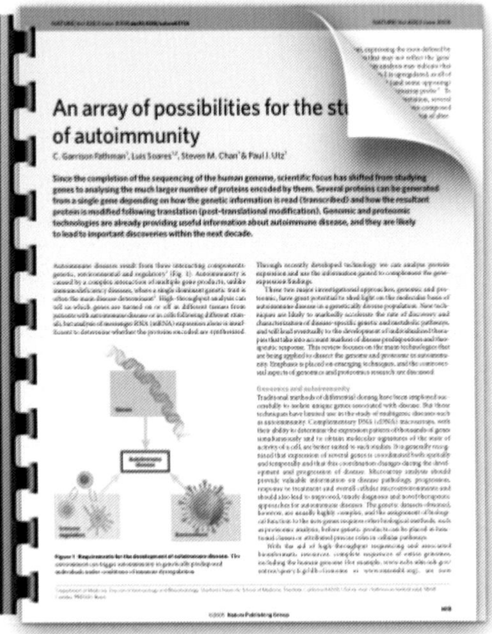

An array of possibilities for the st[...]
of autoimmunity

C. Garrison Fathman[1], Luis Soares[1,2], Steven M. Chan[1] & Paul J. Utz[1]

Since the completion of the sequencing of the human genome, scientific focus has shifted from studying genes to analysing the much larger number of proteins encoded by them. Several proteins can be generated from a single gene depending on how the genetic information is read (transcribed) and how the resultant protein is modified following translation (post-translational modification). Genomic and proteomic technologies are already providing useful information about autoimmune disease, and they are likely to lead to important discoveries within the next decade.

Programs to Read PDF files

There are many of these, some free, others are paid. It can be expensive if you want full functionality in terms of editing, for example:

- Adobe Acrobat Reader and Adobe Acrobat Pro
- Preview

Mac OS X comes with *Preview*, a document and image viewer. It will open:

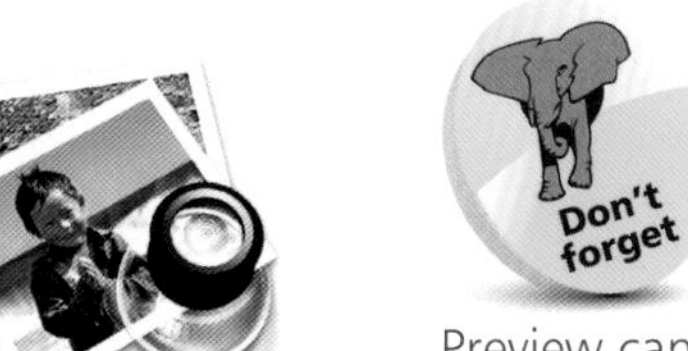

- PDFs
- Images
- Many other types of documents

Preview allows minor editing, cropping, rotation, etc.

Don't forget

Preview can open many types of file – not just PDFs.

Dropping PDF files into other types of document

Did you know you can drop a PDF file on a Word or Pages document, and even PowerPoint or Keynote? Simply drag the PDF file onto an open Word window and the PDF will be embedded within the Word file. There are many other programs that can handle PDFs – if in doubt try dropping a PDF onto a document window.

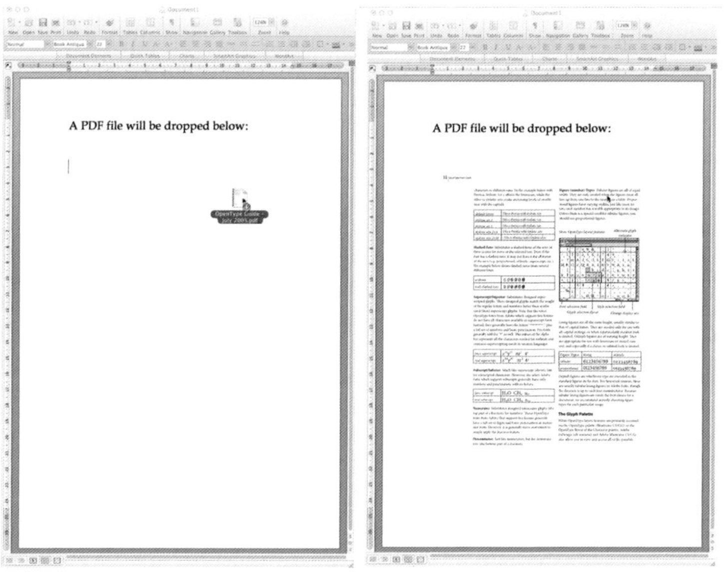

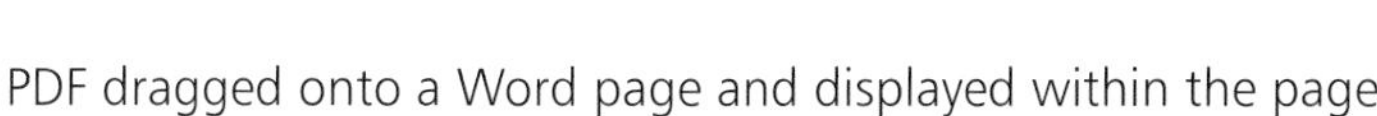
PDF dragged onto a Word page and displayed within the page

Opening PDF in Preview

To open a PDF document

1. Select the PDF you wish to open
2. Double-click and Preview opens the file automatically
3. Alternatively, you can right-click and select **Open with**

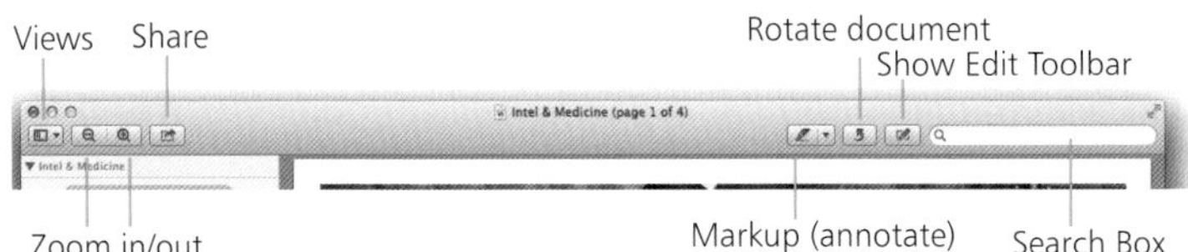

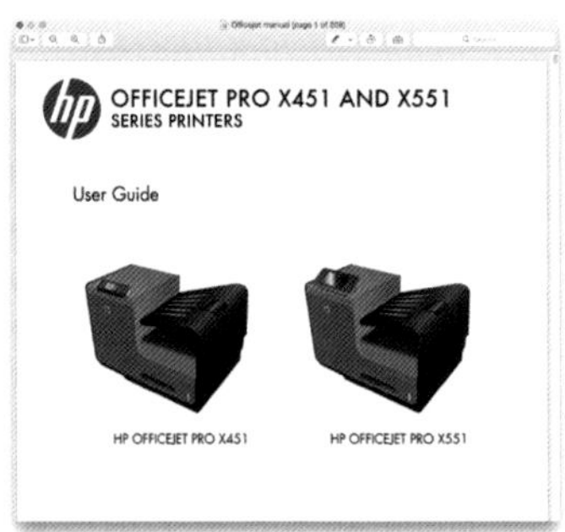

Basic page mode

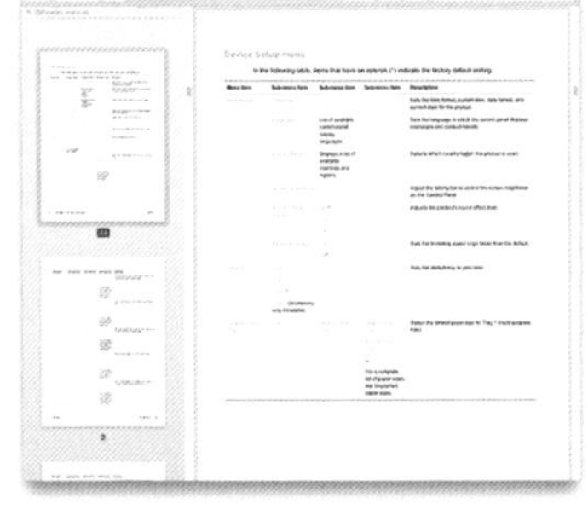

With thumbnails

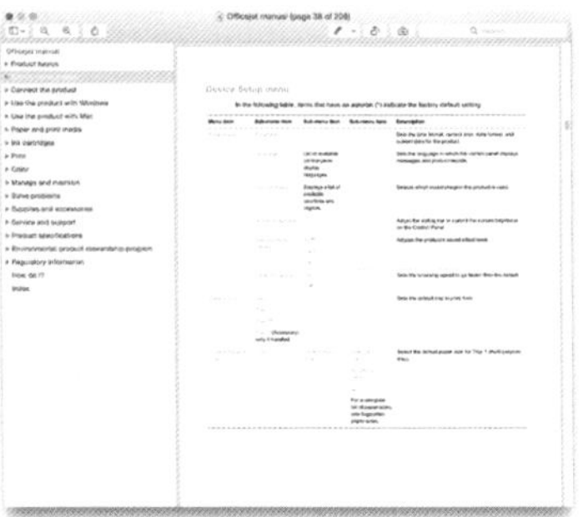

Contents view

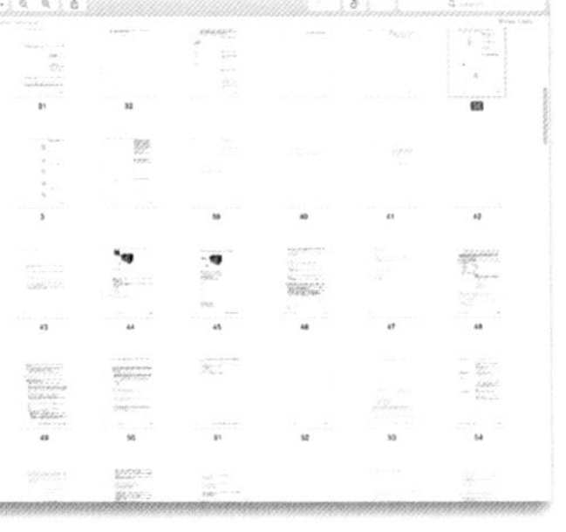

Contact sheet

Add Text to PDF

Annotating PDF files

You can use Preview to annotate a document, adding text boxes, thought bubbles, arrows, and other symbols. This is useful if someone sends you a PDF of a document they're working on. You can then add your thoughts and comments to the document directly and email the document back, and they can incorporate your changes within the master document with the program they used to generate the PDF.

For example, if they're working on a Word document they can generate a PDF from within Word, and send that to you.

You can then add your comments, and they can then make the changes to the Word file based on your comments.

Preview lets you add bookmarks, strike through text, underline text, add shapes, speech and thought bubbles.

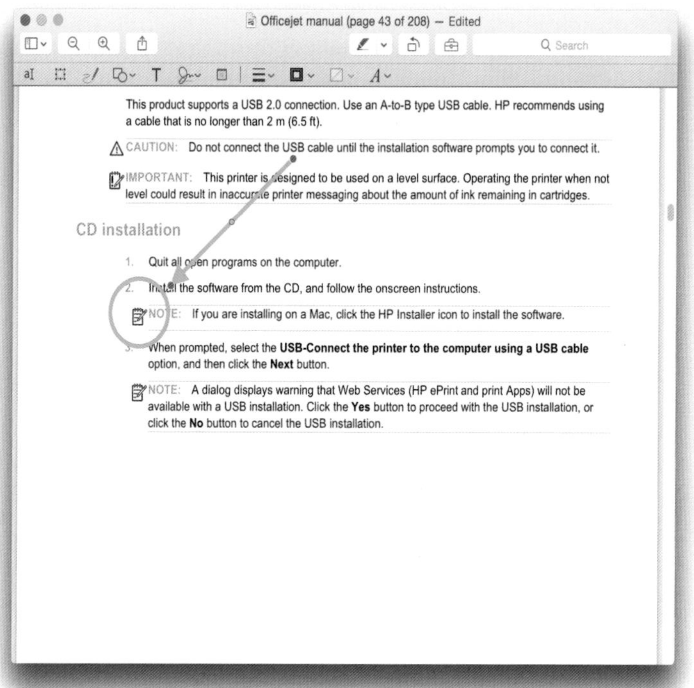

Because you can edit and annotate PDFs using Preview there is no need to buy expensive PDF-editing apps.

Creating a PDF

Creating a PDF using a Mac is very easy.

1. Within your program (Word, Pages, Photoshop, Excel, etc.) select **Print**

2. At the bottom left of the Print dialog box click the PDF dropdown menu

3. Choose **Save as PDF...**

4. Name the file and select the destination for the save

Creating a PDF using a Mac is as simple as printing.

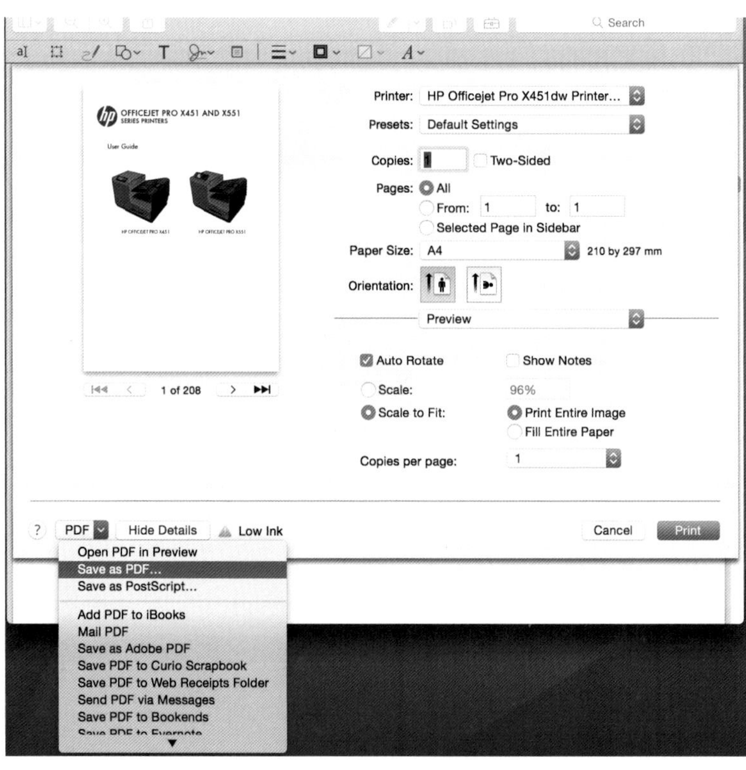

Making PDFs Secure

You can password-protect PDFs so that only those people with the password can open the document.

1. Choose Security options
2. Click **Require password** to open document
3. Type in the password then verify it
4. You can password-protect the editing of the document by using the settings in the dialog box

For a PDF that contains sensitive information consider password protecting it.

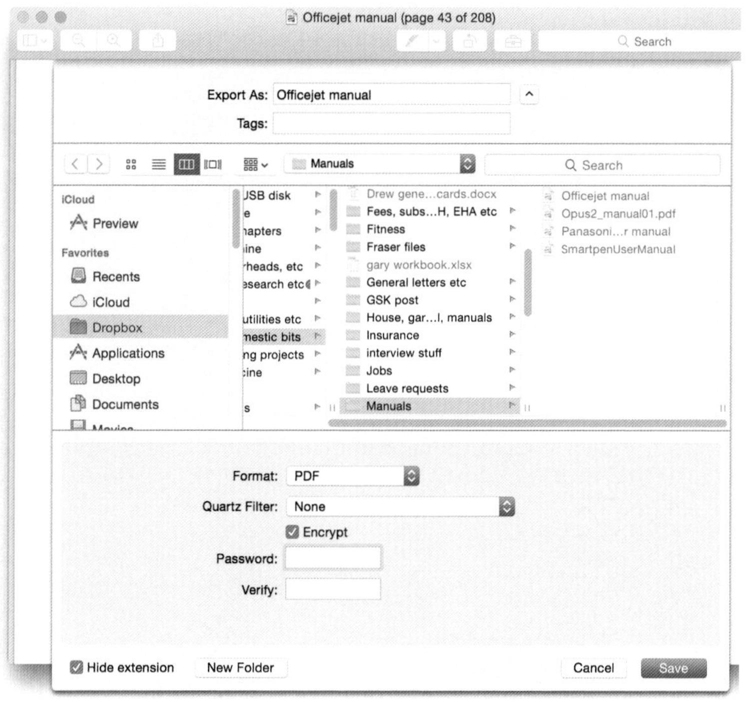

Emailing PDF files

1. Create your PDF
2. **Open Mail** or other email program
3. **Drop PDF onto email** (or attach using **⌘ + Shift + A**)
4. Send email
5. Alternatively, within the Print dialog box select **PDF > Mail PDF**
6. A new email will open
7. Address it, add subject and email content and click **Send**

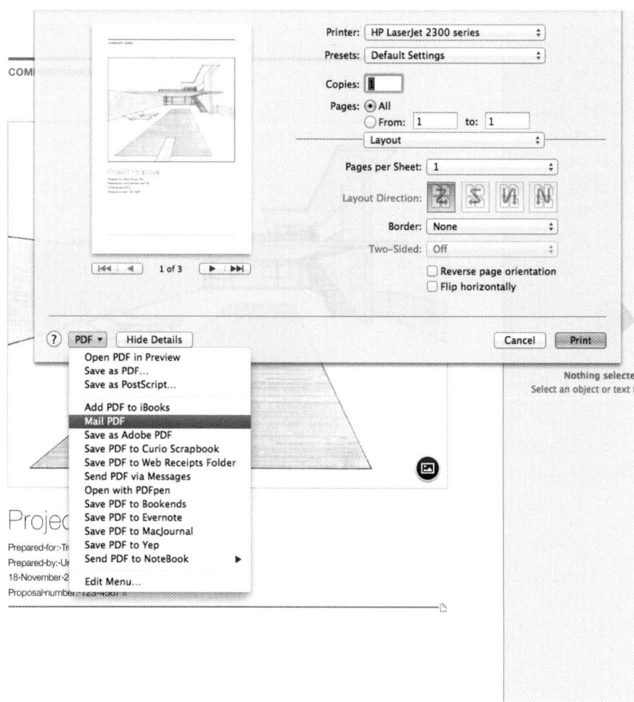

Acrobat Reader

This is a free PDF reader from Adobe with limited editing tools. Because Macs come with Preview there is little need for most Mac users to download Acrobat Reader. Preview is fast and has sufficient capability for most people.

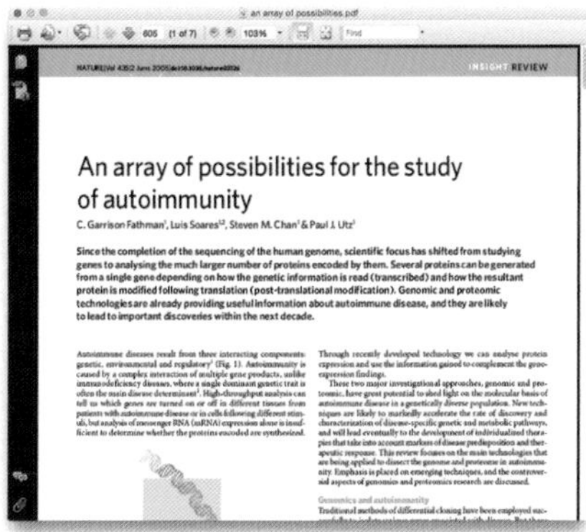

Skitch

This is a freeware program which allows you to annotate PDFs quickly. It is more fun than Acrobat or Preview.

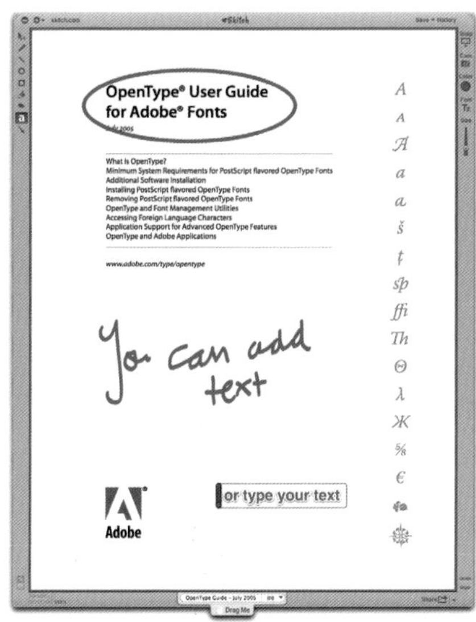

Skitch is a great free app for marking changes and annotating PDFs. You can download it from **skitch.com**

Handoff

Yosemite has a new feature called Handoff which provides continuity for your work. If you start writing a document in Pages, Numbers, or Keynote on your Mac you will see a new icon at the bottom left of your locked iOS device screen. This means you can carry on editing your document on your iOS device, and vice versa. It also works with Safari and if you browse to a website on the iOS device you can pick up where you left off using the Mac.

At the time of writing apps that work with Handoff are Mail, Calendar, Messages, Notes, Reminders, Maps, Safari, Apple Keynote, Numbers, and Pages. It also works with the third-party app GoodReader.

Using Handoff

1. Make sure Bluetooth is on and you are signed into your iCloud account on the iOS device and Mac

2. Start working in Pages or another compatible app on the Mac. You should see the app's icon on the lock screen of your iOS device

3. Or start working on a document on the iOS device and the app's icon will pop up on the left side of the Dock. Click the icon and continue working on the document on the Mac

Here you can see the Safari icon at the bottom left of the lock screen on the iPhone (Safari was opened on the Mac)

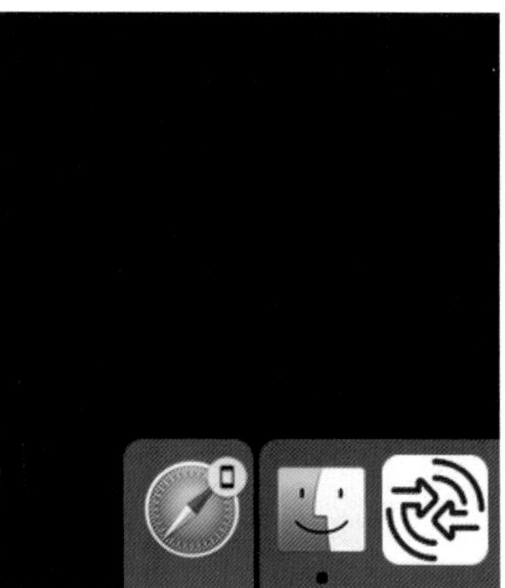

Here you can see the Safari icon to the left of the Dock because Safari was opened on the iPhone.

4 Mastering Email

Apple Mail *comes as part of OS X. It is a powerful and flexible email client.*
In this chapter we will look at the basics of Mail *and how to get the best out of the program.*

The Mail Window

You might spend a fair bit of time writing and sending emails so it's worthwhile getting to know the layout of Apple's email program, Mail.

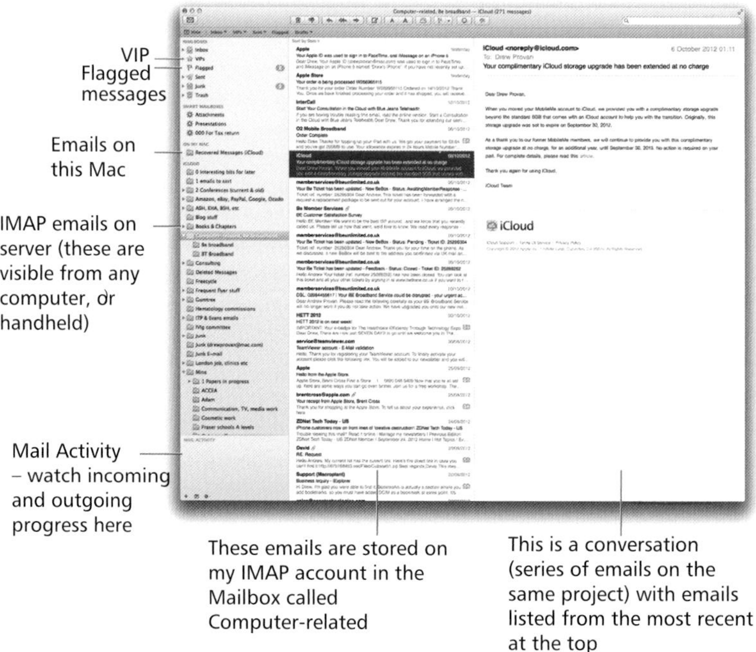

The basic structure of an email is:

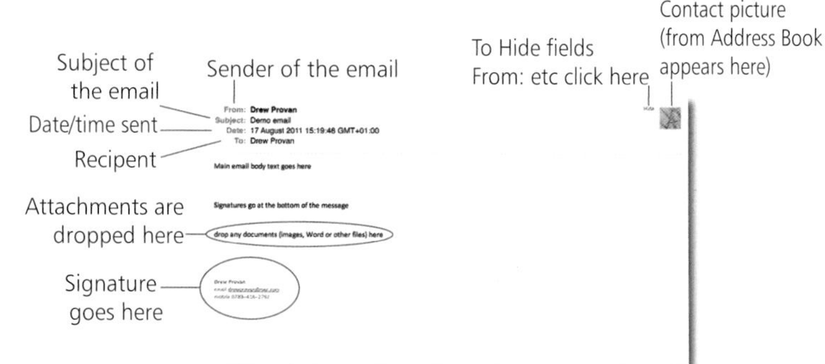

Add an Email Account

You cannot send or receive email until you set up an account. You can add others later but for now, let's just add one account.

1. **Launch Mail**
2. Go to **Mail menu > Preferences > Accounts**
3. Click **+** to add an account (click **–** to remove an account)
4. Enter your name, email address and password for that email account then click **Continue**

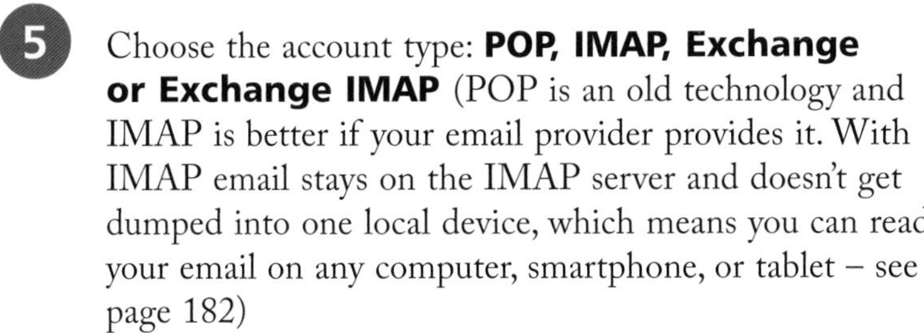

5. Choose the account type: **POP, IMAP, Exchange or Exchange IMAP** (POP is an old technology and IMAP is better if your email provider provides it. With IMAP email stays on the IMAP server and doesn't get dumped into one local device, which means you can read your email on any computer, smartphone, or tablet – see page 182)

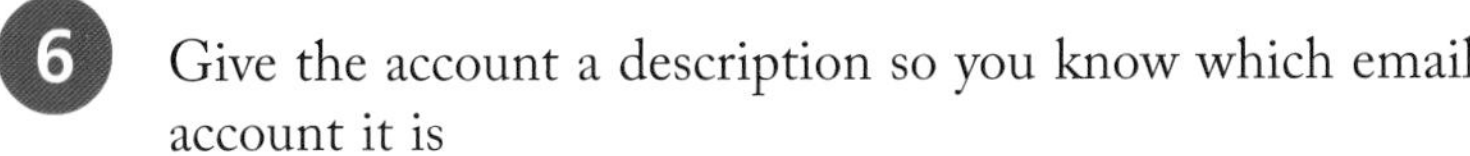

6. Give the account a description so you know which email account it is
7. Enter **Incoming Mail Server,** e.g. imap.gmail.com
8. Then enter **User Name** and **password** and click **Continue**

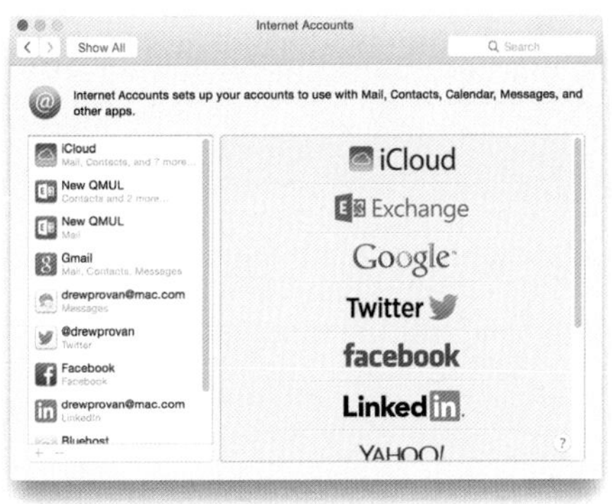

Try to use IMAP email whenever possible.

Create an Email Message

1. Type ⌘ **+ N** or go to **File New Message**
2. A new email window will open
3. **To:** add the recipient's email address
4. **Cc:** add anyone you want to receive a copy
5. **Bcc:** if you want to send a blind carbon copy (the "To:" recipient won't see this email address) add that person's email address here
6. **Subject:** add something brief which describes the topic of email

If you want to send an email to someone and include (secretly) a third party but not let the main recipient know, add the third party's email address to the Bcc: box.

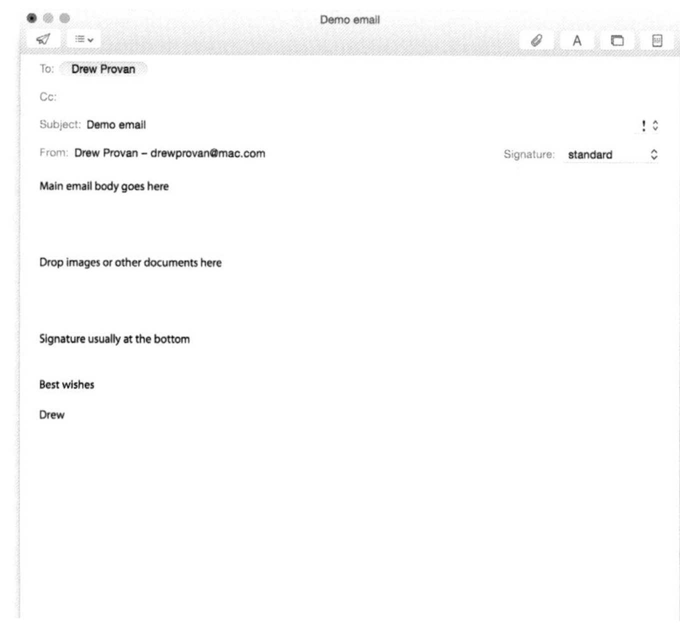

Send an Attachment

You can send most types of file by email. Be careful not to send huge attachments – generally up to 2MB is okay.

Add attachment

Drop onto email body

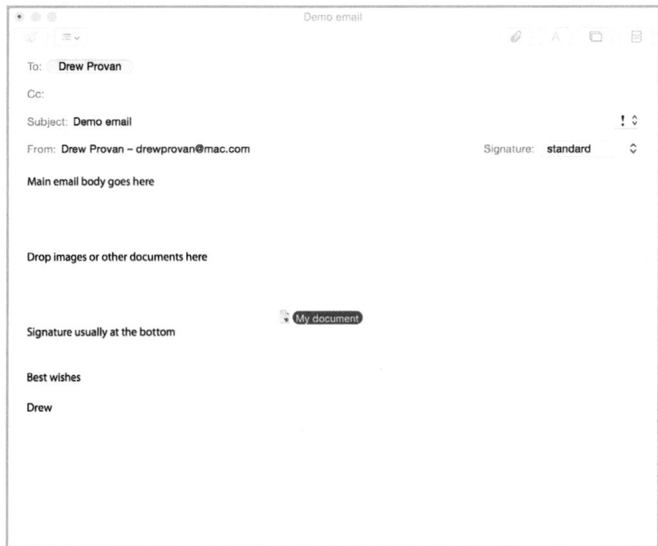

2 Or click the **paperclip** icon and locate the file you want to send

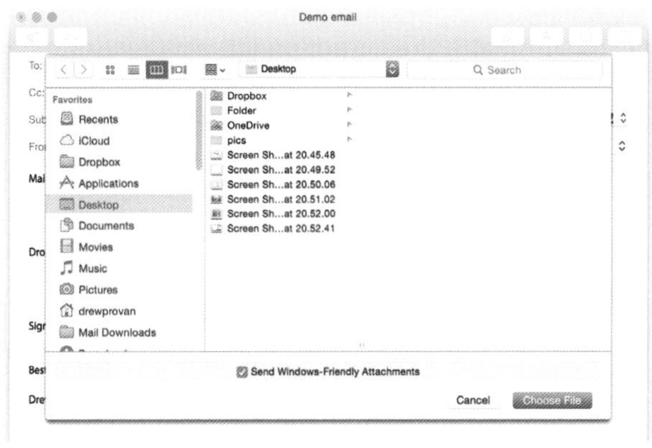

Receive Email Attachments

People often send you email containing attachments. Sometimes you can see the attached file in the email, e.g. photos. However, you may need to download the attachment first and then open it.

You can tell an email contains an attachment from the paperclip icon in the email window.

You can change the way Mail sends you notifications by going to System Preferences > Notifications and selecting Mail.

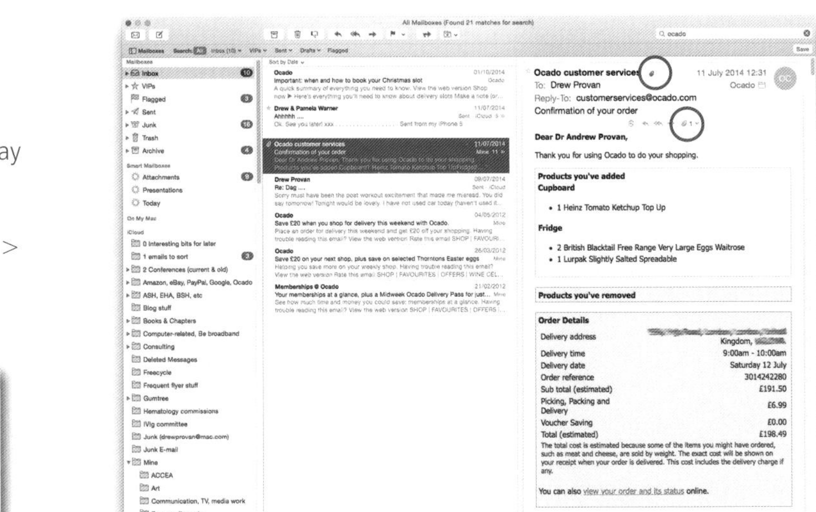

Click the **Save** dropdown to save the attachment:

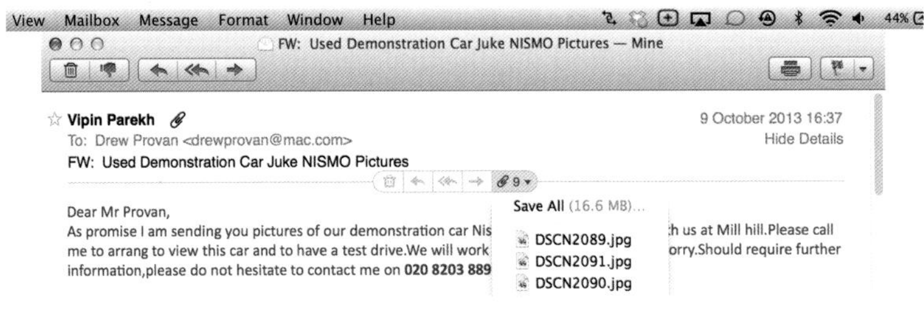

Reading Emails

All your emails will be listed in the middle pane of the email window. If you click on one email its contents will be shown in the rightmost pane. You can quickly read through your emails by moving up and down through the middle pane using the up and down arrow keys.

Reply to an email

1. Tap the **Reply** or the **Reply All** button on the mail toolbar
2. A reply window will open and the cursor will be at the top of the text area
3. Write your reply and hit **Send**

Click here to reply to sender

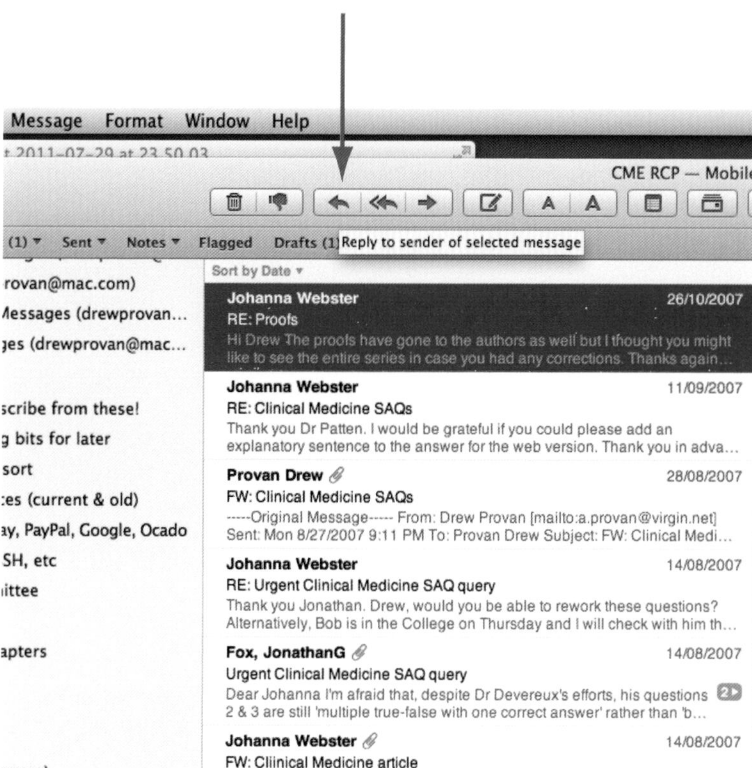

Message Format Window Help
CME RCP — Mobile
(1) Sent Notes Flagged Drafts (1)
Reply to sender of selected message
Sort by Date
rovan@mac.com)
Messages (drewprovan...
ges (drewprovan@mac...
scribe from these!
g bits for later
sort
tes (current & old)
ay, PayPal, Google, Ocado
SH, etc
nittee
apters
Johanna Webster 26/10/2007
RE: Proofs
Hi Drew The proofs have gone to the authors as well but I thought you might like to see the entire series in case you had any corrections. Thanks again...
Johanna Webster 11/09/2007
RE: Clinical Medicine SAQs
Thank you Dr Patten. I would be grateful if you could please add an explanatory sentence to the answer for the web version. Thank you in adva...
Provan Drew 28/08/2007
FW: Clinical Medicine SAQs
-----Original Message----- From: Drew Provan [mailto:a.provan@virgin.net] Sent: Mon 8/27/2007 9:11 PM To: Provan Drew Subject: FW: Clinical Medi...
Johanna Webster 14/08/2007
RE: Urgent Clinical Medicine SAQ query
Thank you Jonathan. Drew, would you be able to rework these questions? Alternatively, Bob is in the College on Thursday and I will check with him th...
Fox, JonathanG 14/08/2007
Urgent Clinical Medicine SAQ query
Dear Johanna I'm afraid that, despite Dr Devereux's efforts, his questions 2 & 3 are still 'multiple true-false with one correct answer' rather than 'b...
Johanna Webster 14/08/2007
FW: Cliinical Medicine article

Beware

Don't overuse the Reply All. It gets very wearing seeing dull emails endlessly circulated around a group.

Hot tip

You can go to the top of your Inbox list by clicking the sort bar at the top of the message list!

Mailbox Folders

Like snailmail, emails should be filed or trashed or your Inbox will become overloaded. You should develop a system where you can file your emails in mailboxes.

iCloud is cloud storage provided by Apple. The use of iCloud allows apps to sync across devices such as Mac, iPhone, iPad and iPod Touch.

Create mailboxes for storing emails. Don't leave them all in your Inbox!

Create mailboxes

1. In Apple Mail go to **Mailbox > New mailbox**

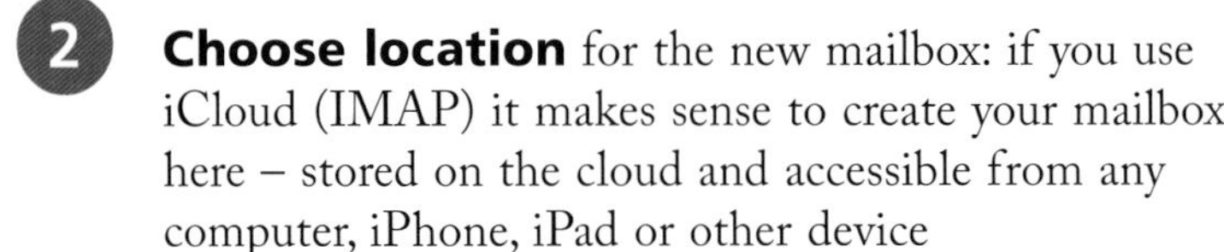

2. **Choose location** for the new mailbox: if you use iCloud (IMAP) it makes sense to create your mailbox here – stored on the cloud and accessible from any computer, iPhone, iPad or other device

3. Give the mailbox a **name,** e.g. Personal, Banking Holidays, Work, Family, etc.

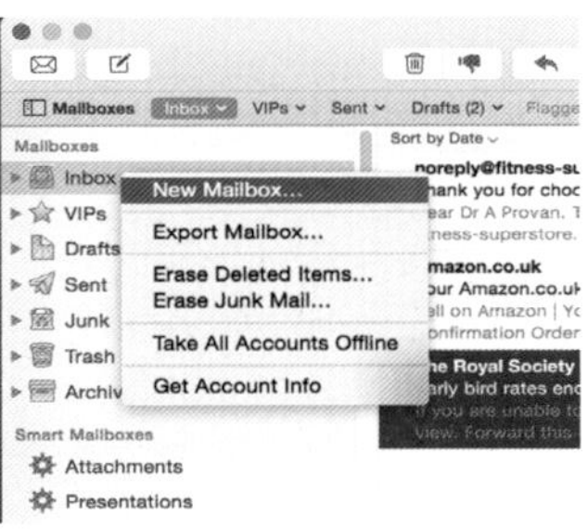

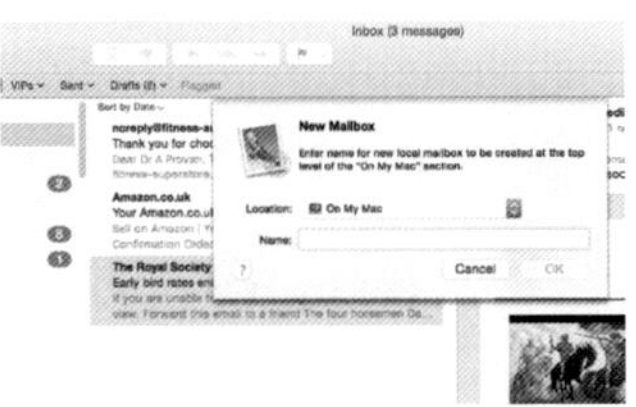

4. You can create as many mailboxes as you need (you can also create mailboxes within mailboxes)

5. Once created, file your emails!

Smart Mailboxes

If you regularly receive emails from your bank or other senders and you want to store these in a mailbox, you can drag them there or you can create a *rule*. The rule would tell Mail that any email from your bank (e.g. containing the address *hsbc.com*) gets moved to the Smart mailbox called Bank automatically. All the work is done for you by Mail.

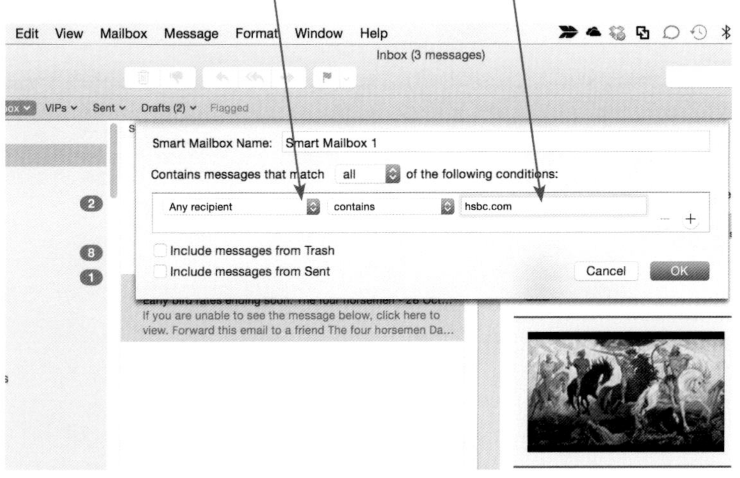

Smart Mailboxes do all the sorting for you!

This is similar to creating smart playlists in iTunes.

Using Markup to annotate a picture in an email

You can drop a picture into an email and annotate using the tools in Markup (text, arrows, circles, etc). Just drop a photo into the email, click once on the photo and then click the Markup menu. The Tools needed for marking up the image will be displayed.

You can now annotate images added to your emails using Markup.

Searching Mail

Search

The mail toolbar contains a search box at the top right. If you want to search for words within the email body, or for emails from a particular sender, type your search string into the search box.

You can select whether to search all your emails or just specific folders.

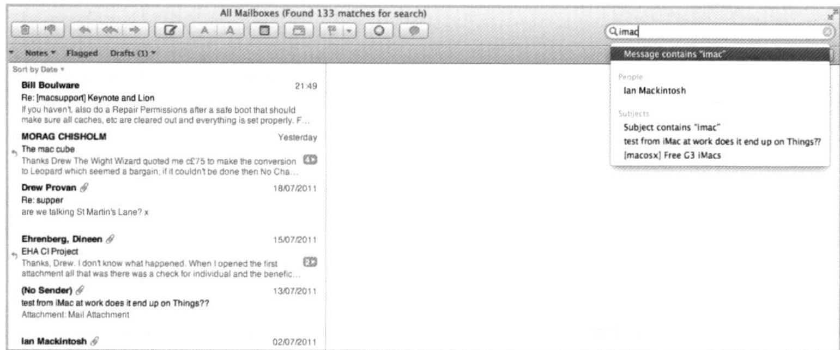

Flag emails

Sometimes you want to mark an email to read later. Apple Mail uses a system of colored flags which can be applied to emails.

These will then be moved to the flagged email mailbox making it easy for you to review these emails at a later time.

Flag your emails so you can easily find them later.

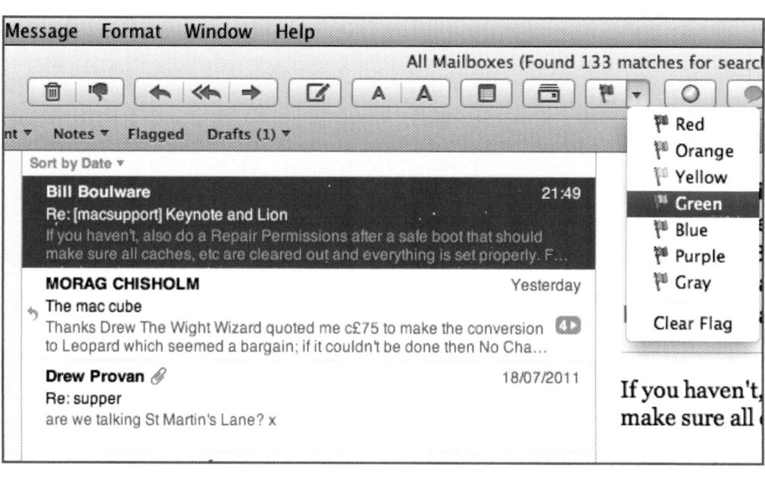

Change Fonts and Colors

If you do not like the default fonts or colors you can change these by:

1. Going to **Mail Preferences**

2. Selecting **Fonts & Colors**
3. You can change the message list font, the message font, the note font, and the fixed width font. You can also change the color of the quoted text

Adding a signature to your email

You can add a signature (usually your name along with some contact details) by hand with every email, or you can set up a signature and have that added automatically at the end of your emails.

1. Go to **Mail > Preferences > Signatures**
2. Click the **+** button and enter your signature text in the window

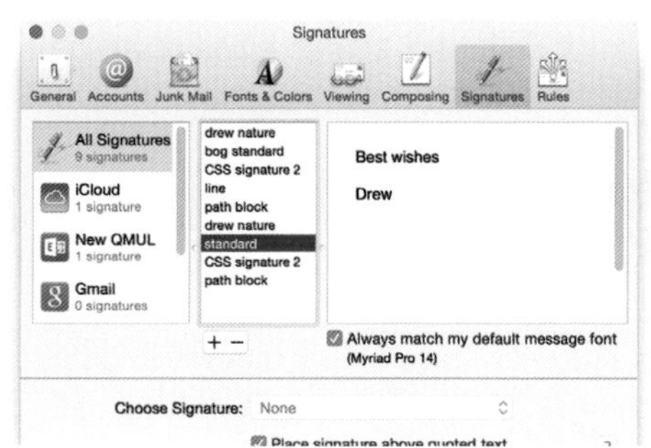

3. Assign it to email accounts by dragging the signature onto the account name

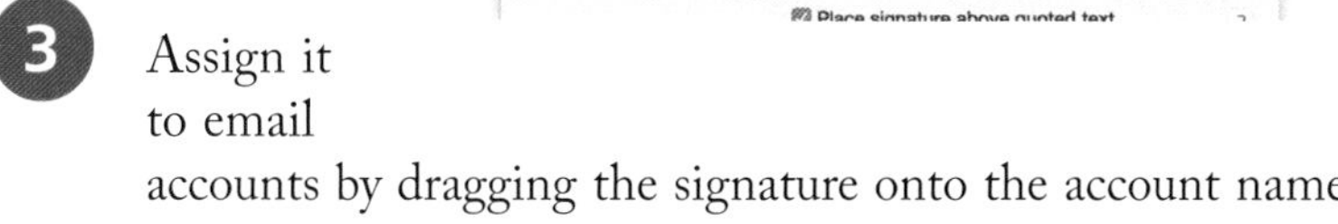

Set up at least one signature for your email to avoid having to type this in every time.

VIP List

If you want to make sure the emails from your boss or partner (for instance) are easy to find, you can make them VIPs. This marks their emails as VIP as they are received and places them neatly in a special folder in Mail called **VIPs**.

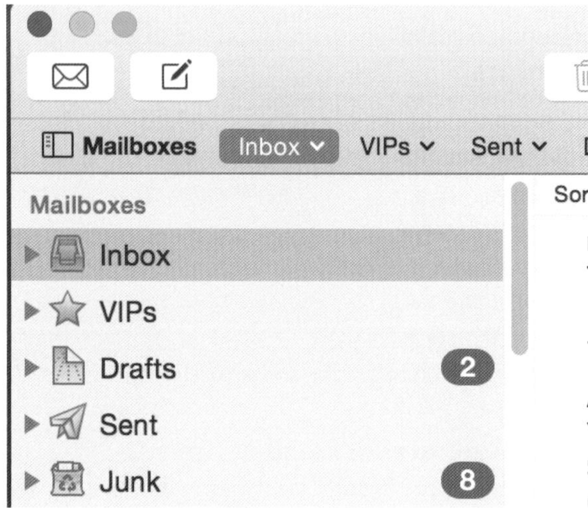

Add a VIP

1. Open an email from the person you want to add to the VIP list

2. **Click on their email address** and select **Add to VIPs** from the dropdown list

3. All emails from that address will be added to the VIPs mailbox automatically

5 Surf with Safari

Safari *is a full-featured web browser. It is clean and fast. OS X Yosemite brought even more features to* Safari, *and for the majority of Mac users,* Safari *is the only browser you will need.*

Go on Safari

Yosemite has brought with it a brand new version of the Safari browser. There have been some layout changes but it remains a fast and easy browser to use.

Layout of Safari window

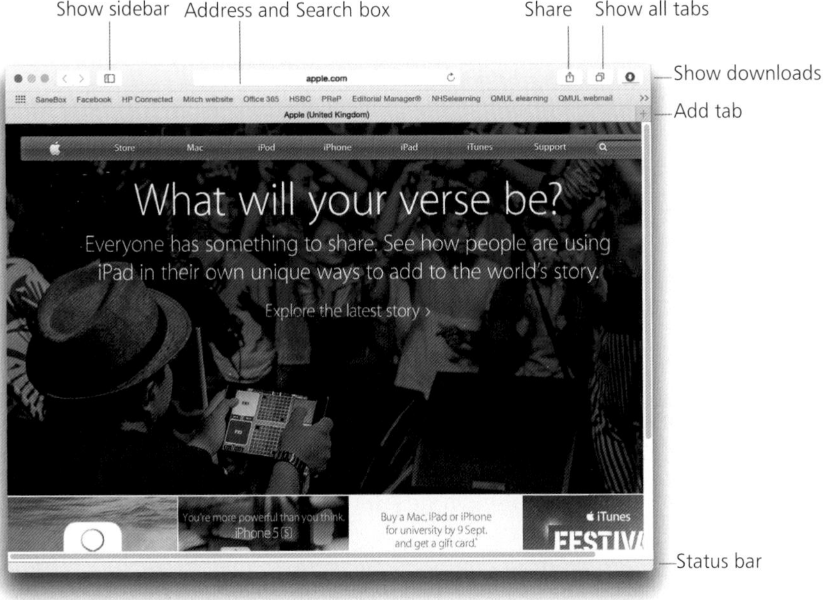

Like Google Chrome, Safari now has a unified search and address box.

Set Homepage

You may not want Safari to open at Apple's Homepage each time you launch the program.

1. Go to file **Preferences > General**
2. Where it says **Homepage:** delete the Apple URL (*Uniform Resource Locator*, i.e. a web address) and enter the URL of the page you want to see when you start Safari

You can change the Homepage (i.e. the web page that opens when you launch Safari) to anything you want.

Full-Screen Browsing

The Safari window can either float on your desktop, which is the standard mode for most computers, or you can make Safari fill the entire screen. *Note*: most programs can be used in full-screen mode.

Activate full-screen mode

1. With the Safari window open, click the green button at the top left of the window

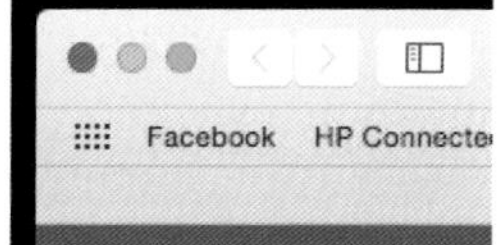

Deactivate full-screen mode

1. Press **Esc**

To exit full-screen mode in any program tap the Esc key.

Switch between pages

1. **Swipe** Left or Right using **two fingers**

Zoom in/out

1. **Double-tap** with two fingers
2. Or **stretch** to zoom in or **pinch** to zoom out

How to exit full-screen browsing

1. Type **Esc**

Use DuckDuckGo if you want your browsing to be private.

Private browsing

Safari provides more secure browsing using DuckDuckGo as its search engine. To use this go to **Safari > Preferences > Search**.

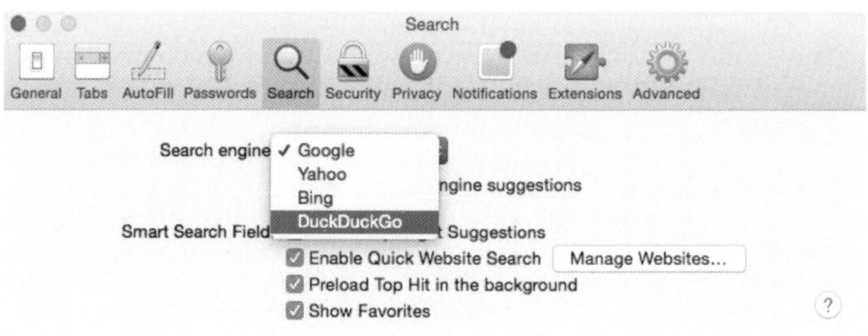

Reading List

In the past, if you wanted to save a page to read later you had to save this as a bookmark. With OS X Yosemite, the latest version of Safari allows you to save pages to a Reading List. This means your pages are easy to find, and it also avoids cluttering up your Bookmark list.

Save page to reading list

1. Go to **Bookmarks > Add to Reading List**
2. Or type **Shift + ⌘ + D**
3. Or go to Share icon (top right) and clilck **Add to Reading List**

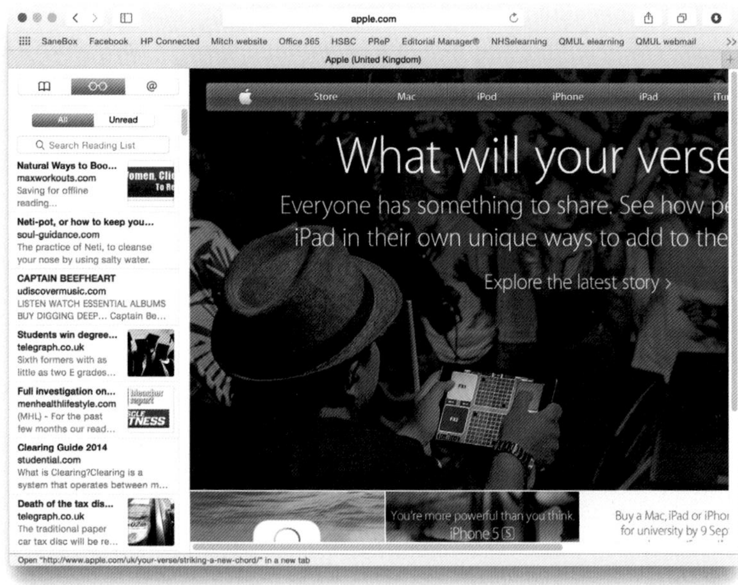

Search the Internet

Safari has a search box at the top right of the window. Google is the default search engine but you can change this to Yahoo! or Bing.

Changing the search engine from Preferences

1. Open Safari and go to **File > Preferences**
2. Go to the **Search** tab
3. Change from Google to Yahoo! or Bing

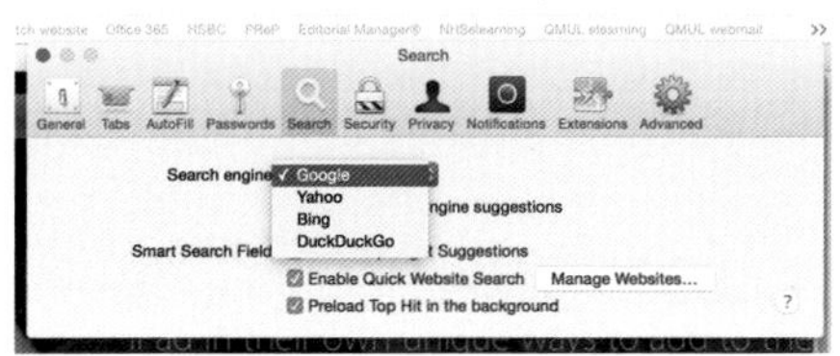

You can switch from Google to Yahoo! or Bing as your search engine.

Bookmarks

It is a good idea to keep the sites you visit frequently as bookmarks. These can be stored in the Bookmarks Menu or on the Bookmarks Bar – this gives you fast access to frequently-visited sites.

To save current page as bookmark

1. Go to **Bookmarks > Add Bookmark...**
2. Or type ⌘ **+ D**
3. When you see **Add Bookmark** click the dropdown menu and choose from the options **Favorites** or **Bookmarks Menu**
4. Navigate to the folder where you want to store the bookmark and the bookmark will be saved there

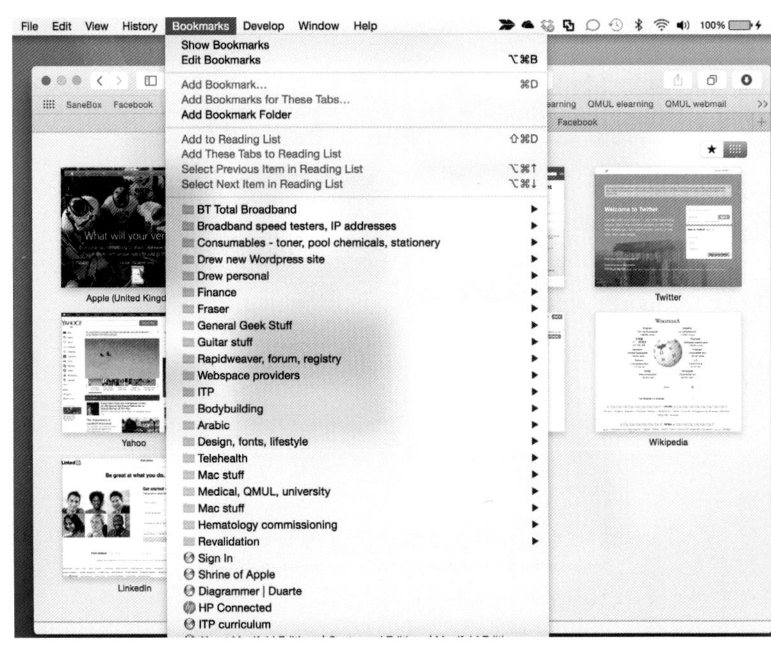

Organizing Bookmarks

Much like email, you need to create folders for your bookmarks so you can save your bookmarks according to topic, e.g. Personal, Music, Fitness, etc.

Organize bookmarks

1. Go to **Bookmarks > Edit Bookmarks**
2. Or type **Option + ⌘ + B**
3. Click on the **Bookmarks Menu** in the left pane
4. To add a new folder click **+**
5. Enter the name for the new folder

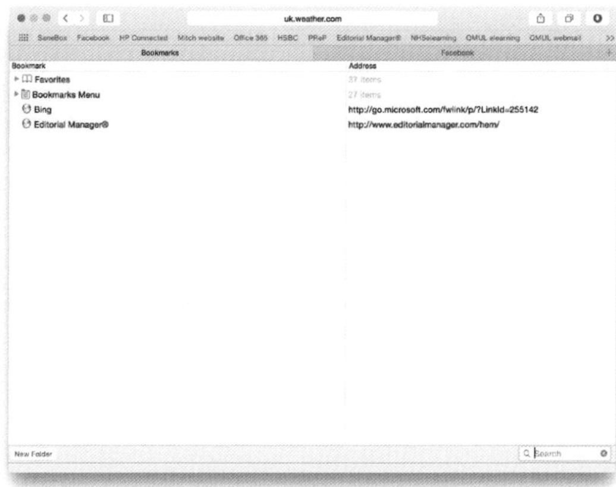

Organize your Bookmarks or you'll end up with a huge list of disorganized links! Make folders for different topics.

Deleting bookmarks folders

1. Type **Option + ⌘ + B**
2. Use the delete key to remove the folder you wish to remove

Importing Bookmarks

You may have been using another browser, Mac or PC and want to import all your previously-saved bookmarks.

Import bookmarks

1. Using your previous browser, export your bookmarks (for most browsers this is achieved by going to **File > Export Bookmarks...** and saving this file to the desktop)

2. On your new Mac open Safari and go to **File > Import From**

3. Find the export file you made previously and click **Import**

Use iCloud to sync all your bookmarks across your devices (see page 188).

Browsing Using Tabs

Tabs represent different web pages and make browsing multiple pages faster and much easier. Each page is represented by a separate tab at the top of the Safari window.

You can jump from page to page quickly by clicking on the various tabs.

To open a new tab

1. Go to **File > New Tab**
2. Or type **⌘ + T**
3. A new tab will appear

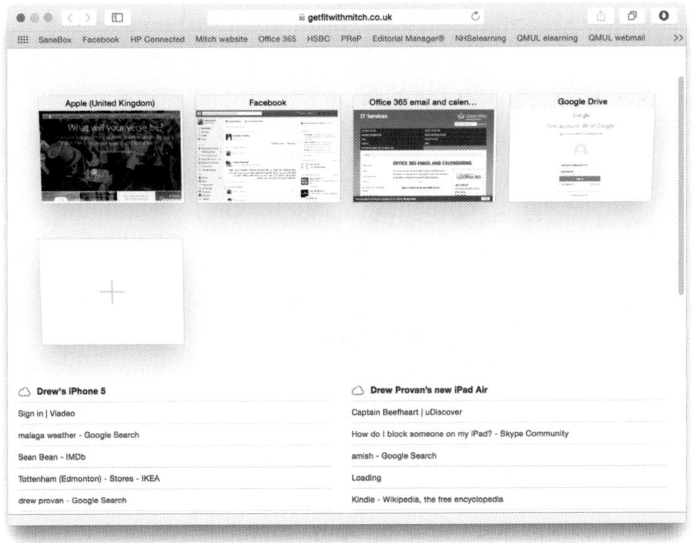

Use Tab View

1. Click the Tab view icon

Making Browsing Secure

Browsing the web involves interacting with various websites, accepting cookies and pop-up windows. When you go online you leave a trail which can potentially make you vulnerable to attacks by hackers.

Safari makes it very easy to clean up your browsing history, cookies and other items.

Don't forget

Cookies are small files from a website which enable the site to remember you. Pop-up windows are built into some websites. These do not require you to click anything; they simply pop up on their own.

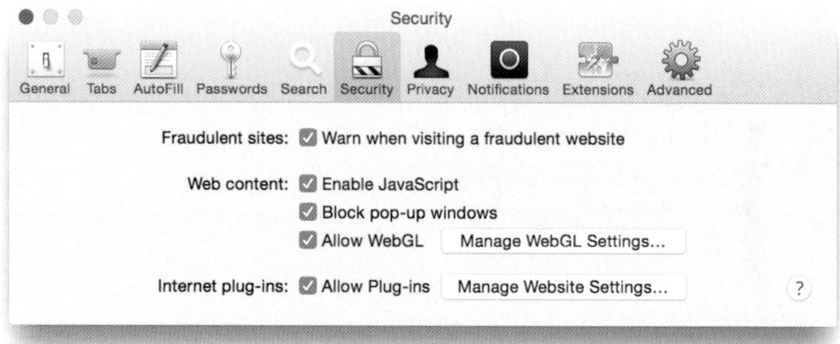

Reset Safari (see page 217) from time to time to clear out temporary files and delete cookies!

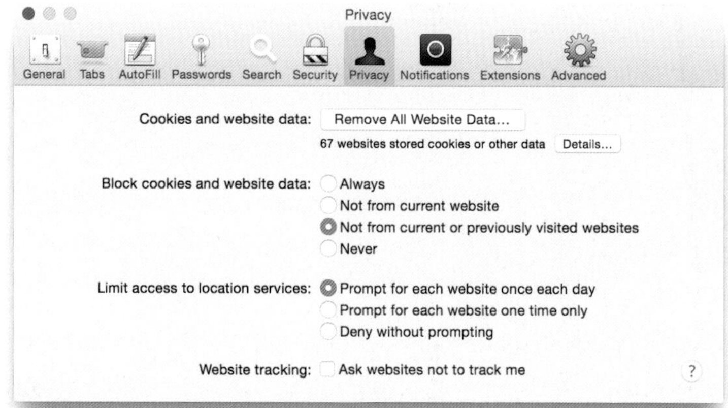

6 Calendars and Contacts

We all keep diaries and contact lists. The apps Calendar *and* Contacts *integrate well. In this chapter we will look at how best to use these so you get the most out of the apps.*

Calendar

Calendar is the Mac OS X calendar program. You can create events (appointments), set alarms, and add recurring events. You can also add appointments to Calendar directly from Mail.

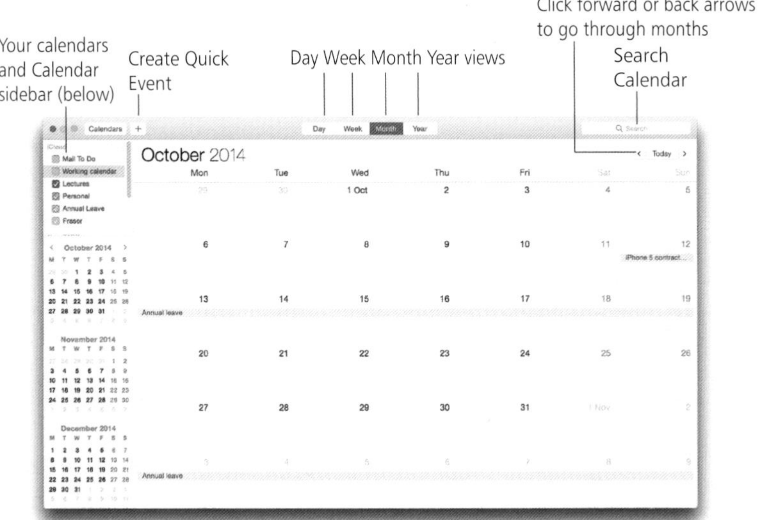

Set your default calendar

If you have more than one calendar you can tell Calendar which one should be used for new events.

You can also set up the first day of the week, day start and end time, as well as default time for event alerts.

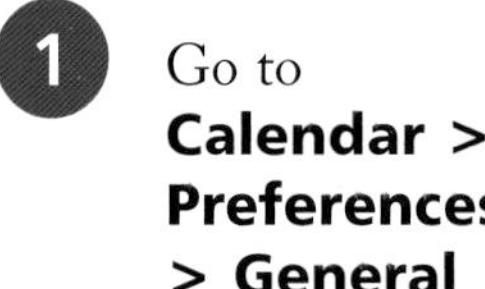

1. Go to **Calendar > Preferences > General**

Calendar Views

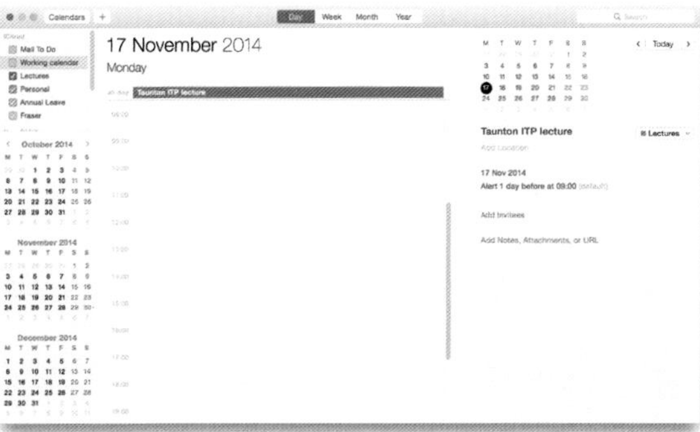

Calendar Day view

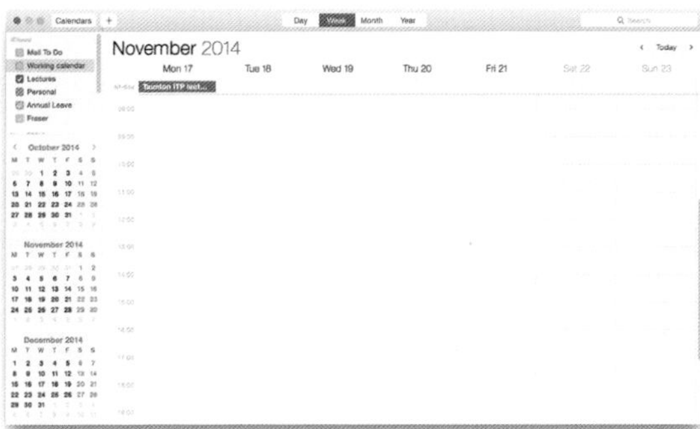

Calendar Week view

Calendar Year view

Add an Event

1. **Open Calendar**
2. **Double-click** on the date of the event
3. A new event window will open
4. **Add details** of event
5. Make sure the start and end dates are correct
6. **Add the time** if necessary
7. If recurrent (e.g. birthday) click the **repeat** dropdown menu and select **every year**
8. Add **invitees** if you want to send email invites
9. If the appointment is an all-day appointment, check the **all-day** box
10. If you have multiple calendars (e.g. Work, Home) ensure the event is assigned to the correct calendar

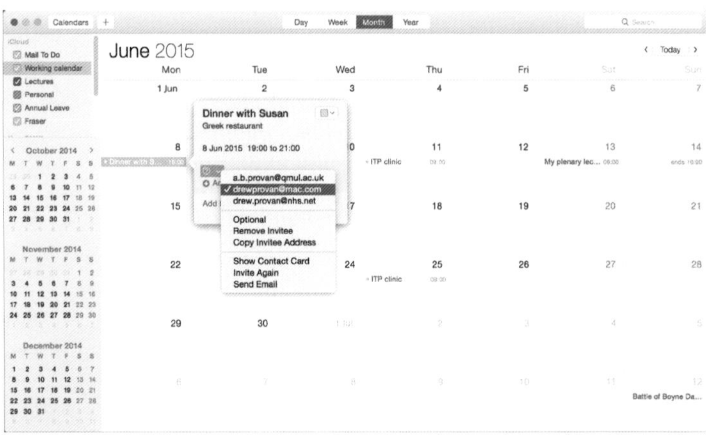

Edit an Event

1. **Double-click the event**
2. Or click once on the event then type **+ ⌘ + E**

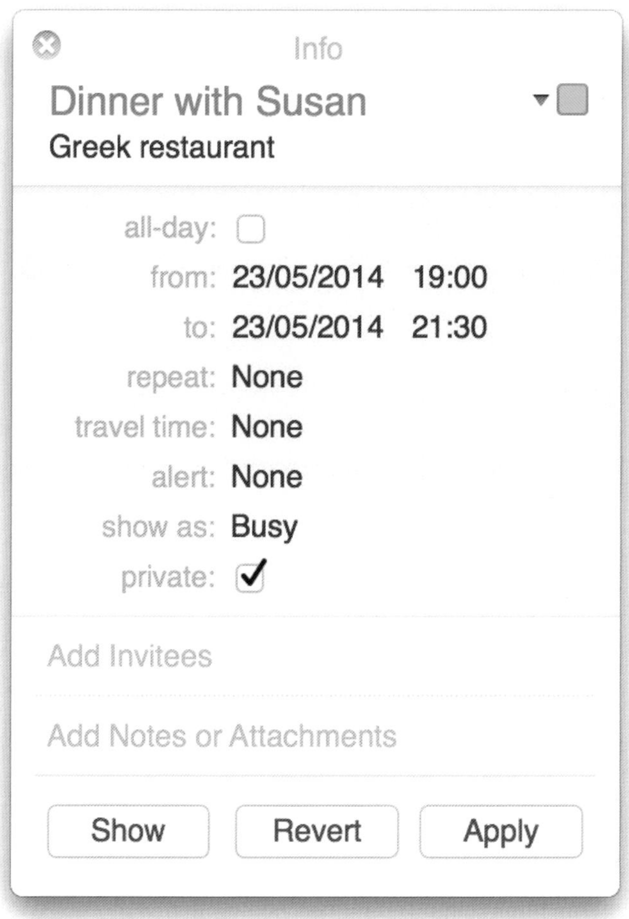

Create Quick Event

You can create an event quickly by clicking on the + symbol at the top left of the Calendar view:

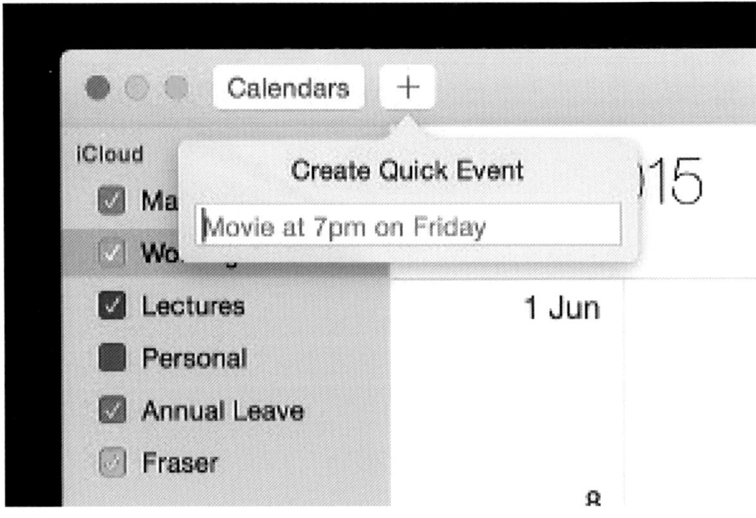

Hot tip

Events can be dragged around the calendar to different days and times.

Add location

If you add a postcode or zip code or even a description of the location, Calendar will find it and show you a map of where you are going.

NEW

Calendar will now show you a map of your location if you provide an address or ZIP code.

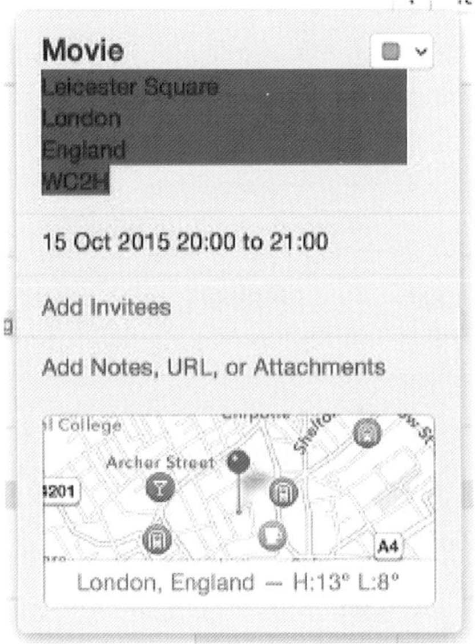

Multiple Calendars

What is the point of having multiple calendars? You may want separate calendars for work and home. You can add almost as many calendars as you want. Multiple calendars are useful if you want to print off or view only work-related events or home-related events.

Add new calendar

1. **File > New Calendar**
2. Or type **Option + ⌘ + N**

Personalize your calendars

1. Click **Calendars** on the toolbar
2. Select a calendar
3. **Right-click** on the one you want to change
4. Select **Get Info**
5. You can **rename** and change the **color**
6. You can also use this window to **publish** a calendar online (e.g. let work colleagues view the calendar)

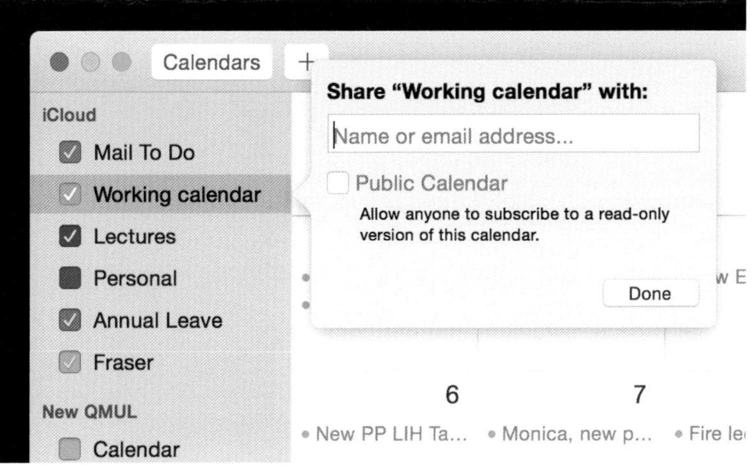

Sending Invites

If you are setting up an appointment where other people need to attend, you can send invites to people who are in the Contacts. If you want to invite people who are not in the Contacts you can simply type their email address into the invitees box.

To send an invite

1. Edit the event (**double-click** then edit or use the Inspector)
2. Click the box next to **invitees**
3. Enter the first name or the surname, and a list of names from those in your Contacts will appear
4. Choose the correct email address
5. For multiple invitees, separate these with a comma
6. Click **Send** and the invite will be sent

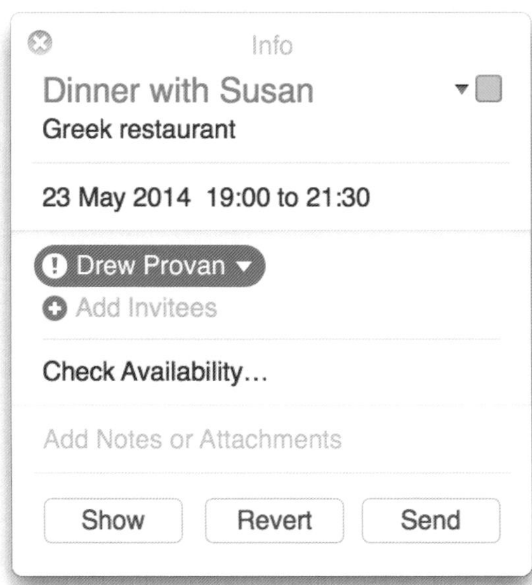

Searching Calendar

If you want to search Calendar but you have many appointments it is generally easier to let Calendar find them rather than trying to find them manually.

1. Go to **search box** at the top right of the Calendar window
2. Enter the search term
3. The results will be displayed at the bottom of the Calendar window

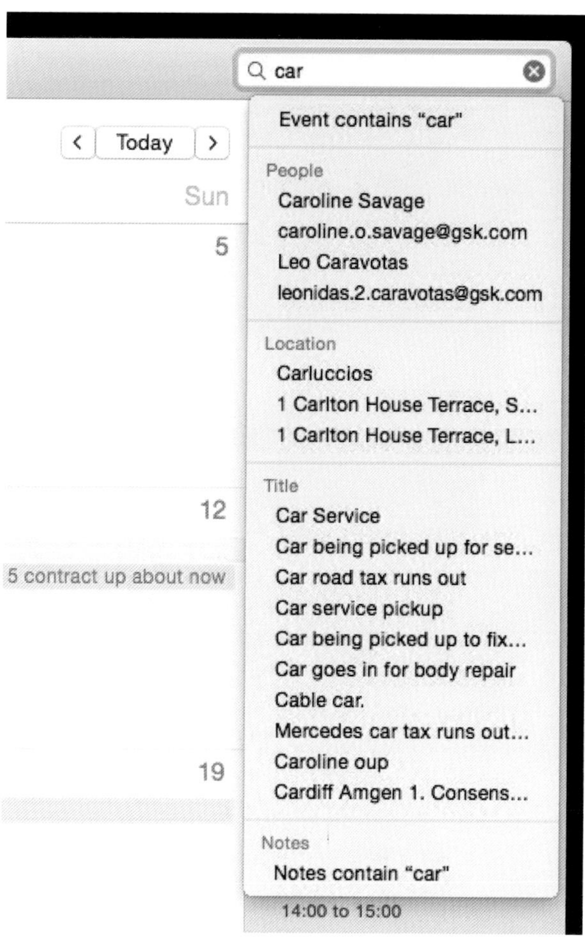

Contacts

With OS X Yosemite, Contacts has been completely redesigned to look very much like Contacts on the iPad.

Make sure the Address Format is correct

Your address layout may be incorrect unless you tell Contacts which country you are in.

1. Go to **Contacts > Preferences > General**

2. Use dropdown menu next to **Address Format** to specify your country

Check the address format before you add contacts, or the address format may be incorrect for your country.

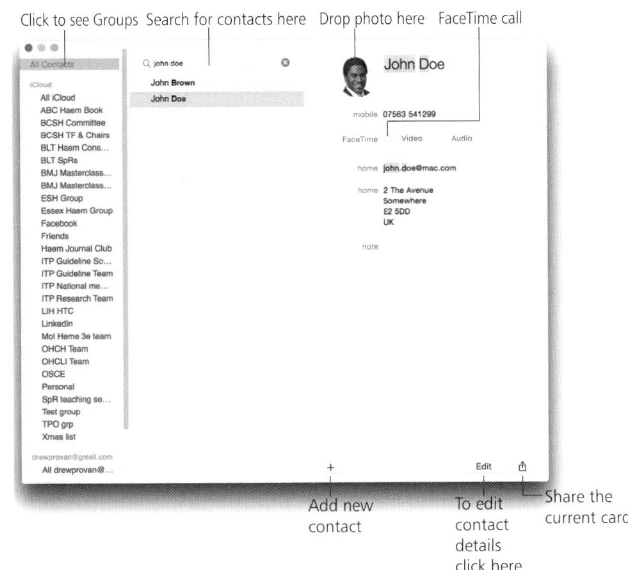

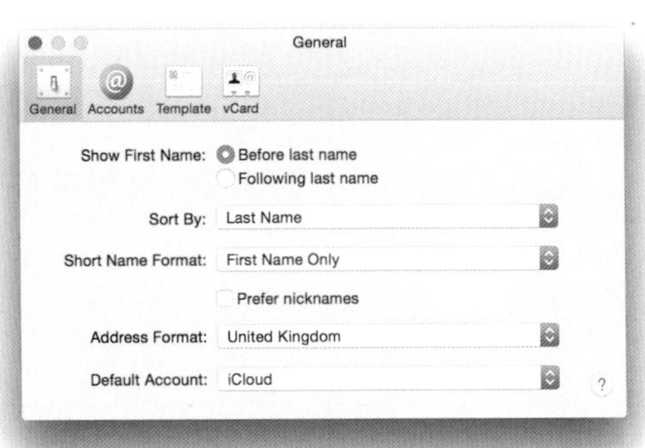

Add a New Contact

1. Go to **File > New Contact**
2. Or type ⌘ **+ N**
3. Enter the contact's first and last names
4. Enter company name if necessary
5. Enter phone numbers – home, work, mobile – you can change the order of these by using the dropdowns, e.g. change mobile to work if you want the phone numbers listed in a different order to the default
6. Add one or more email addresses
7. Add work or home addresses
8. You can **add a photo** by dragging a picture onto the photo box
9. When complete, click **Done**
10. To edit a contact's details click **Edit**
11. To email your contact details to someone else click **Share**

Add a photo to your most popular contacts.

Remove a contact

1. Select the name of the contact you wish to delete
2. Use the **Delete** key
3. Or go to **Edit > Delete Card**

Add a Contact From Email

If you want to add someone who has emailed you to your contacts

1. In Mail, **click once on the email** from the person
2. Go to **Message > Add Sender to Contacts**
3. To edit their details, click **Edit**

Send Again	⇧⌘D
Reply	⌘R
Reply All	⇧⌘R
Forward	⇧⌘F
Forward as Attachment	
Redirect	⇧⌘E
Mark	▶
Flag	▶
Archive	^⌘A
Move to	▶
Copy to	▶
Move Again	⌥⌘T
Apply Rules	⌥⌘L
Add Sender to Contacts	

Contacts Groups

Sometimes you want to email a group of people on a regular basis. Rather than adding each person's email address to the email it is much easier to make a group, add their names to the group and simply email the group each time.

1. Go to **File > New Group**
2. **Name** the Group
3. Add contacts to the group by clicking All Contacts at the top of the Contacts, then go through your list of contacts and **drag them onto the group** you have just created

7 Photos and Videos

iPhoto, iMovie *and* DVD Player *make it fun to create and share movies. We will look at how to import still photos and movies into their respective programs, then have a look at how we can share these with our friends and family.*

Programs for Viewing Photos

The Mac has a number of inbuilt programs for viewing photos:

- iPhoto
- Preview
- Image Capture

Other programs can also be used to view photos:

- Safari (see page 66)
- TextEdit (see page 33)

With these programs you may need to drop the photo onto an open Safari or TextEdit window or you can right-click the photo and choose **Open with...** then choose **Other...**

Image capture will let you view photos if you connect an iPhone or digital camera to your Mac

Safari and other browsers will let you view photos and movies – just drop them onto a Safari window

Preview is a fast photo app with some editing facilities

iPhoto

This program comes with OS X and is the default photo (image) viewing and editing program. It is not as powerful as Apple Aperture or Adobe Photoshop but has sufficient options for most people.

iPhoto probably has enough editing tools for most users.

You can use iPhoto to

- Import your photos
- Create albums
- Edit your photos (Crop, Rotate, Straighten, and other functions)
- Create slideshows and books which you can upload to Apple to be made into printed photo albums

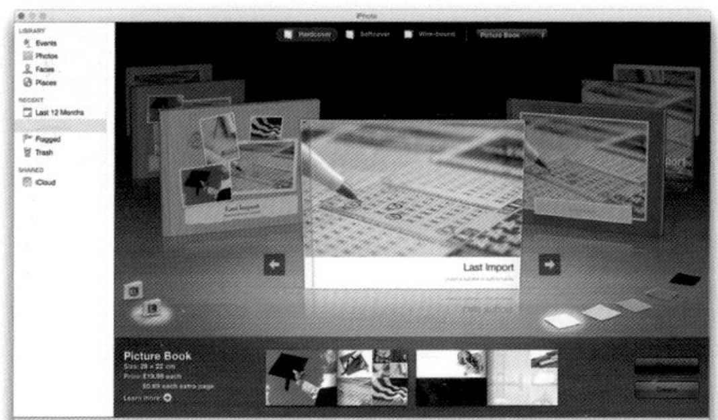

Click the Share icon to share your photos by email, Facebook and other sharing options.

- You can also create Calendars or cards

Opening iPhoto

You will find iPhoto in the Applications folder or you can use Launchpad.

1. After opening iPhoto you will be asked a few questions to see whether you want to import your photos every time you connect a digital camera, allow iPhoto to use geotagging so you can see where your photos were taken, and other options

2. Answer **Yes** or **No** to these questions (in general it is better to answer Yes)

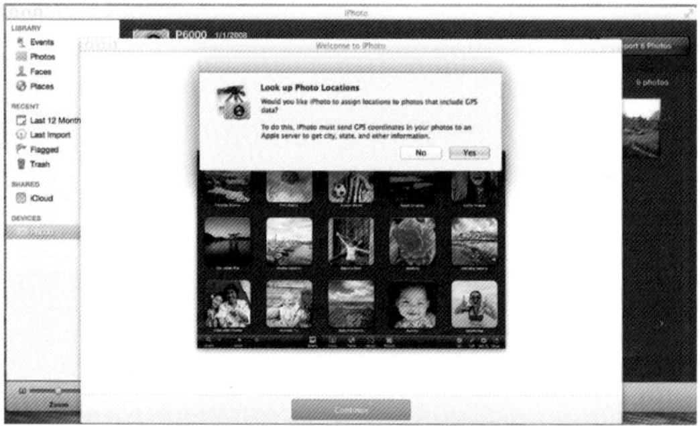

3. iPhoto will then open and you will see a layout similar to the one shown below

Importing Photos

You can import using several methods:

- **Attach a digital camera** to the USB port
- **Insert an SD card** into an SD card reader

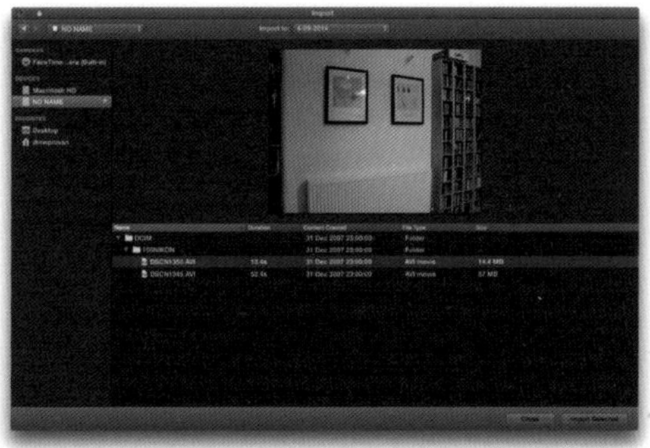

- You can also copy photos from an external drive, including **USB, CD or DVD**
- You can **drag photos** from any folder on your Mac onto the iPhoto window

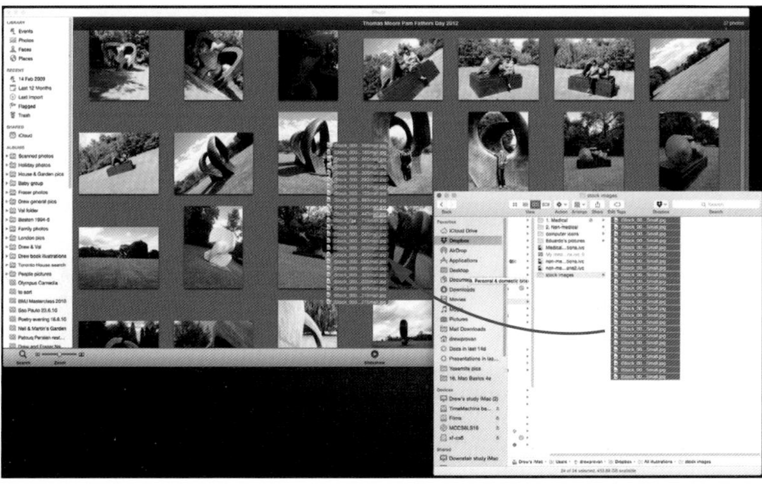

- You can also import using **File > Import to Library...**

Create a New Album

Once you have your photos imported it is best to create albums so you can keep related photos together. Otherwise you will have to scroll through hundreds of photos to find the ones you want.

1. Go to **File > New Album**

2. Change the name from **untitled album** to something more meaningful

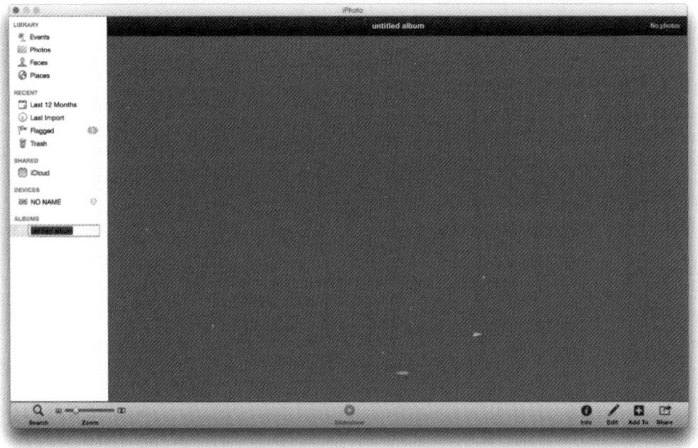

You can share your photos across all your devices including iOS devices if you switch on Photo Stream in the iCloud System Preference.

Sorting photos into albums

1. View the album by **clicking on the album name**

2. Only the photos within that album will be shown in the main window on the right

Viewing all photos

1. Click **Photos** in the left-hand pane and all photos are shown

View events

1. A collection of photos imported together are grouped into an event. The event will initially be shown as a date that you can change to something more useful such as Holiday 2014

Editing Photos

1. **Double-click** a photo – the photo will open and occupy the main window

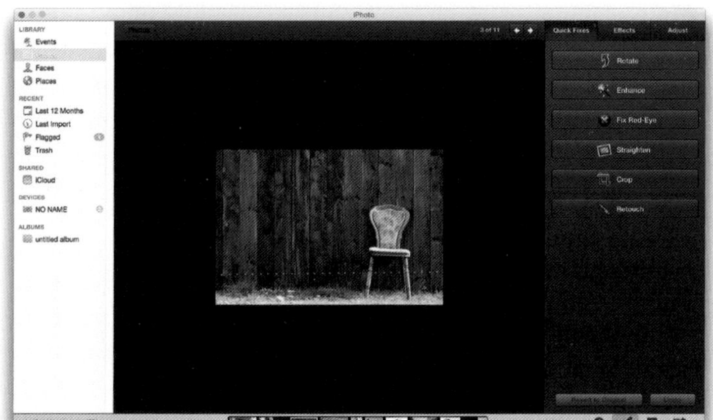

2. Click **Edit** and make changes (rotate, fix red-eye, etc.)
3. **Double-click** the photo when finished
4. Check out the Effects and Adjust options too

Viewing iPhoto in full-screen

1. With iPhoto open, click the full-screen icon (green button to left of window)

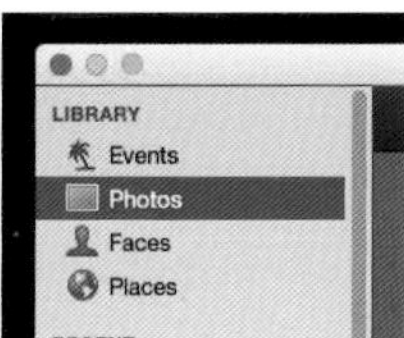

2. iPhoto will now fill the screen
3. To return to normal view tap **Escape**

Videos on the Mac

The Mac is great for viewing videos, and using software that comes with OS X Yosemite you can create your own movies using iMovie. There are other programs on your Mac that can play video, including:

- DVD Player
- QuickTime Player
- iTunes
- You can also drop movies onto a Safari (or any browser) window and play them there

iMovie comes as standard with OS X and is a great app for editing your movies

DVD Player is the default app for viewing commercial DVDs

QuickTime Player is a versatile app for viewing movies. You can also use the program to record screencasts (movies of your screen, e.g. if you want to make a screen demo)

iTunes is the portal for music and movie purchase, but the program can also be used to view movies you have added to its library or purchased from the iTunes Store

DVD Player

Insert a commercial DVD into the optical drive of your Mac. DVD Player will recognize that you have inserted a movie DVD and will open and play the movie.

You will be prompted to accept the DVD region for that disc.

- If you are in North America you should make sure the **Region Code is 1**
- If you are in Europe the **Region Code should be 2**
- The Mac *cannot* be made multi-region, i.e. you cannot play discs from different regions
- You can only change the Region Code **5 times** and from then on the region code remains fixed at that region permanently

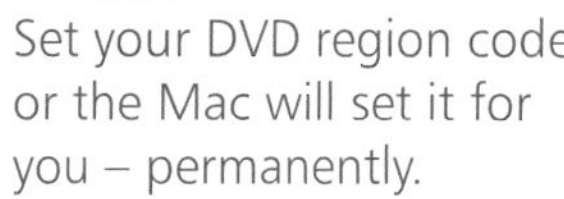

Set your DVD region code or the Mac will set it for you – permanently.

Editing Your Own Movies

You can import your home movies into iMovie and then edit them here.

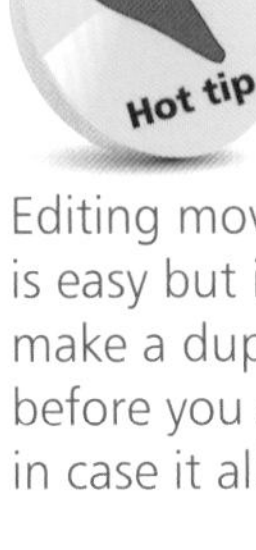

Editing movies in iMovie is easy but it's best to make a duplicate copy before you start editing in case it all goes wrong!

Import movie

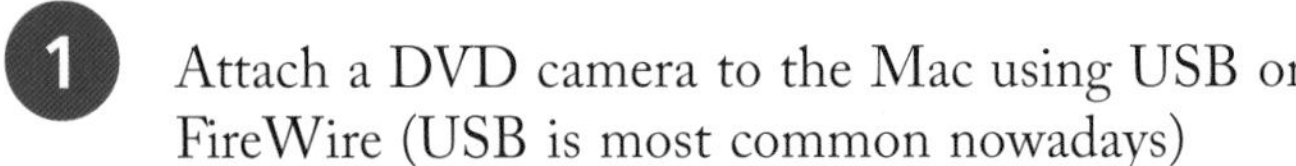

1. Attach a DVD camera to the Mac using USB or FireWire (USB is most common nowadays)

2. **Open iMovie**

3. Import the video by clicking **Open Camera Import Window**

4. Or go to **File > Import from Camera...**

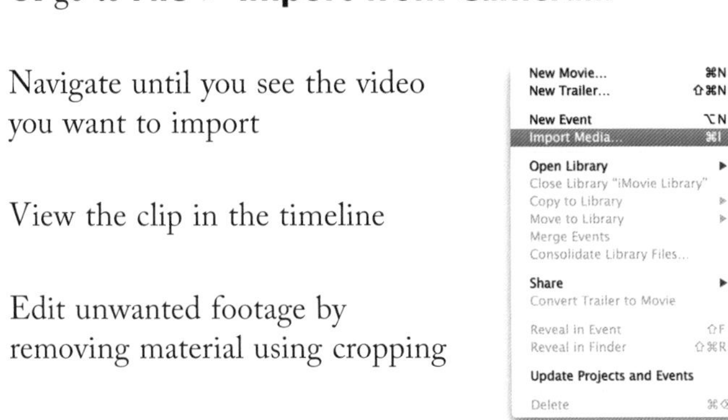

5. Navigate until you see the video you want to import
6. View the clip in the timeline
7. Edit unwanted footage by removing material using cropping
8. Save the movie project (this file will not be playable yet), add titles and other effects such as scrolling titles to the movie using the **Title** window options

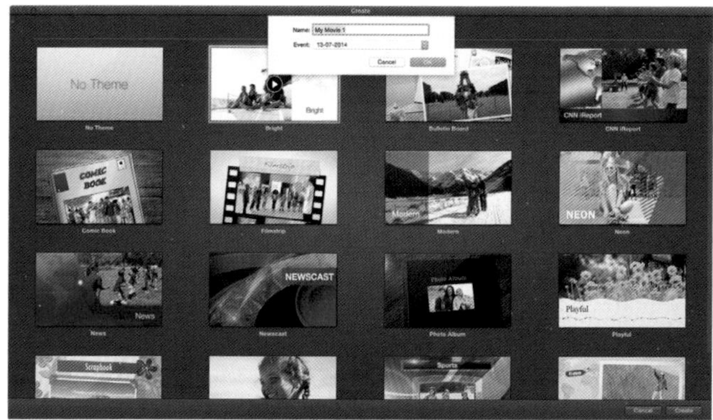

Select theme for the new project

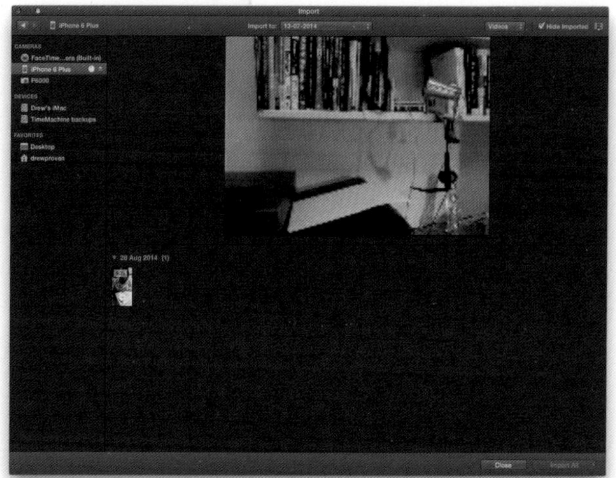

Importing video from an iPhone

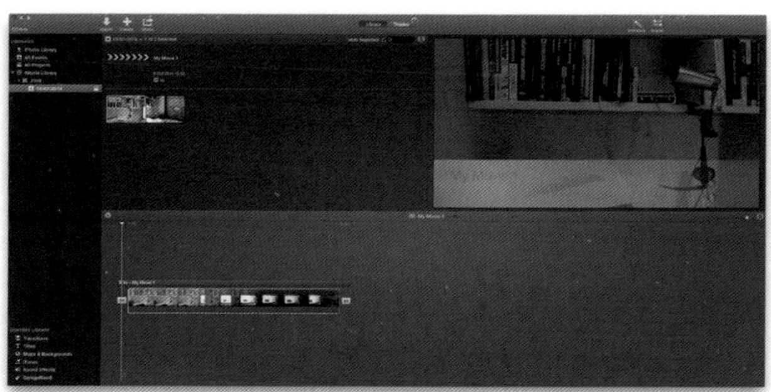

Drag the bars on left and right to crop and perform other edits

Sharing Your Movie

Once complete, you will want to export your movie onto a DVD or file so that others can appreciate your efforts!

Apple makes movie-sharing easy from within iMovie.

1. If you are happy with your video, audio, theme, credits, etc. click **File > Finalize Project**
2. iMovie will create an HD 1080p movie
3. You can then export this in a large number of optimized formats, e.g. YouTube, Facebook, and others
4. Or you can save in a format that iDVD will recognize and play

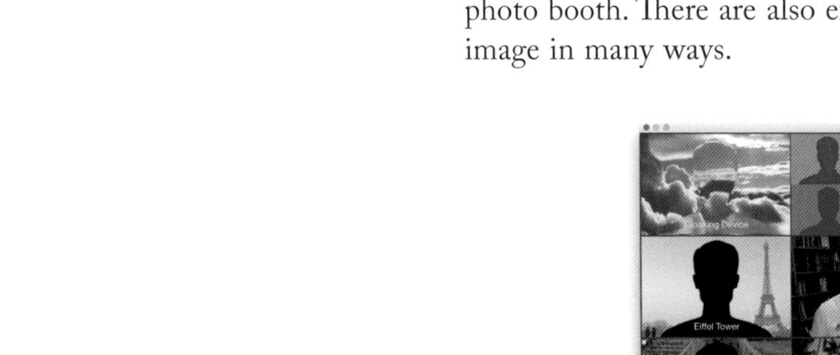

Photo Booth

This app lets you take passport-type pictures similar to a real photo booth. There are also effects which distort and change the image in many ways.

8 The World of iTunes

iTunes *is at the heart of every Mac and iOS device like the iPhone, iPad, and iPod Touch. It's worth spending time learning to navigate your way around the* iTunes *interface, since so many other functions rely on it.*

What is iTunes?

iTunes is an app that is the central hub for iPhone, iPad, and iPod integration, purchasing and playing music, films, podcasts, and other content.

You can import your audio CDs. Genius will suggest other music based on your current iTunes library.

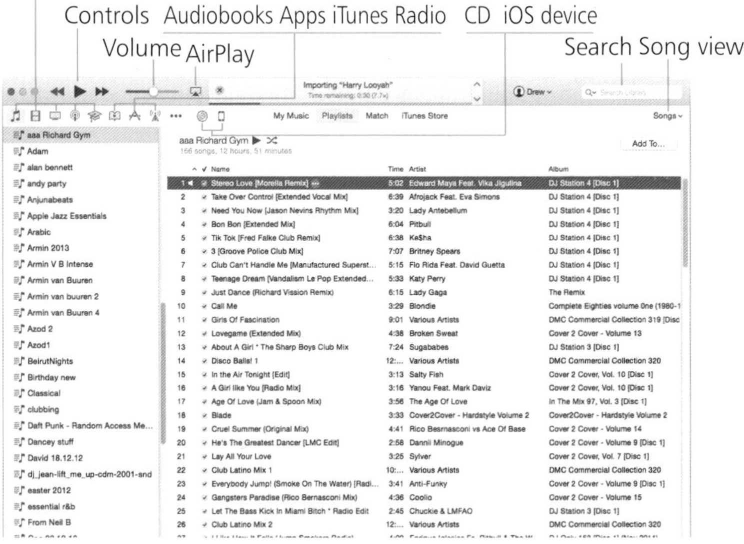

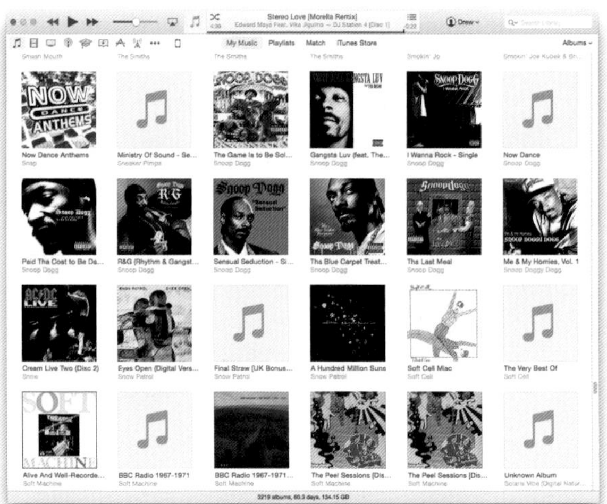

iTunes showing Album view

Importing Audio CDs

It is very easy to import your CDs into iTunes.

1. **Insert CD** into the optical drive
2. iTunes will show the CD contents
3. You will be asked "*Would you like to import the CD into your iTunes library?*"
4. Click **Yes** to import all
5. Or **uncheck** any tracks you do not want to import
6. iTunes will import tracks
7. You will hear a chime when the import is complete
8. **Eject the CD** by dragging to the Trash, or click the eject symbol in the left pane in the iTunes window

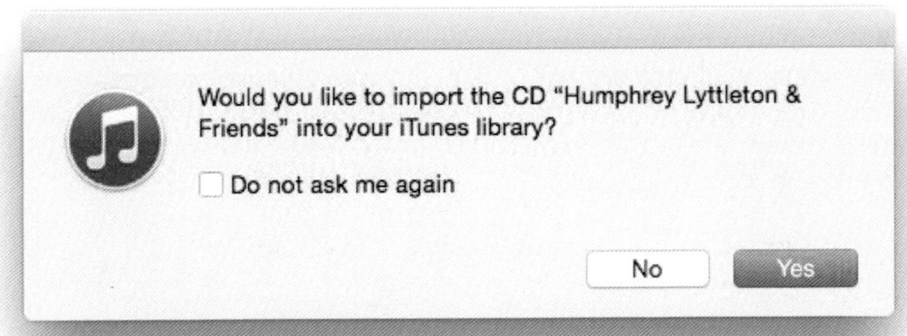

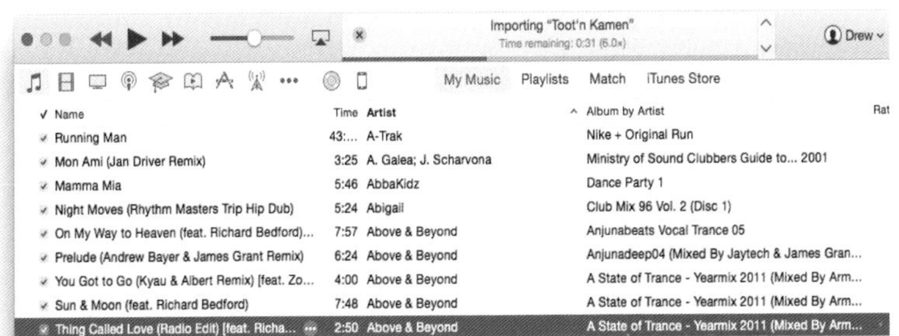

iTunes Preferences

It is worth checking out the preferences, since you can change the import formats and set up many other features within the Preferences section.

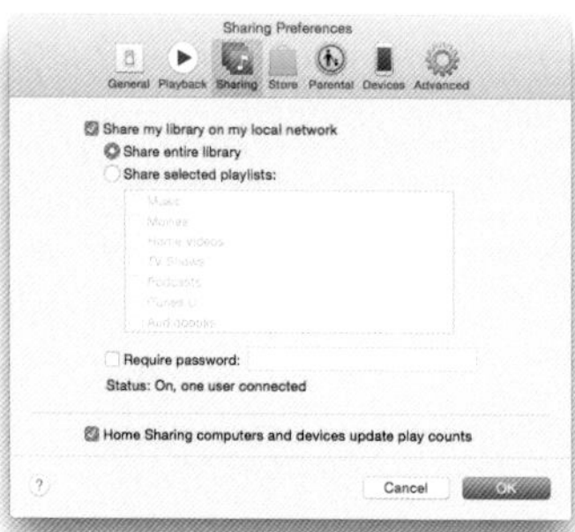

Select this if you intend to allow others to listen to your iTunes content

Controls iPod, iPhone, and iPad sync

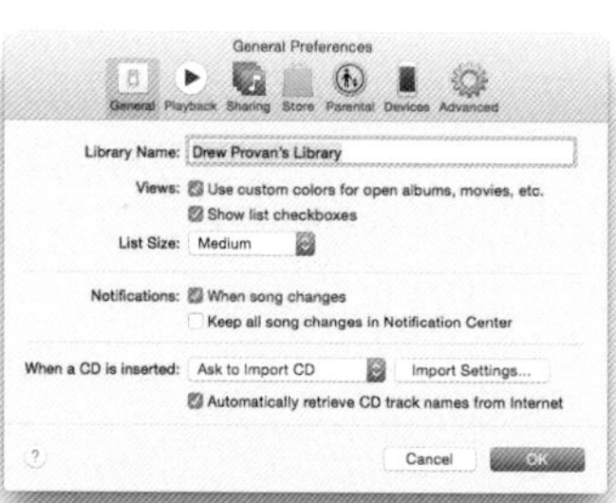

Tell iTunes what to show, e.g. Movies, TV shows, etc. – the default settings are fine for most people

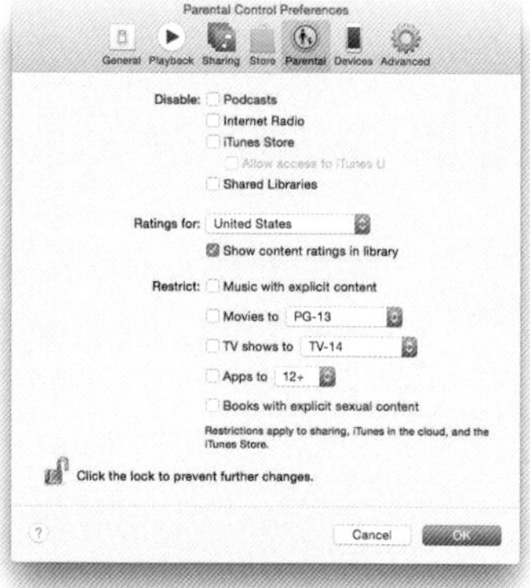

This is useful for parents to prevent children accessing inappropriate content

Allows crossfading of music if you like this effect – sound check will make all tracks the same volume (avoids having some tracks which are really loud)

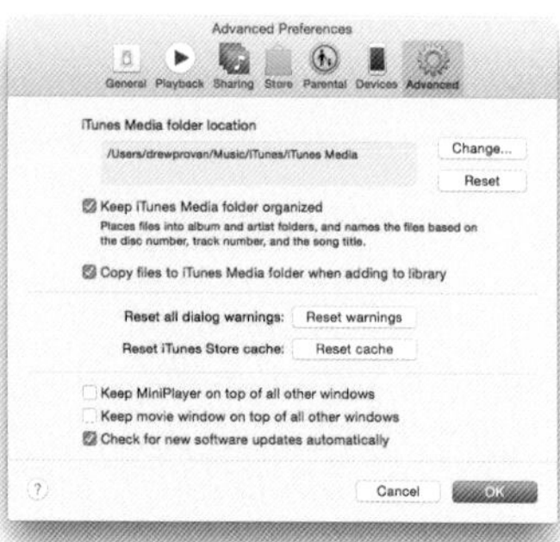

Allowing iTunes to organize your media folder is very useful – if you don't you will have media files scattered all over your hard drive

Playing Audio

1. **Open iTunes**
2. **Find artist/album/song** you want to play, select this (click once) then select the play icon
3. Or **double-click** the track
4. Or **tap the spacebar**
5. Finding music tracks in your library is easy – you can type the name of the artist into the **search box** at the top right of the iTunes window
6. Or you can **select a column**, such as Artists, and type the first couple of letters of the artist's name

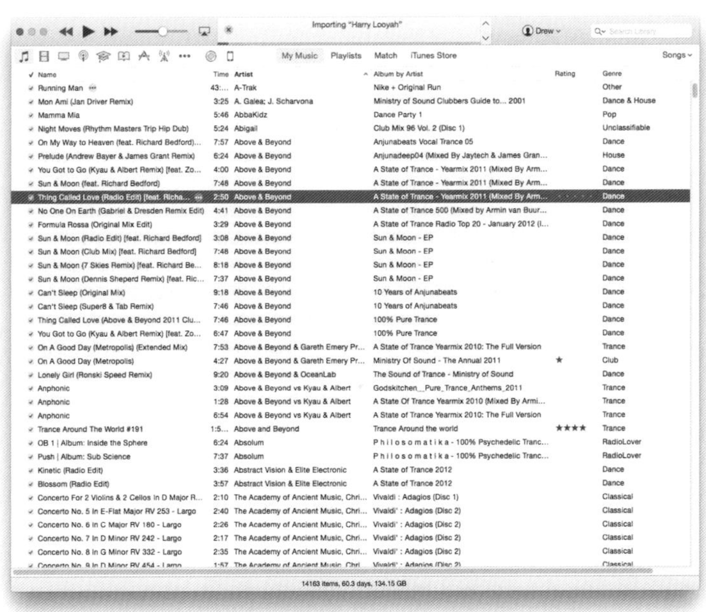

Buying Music from iTunes

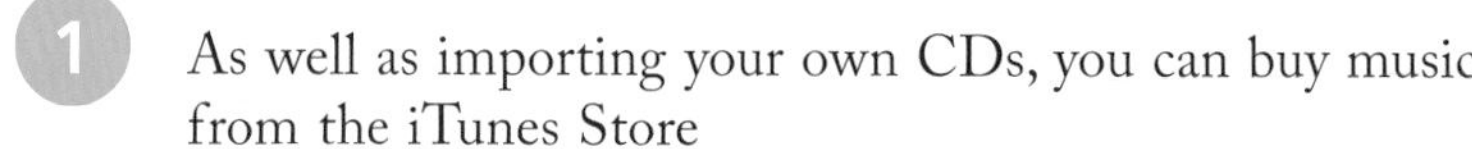

1. As well as importing your own CDs, you can buy music from the iTunes Store

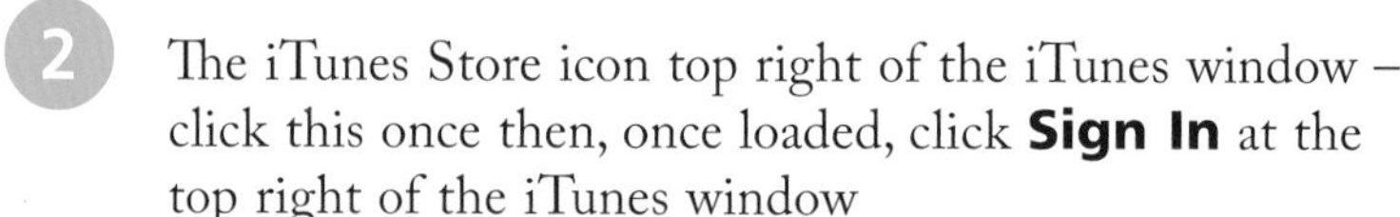

2. The iTunes Store icon top right of the iTunes window – click this once then, once loaded, click **Sign In** at the top right of the iTunes window

3. Enter your **Apple ID and password**

4. If you don't have an iTunes account, iTunes will help you set one up

5. You can find new music by browsing the main page, or click the music tab at the top of the window, or search for specific songs or artists using the search box

6. Once you have identified the music you want to purchase, click **Buy Album,** or to buy individual songs rather than albums click **Buy** next to the right of the song title

You need to set up an iTunes account before you can buy anything from the iTunes Store.

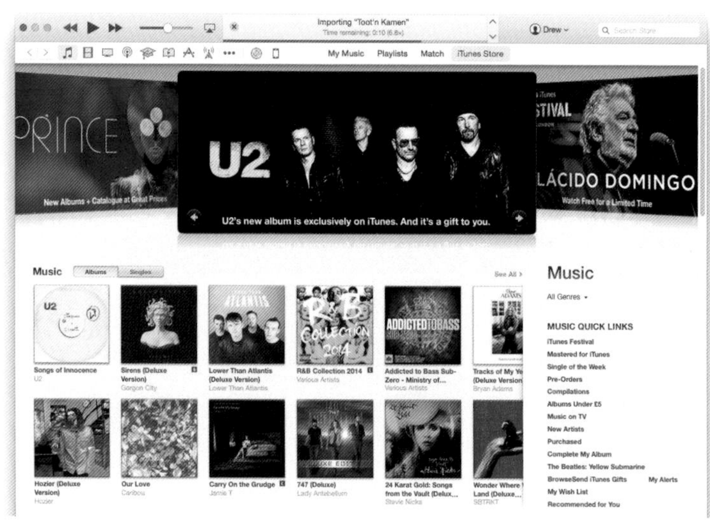

Pause and Skip

This is pretty much like any music player, with icons for Play, Pause, Skip Back, Skip Forward, Rewind, and Fast Forward.

Controls are found at the top left of the iTunes window

Skip to previous track if clicked once. Click and hold to rewind through current track

Play or pause (turns to Play icon when paused and Pause icon when playing)

Skip to next track if clicked once, or fast forward through currently-playing track

iTunes Preferences

There are many user-configurable options if you go to **iTunes > File > Preferences**.

General Preferences (shown here)

- Use this to decide what iTunes should show (Movies, TV Shows etc.)
- Text size
- Decide what happens when you insert a CD into the Mac
- Download missing artwork
- Other options

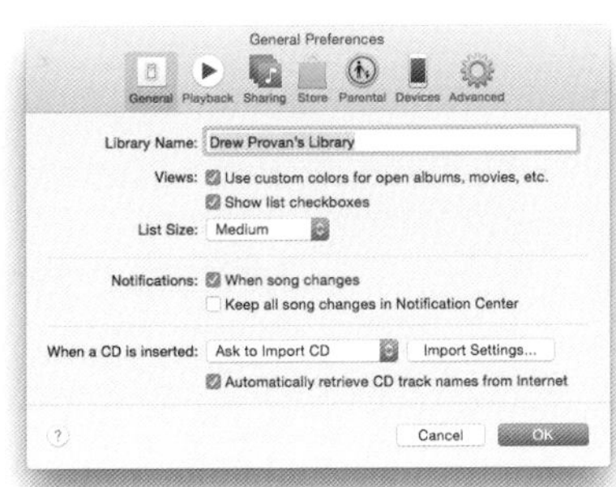

Playlists

It is worth getting to grips with playlists since you may have an iPhone, iPad or iPod and want some music on these devices. Your whole music library probably won't fit onto your device but by creating playlists you can sync specific playlists to the devices.

1. Click the **+** symbol at the bottom left of the window or go to **File > New Playlist** or type **⌘ + N**

2. You will see *untitled playlist* appear at the bottom of the playlist group

3. Give the new playlist a **name**

4. To get songs into your playlist, find them in your main music window and **drag** them to the new playlist you have created

5. When you sync your iPhone or other device to your Mac, make sure that the playlists you want to sync are checked in the sync options window

6. To remove music from playlists, select the songs you wish to remove and **tap the delete key**. *Note:* your original music files remain in the main music library and have not been deleted even though you have deleted them from the playlists

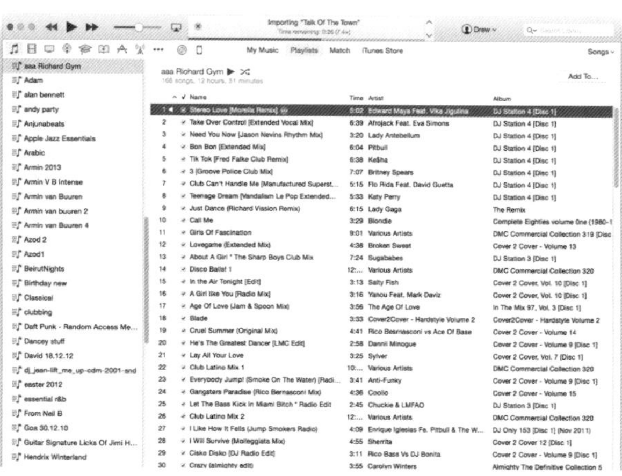

Smart Playlists

People don't use these often enough! They are very easy to set up.

Why are smart playlists so useful?

Basically, you set the rules, e.g. any track with a five star rating automatically gets added to the smart playlists. This saves you having to drag songs to the playlist manually.

To remove songs, simply change the star rating for the song and the song will be removed from the smart playlists.

Smart Playlists make it simple to update your playlists with new music.

1. Go to **File > New Smart Playlist...**
2. Or type **Option + ⌘ + N**
3. You will then see the rule window
4. Choose something like **Rating contains 3 stars**
5. Make sure **Live Updating** is checked
6. **Name** the smart playlist
7. Then go to your music library and assign some music with three star ratings
8. You will see these have been added to the smart playlist

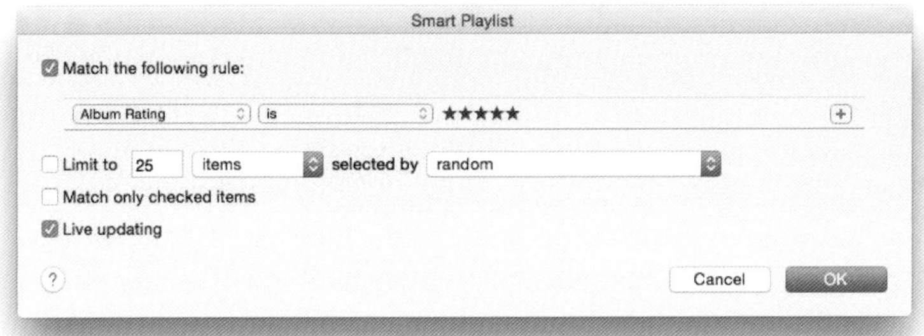

Changing iTunes Views

As well as the standard iTunes view (see page 100) you have a couple of other options.

You can view iTunes as

- Songs view (*was* List view)
- Albums list
- Artists and Genres views
- Playlists view

Songs view (default)

Albums view

Artists view

Playlists view

Column options

You can choose which columns are displayed in the list view. Select the columns you would like to display by clicking the check boxes for those columns.

Genius

Genius creates playlists based on songs in your iTunes library. For example, if you are playing a jazz track, Genius will create a jazz playlist for you using music already in your library.

1. **Choose a song** to play
2. **Right click** on the song
3. Choose **Create Genius Playlist**
4. The new Genius Playlist will appear in the left pane under Genius

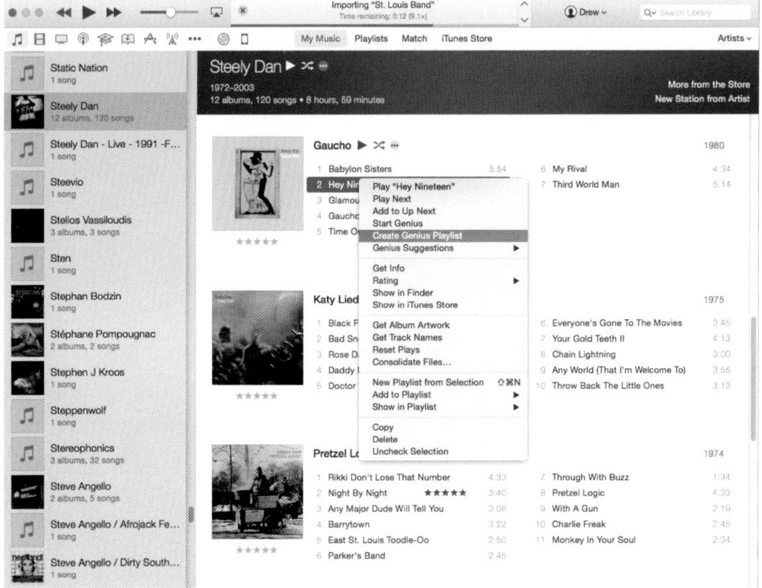

If you are bored with your playlists let Genius generate a playlist for you. You will hear music you don't generally listen to.

Sharing Your Music

You can share your iTunes library over a wireless network. Any Mac or PC on the same network can see and play your music but they cannot (easily) copy the tracks onto their computer.

1. Your Mac needs to be running in order to allow sharing
2. Go to **iTunes > Preferences > Sharing**
3. Select **Share entire library** or **Share selected playlists**
4. You can **password protect** (enter password required into the box Require password). You can also play audio and video on Apple TV if you switch on **Home Sharing**
5. Go to **Advanced > Turn On Home Sharing**

Burning music CDs

This is covered in Chapter 14.

9 Networking the Mac

Networking computers is usually a fairly geeky affair on many platforms. Macs make networking very simple whether it be to other Macs, PCs, printers, or other devices.

Networking is Easy!

Macs can network to other Macs, networked printers, or local networks and use Virtual Private Networks (VPN).

Network System Preferences

Go to **Apple Menu > System Preferences**

2 Look for the network icon

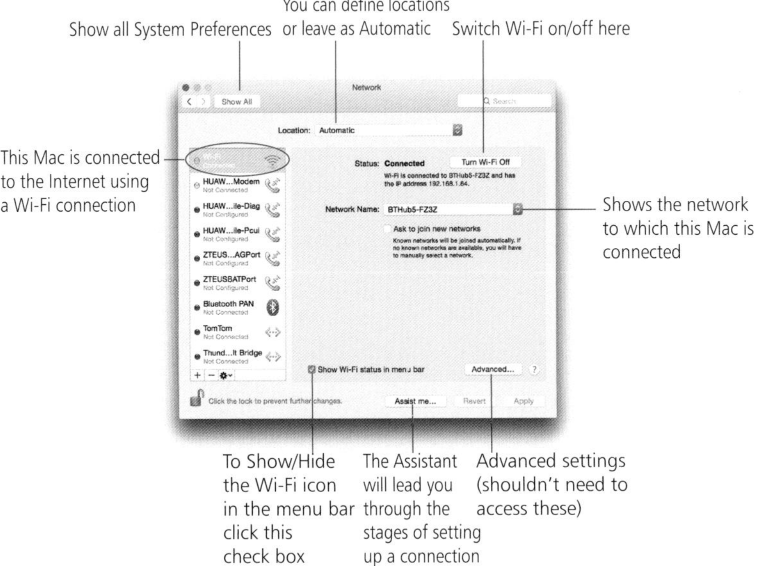

Getting Online

To access the Internet you have the option of choosing a wired connection to a router (Ethernet) or wireless (Wi-Fi).

Setting up a wireless Base Station

1. Using a standard Ethernet cable connect your Mac to the broadband router, AirPort Extreme Base Station or Time Capsule (Apple's router with hard drive inside)
2. Launch **Utilities > AirPort utility**
3. **Scan** for wireless devices
4. Once the device appears in the pane on the left, click **Continue** and the AirPort Utility will lead you through the various settings
5. Check to make sure your Wi-Fi signal is good (shown on the toolbar) and open Safari. Try opening a web page to check that you are connected to the Internet

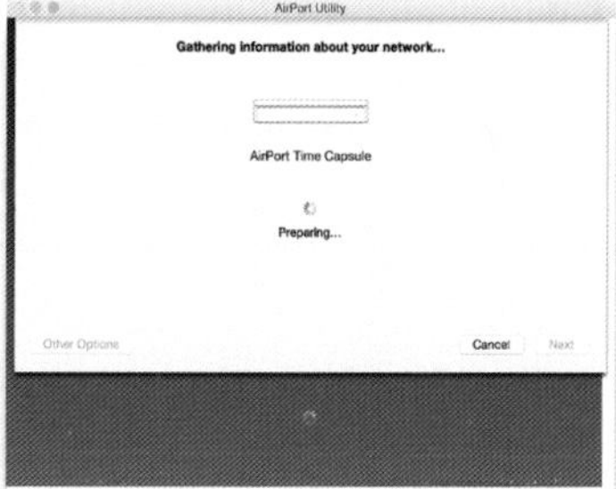

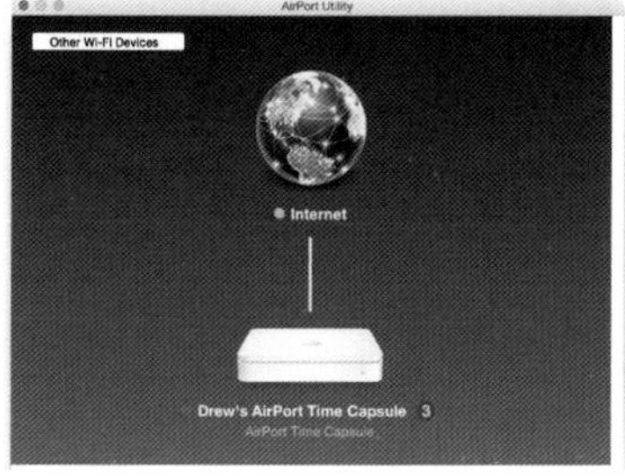

Sharing Internet Connection

Some Internet Service Providers (ISPs) don't like you to share your connection so take care if you decide to share the Internet connection with another computer. *You have been warned!*

Why share an Internet connection?

You may be in a hotel and have a wired connection to the Internet but need to get a second computer or mobile device such as an iPhone or iPad online. The best way to do this is to get a laptop online using the wired connection then set up an *ad hoc* (computer-to-computer) Wi-Fi network from the laptop which the other devices can use.

Sharing an Internet connection is very unpopular with ISPs. Be careful if you decide to allow sharing of your Internet connection.

1. Go online with the laptop
2. Make sure you're connected to the Internet (do a Google search or open any web page)
3. Go to Wi-Fi at the top of the screen and scroll to **Create Network...**

4. Give the network a name or leave as the default

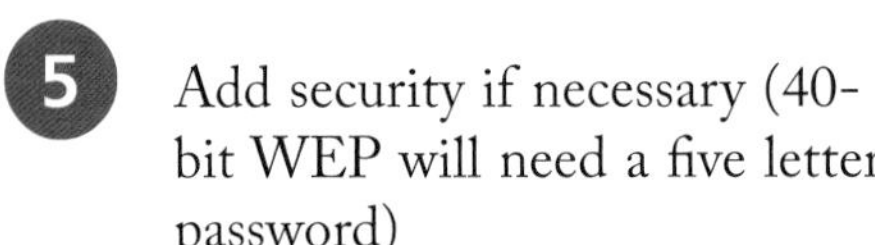

5. Add security if necessary (40-bit WEP will need a five letter password)

6. Click **Create**

7. The Wi-Fi icon will change to

8. Now go to **Apple Menu > System Preferences > Sharing**

9. Click **Internet Sharing** (make sure the dialog box says *Share your connection from Ethernet to computers using Wi-Fi*)

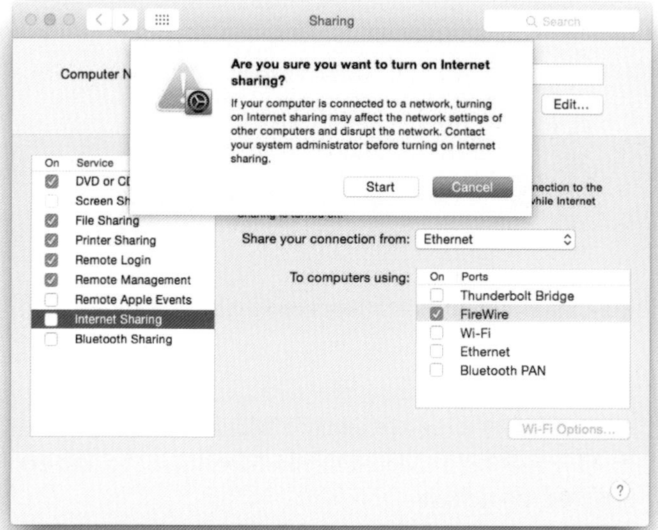

10. Click **Start**

11. The Wi-Fi icon will change to

12. Now check for the Wi-Fi signal using your other laptop, iPhone or iPad. Connect by entering the password you specified when you set the network up

Connecting to Other Macs

If two Macs are on the same wireless network they can "see" each other. This is one way of sharing files, viewing folders and documents on one Mac using another Mac. You can also network to Windows machines but this will not be covered here.

1. On both Macs go to **Apple Menu > System Preferences > Sharing**

2. Make sure **File Sharing** is **ON** (or you will not be able to see any files!)

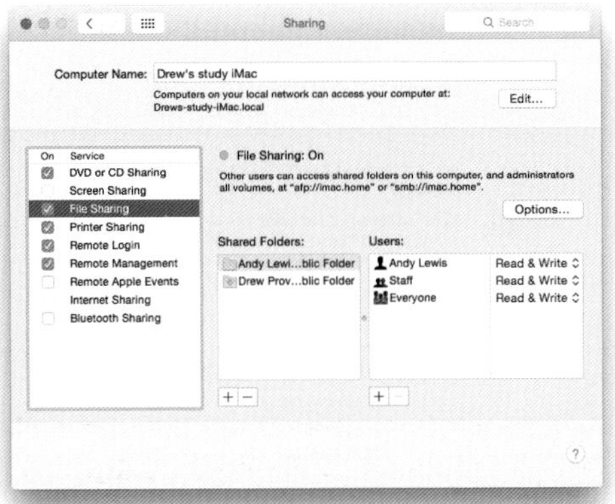

3. Let's suppose we're sitting at a MacBook Pro and want to view files on a iMac. On the MacBook Pro, **open Finder window**

4. Look for the iMac we want to connect to (if not shown under **Shared** make sure both Macs are on the same network)

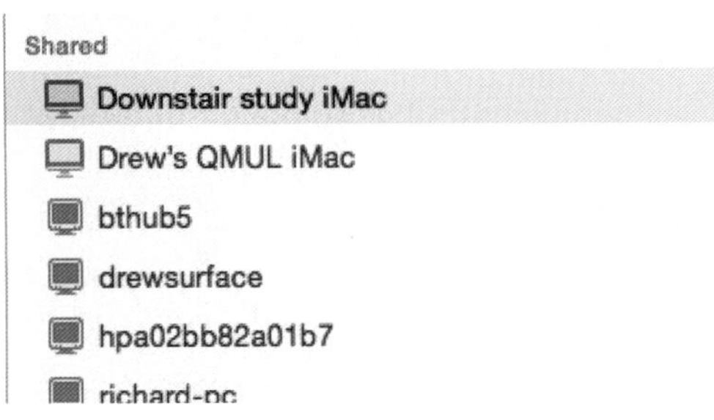

5. Click the iMac icon in the left pane
6. You will then see **Connect and Share Screen...**

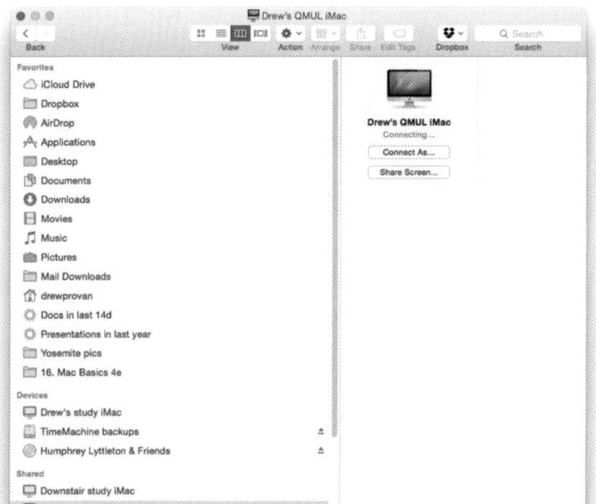

7. Click **Connect**. You may only have **Guest Access** (not very useful) so click **Connect As...** and enter the **username** and **password** for the iMac
8. You should now see all files and folders and you can delete files, or copy across to/from the iMac

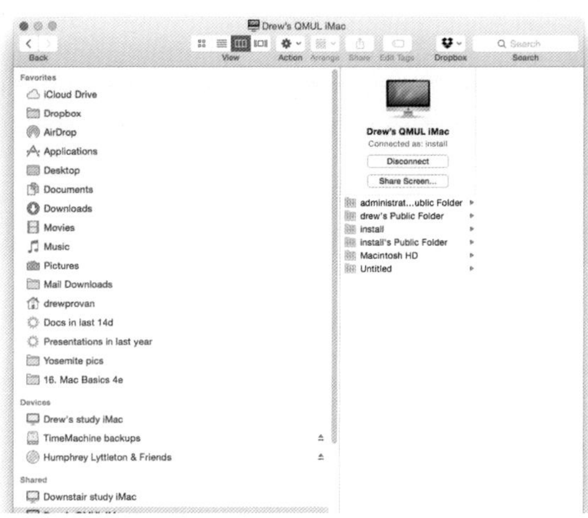

You can share Macs in two ways: file sharing and screen sharing. Screen sharing is useful if you want to see what's on the other person's screen. It is also great if you want to troubleshoot their Mac but you cannot physically get to their Mac.

Screen Sharing

You can share another Mac's screen using several methods, e.g. iChat, Skype, and screen sharing using the same method as file sharing (see page 116).

Let's share a MacBook Pro screen using a MacBook Air, i.e. view the MacBook Pro screen *from* the MacBook Air screen.

Note: both Macs must be on the same network. Screen sharing must be switched on for the Mac screen you want to share. You can check this by going to **Apple Menu > System Preferences > Sharing** and click **Screen Sharing**.

1. **Open a Finder window** on the MacBook Air
2. Click the MacBook Pro under **Shared**
3. Click **Share Screen...**
4. You will be prompted for the password for the MacBook Pro – enter this and the MacBook Pro screen should display on the MacBook Air

You can now copy files and folders in screen sharing using drag-and-drop.

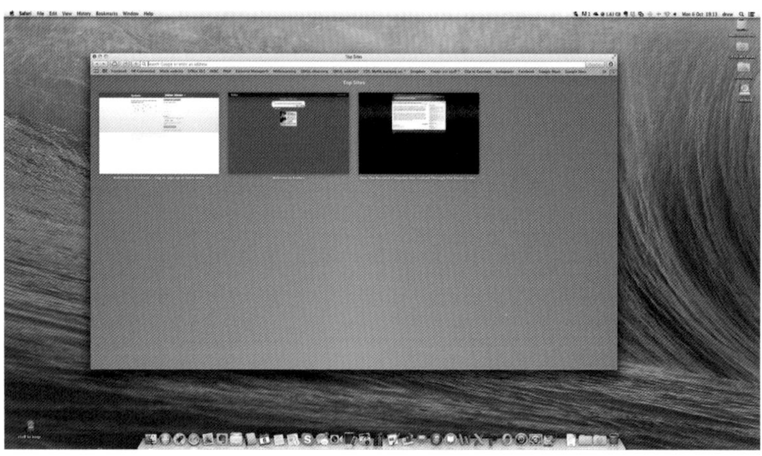

Here you can see the MacBook Pro screen *within* the MacBook Air screen.

In Yosemite (OS X 10.10) you can use drag-and-drop to copy files from the remote Mac to the local Mac, and vice versa!

Share Files Using AirDrop

This is a feature of OS X Yosemite that allows users on the same network to drag-and-drop files onto other Macs. You can AirDrop files between Macs, or iOS devices, or both Mac and iOS device.

How to transfer files using AirDrop

1. Click on **Go** at the top of the screen – **select AirDrop**

2. Or type **Shift + ⌘ + R**

3. An AirDrop window will open showing all Macs or iOS devices on the network

4. To send a file to another Mac **drop the file onto the other Mac's icon** in the AirDrop window

5. The person using the other Mac **must accept** the file before transfer will occur

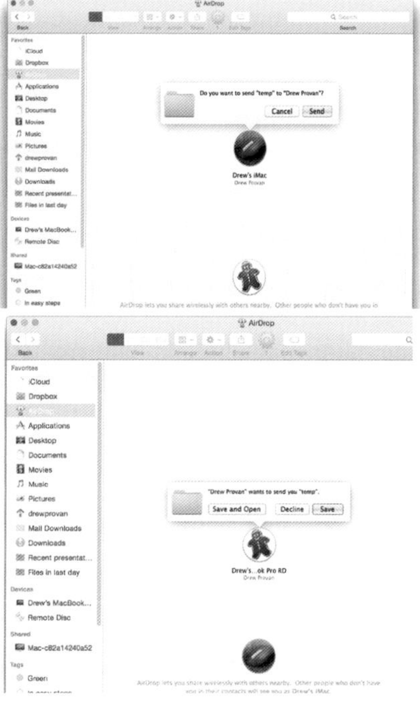

Both Macs must have Wi-Fi switched on to use AirDrop.

You can now use AirDrop between Macs OR between your Mac and iOS device. On your iOS device flick the screen from the bottom to bring up the Control Center and make sure AirDrop is on. On the Mac use the left sidebar to select AirDrop then choose your files or pictures to AirDrop to the Mac.

Wireless Printing

If you're using a laptop in the lounge you may want to print documents without having to leave the sofa!

To print a document wirelessly using a printer connected to another Mac

1. On the Mac with printer attached go to **Apple Menu > System Preferences > Sharing**
2. Make sure the **Printer Sharing** button is **checked**
3. On the Mac with no printer attached go to **Apple Menu > System Preferences > Printers & Scanners**
4. Look for available printers – if none, **click the +** symbol and add the printer connected to the other Mac (i.e. the wired printer connected to the remote Mac)
5. Now, go to your documents and click **Print** – make sure the printer selected is the one attached to the other Mac
6. Collect the printed pages later!

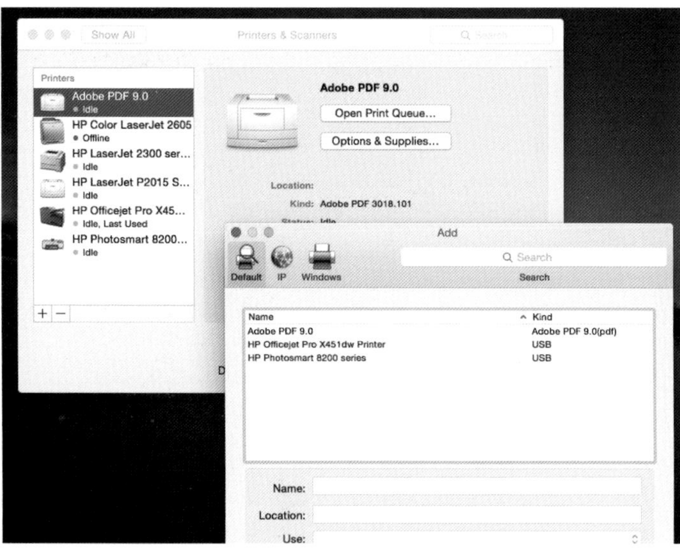

10 Video Chat

Video chatting is incredibly popular, largely due to the arrival of this technology on smartphones and tablets. In this chapter we will look at how to set up video chats in FaceTime, Messages, *and other apps.*

FaceTime Video Chat

FaceTime software is now the Mac standard video chatting app (also found on iPhone, iPad and iPod touch). The software has a very simple interface.

Initially your video image fills the screen but when you connect, your image becomes small and the screen will show the person you are having the FaceTime chat with

Recent FaceTime call contacts are listed here

Video chat using FaceTime

1. **Launch FaceTime** from the dock or the Application folder
2. Enter the name of the contact you wish to FaceTime
3. Click on their name from the list

4. To FaceTime a friend, find their name on the list and choose the method for FaceTime, e.g. iPhone, or using a Mac (select their email address to FaceTime them using their computer)

5. If you FaceTime some people regularly **add them to your Favorites** list. Go to Favorites, click **+** (top right) to add a contact to the Favorites list

6. To call using FaceTime, **click the contact number** or **email**

7. To end the call click **End**

Add people you regularly FaceTime to your Favorites.

FaceTime from Messages

From Messages, click the video camera icon (top right) and choose email or phone number to video chat with someone.

Messages

Yosemite includes Messages which is an inbuilt app which allows you to send and receive SMS and multimedia messages from people using iOS and other types of cellular phone. You can send text, pictures, voice memos and videos easily from your Mac straight to an iOS device or Android.

Sending a text message

1. **Open Messages**
2. Click on the **New Message** icon at the top right. Enter the name or number of the person you want to message
3. Type the text and press **Return**
4. To add a photo or video, drop it onto the message area and press **Return**
5. If you are sending to someone running iOS the message will be sent as an iMessage (your text box will be **blue**). If you are sending to BlackBerry or Android your text box will be **green**

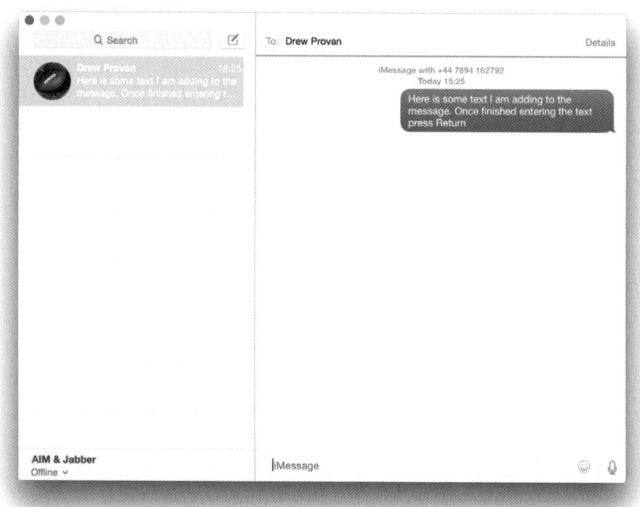

Instead of sending just a boring text message why not include a voice message? Click on the microphone icon and record your voice then send that instead of a text!

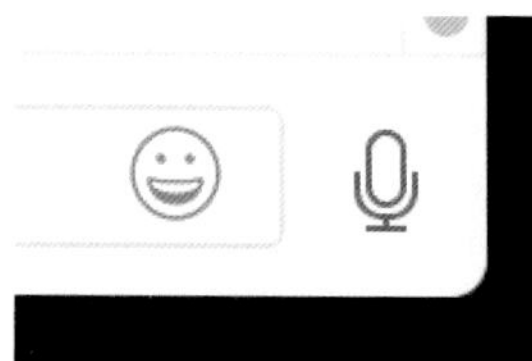

Quick reply

1. If Messages isn't running, you will get a notification after you receive a message (this will appear at the top right of your Mac screen). If you click the notification you will see a Reply box. Type your reply then click Send. You can do this reply without opening the Messages app

2. Click on the New Message icon at the top right. Enter the name or number of the person you want to message

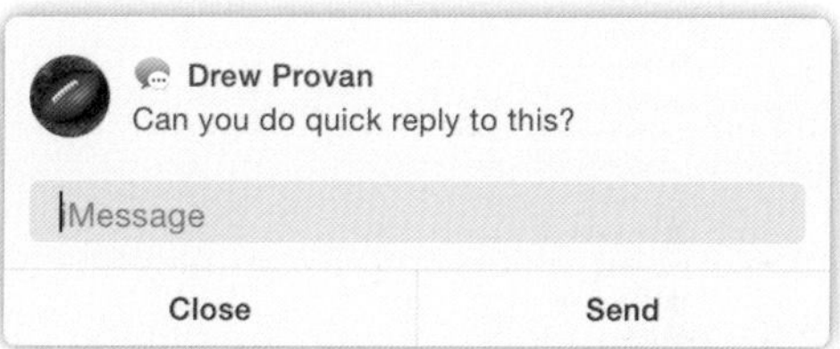

You can now make phone calls and answer calls directly from your Mac! When the Mac detects an incoming call a notification will appear at the top right of the screen.

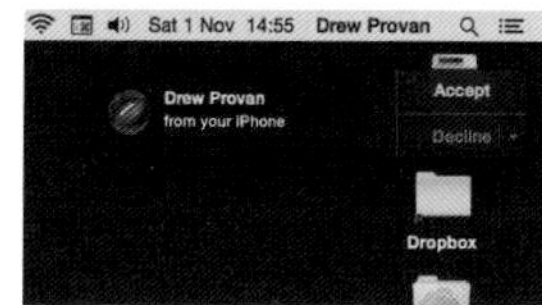

Do Not Disturb

Some message threads have lots of replies and you may not want to see or hear these. Simply click Details then click the box Do Not Disturb.

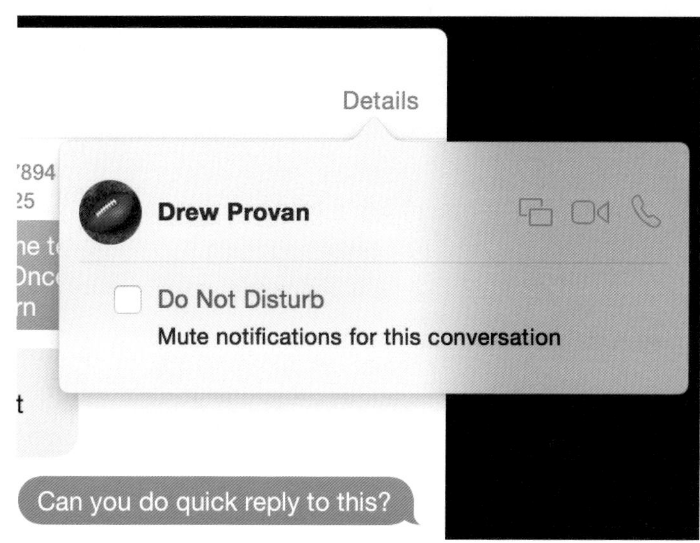

Skype

This is not part of OS X so you need to download the latest version from **skype.com**

Once installed, set up your account. Open the program by clicking the Dock icon or launch from the Application folder.

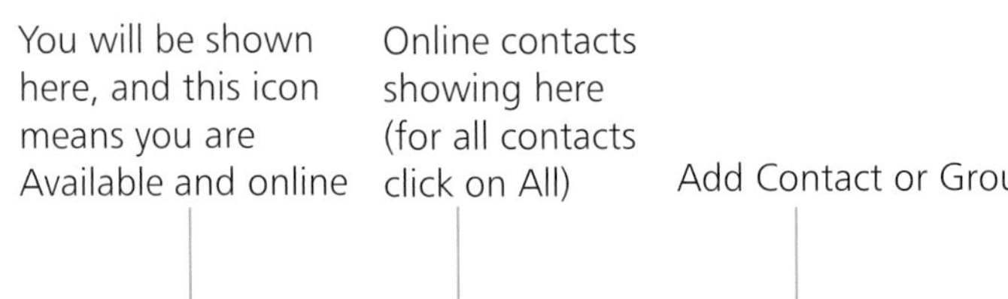

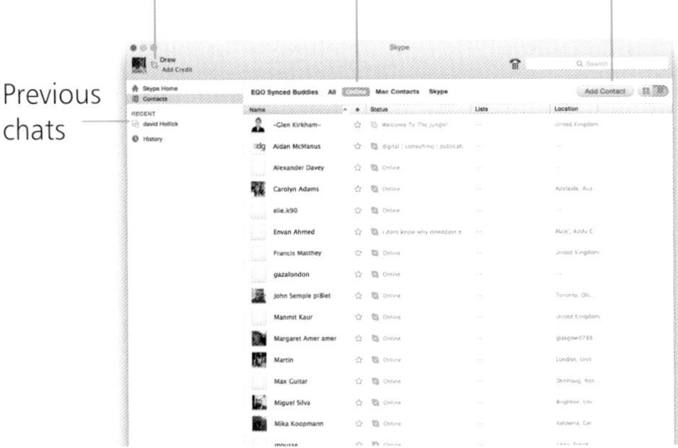

Using Skype

1. **Launch Skype**
2. Your online contacts will be at the top of the screen
3. **Click on contact**
4. You can talk to them using text, video, or audio – you will see the icons for these various options to the right of the screen name

Add contacts

1. Click **+ Add Contact...** or **New Contact Group...**
2. When the search box appears, type in the contact name or search for them online using the search box

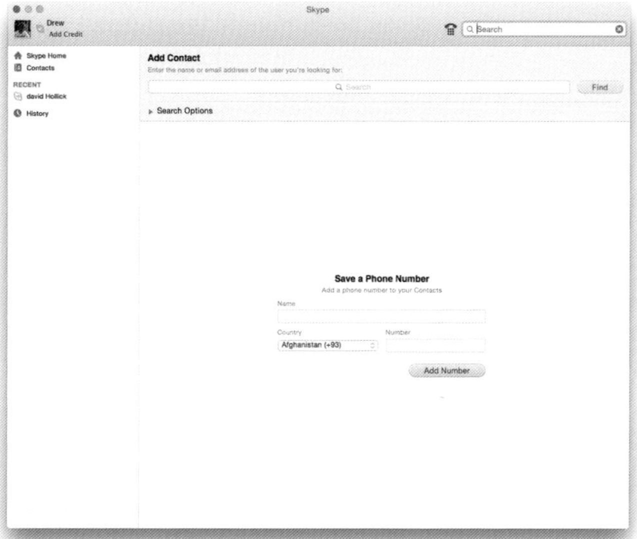

Block contacts

There may be people you do not want to speak to, in which case:

1. **Right-click the contact name**
2. Select **Block** *contact name*

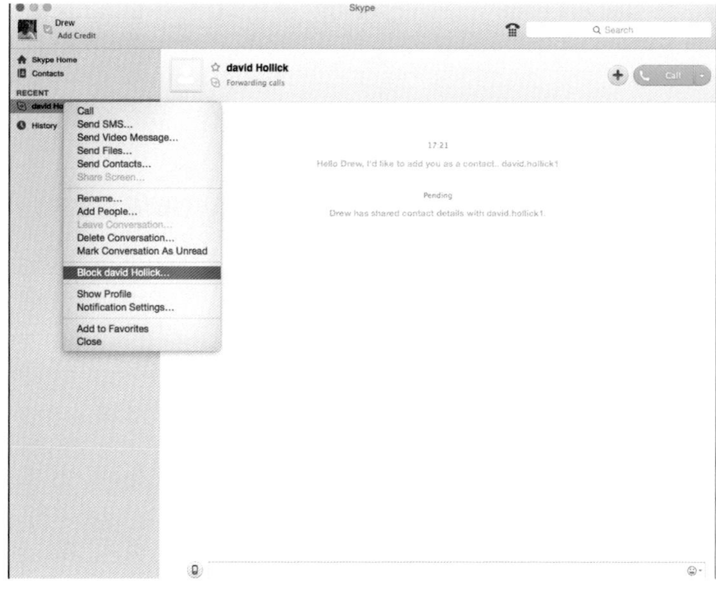

You will occasionally receive invites from strangers on Skype. It is best to block these.

Google Voice and Video Chat

This is a Google app, which runs within Google mail. If not installed, download the plug-in from **google.com/chat/video**

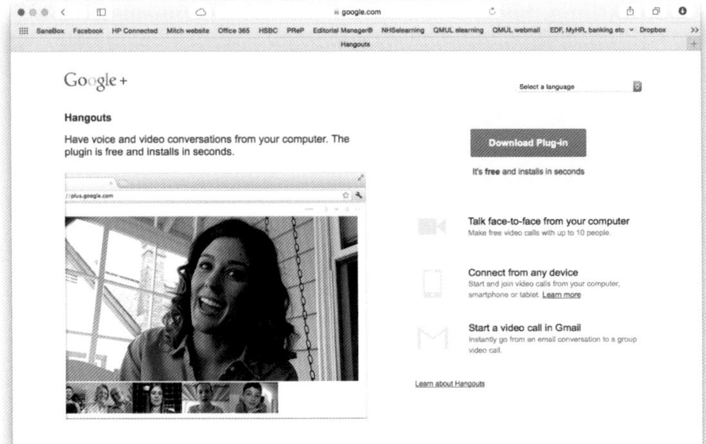

To use Google Voice & Video chat

1. Log in to your Google mail account
2. Make sure you have installed the **Voice & Video Chat** plug-in (*see above*)
3. In the left pane you will see the chat window towards the bottom of the screen
4. Your name will be at the top
5. Set your status to **Available/Busy/Invisible** or create your own custom message

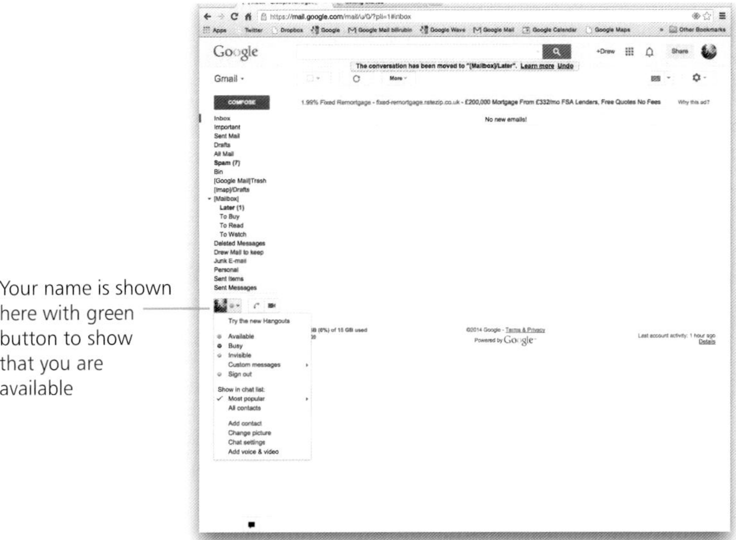

Your name is shown here with green button to show that you are available

Video chat with a contact

1. Select a contact – make sure they are online

2. Click the video icon

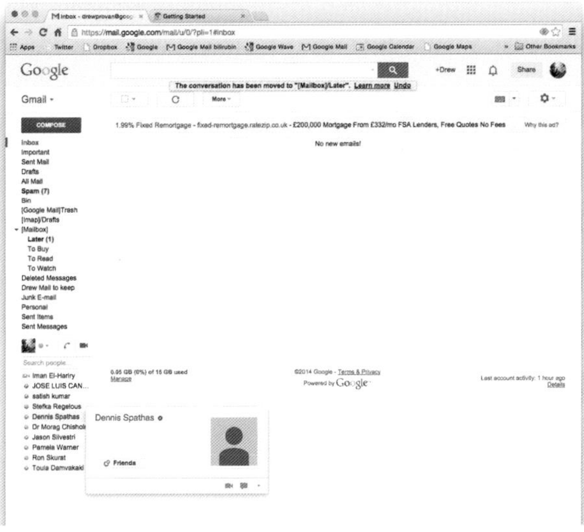

Other Video Chat Options

Facebook video

This is now available and makes it really easy to chat to your Facebook friends when they're online. Simply click on the video icon in the top corner of your Online Friends chat window in Facebook.

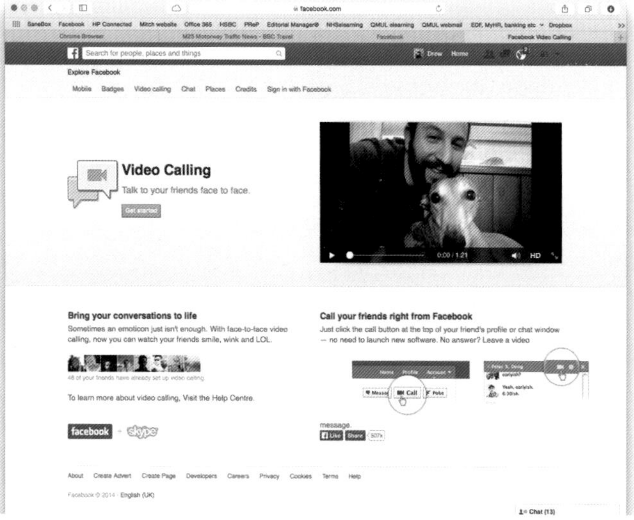

ISPQ video chat

1. Go to **ispq.com/download**
2. **Set up your account** and start chatting
3. Various "Rooms" are available depending on your area of interest
4. Probably best to start in the general area section

11 Personalizing Your Mac

There are many ways in which you can make your Mac work and look just the way you want. This section explores some of the features you can modify.

Name Your Hard Drive

We are dealing here with software personalization – making your Mac run the way you want to with an appearance that suits your taste, rather than talking about hardware, hard drives, adding more RAM, etc.

Naming your Mac's hard drive will make it easier to identify on the network.

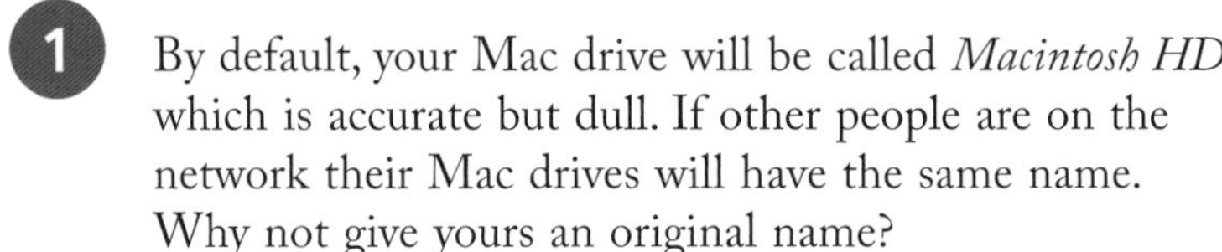

1. By default, your Mac drive will be called *Macintosh HD*, which is accurate but dull. If other people are on the network their Mac drives will have the same name. Why not give yours an original name?

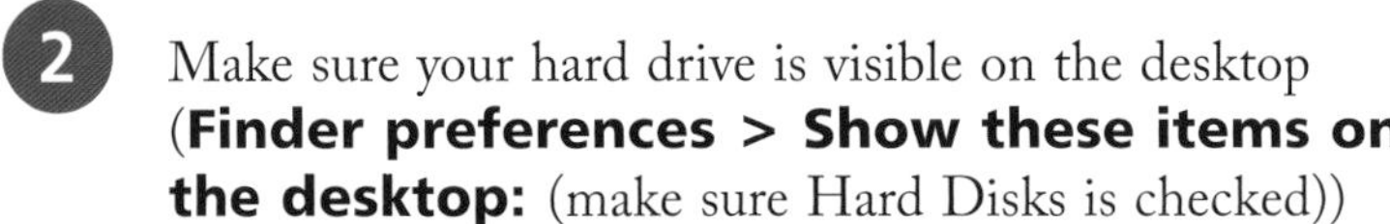

2. Make sure your hard drive is visible on the desktop (**Finder preferences > Show these items on the desktop:** (make sure Hard Disks is checked))

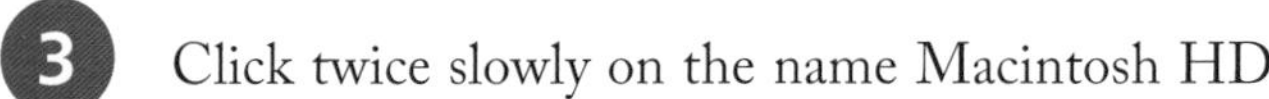

3. Click twice slowly on the name Macintosh HD

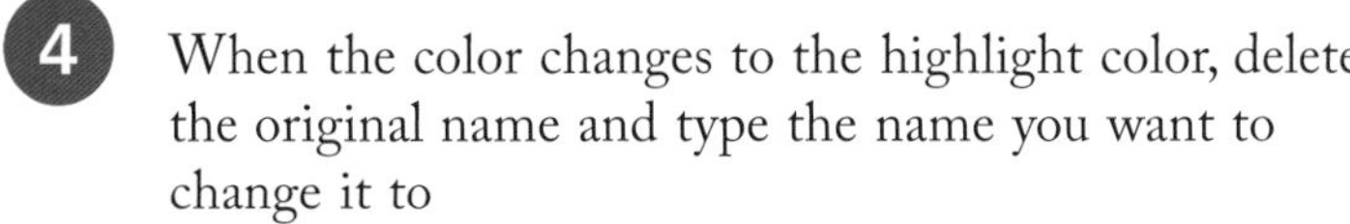

4. When the color changes to the highlight color, delete the original name and type the name you want to change it to

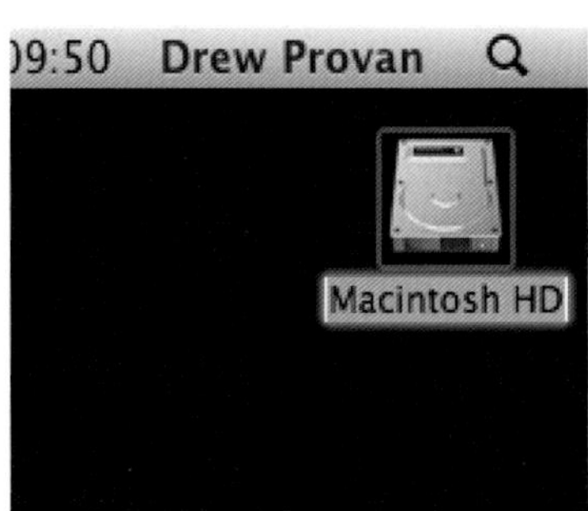

The name Macintosh HD was clicked twice – the color has changed to the highlight color. Start typing the name

I called this Drew's MBA HD (my MacBook Air's HD) so that when I network to the MBA from another Mac, I can be sure I know which drive I am looking at

Using Wallpapers

Wallpapers are photos or images that cover the entire desktop. You can choose plain colors, abstract designs, photos including your own photos.

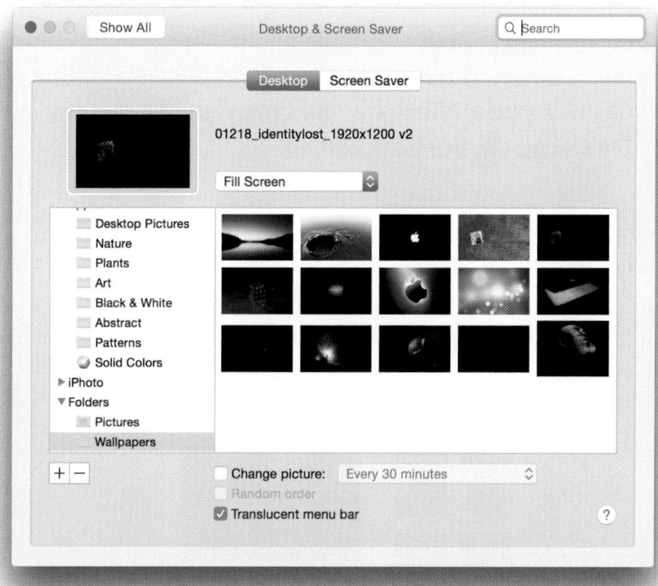

You can choose various options supplied by Apple, including Nature, Plants, Art and many others. You can also choose photos from your iPhoto collection, or you can download artwork from many sites, e.g. **interfacelift.com**

Screen Savers

These have been around for many years, and were intended to prevent your CRT tube screen being burned if you left an image on the screen for a prolonged period. There is probably less need for screen savers today but they remain popular. After a period of inactivity the screen saver kicks in and displays an image, photo, or random animated colors.

1. Go to **Apple Menu > System preferences > Desktop & Screen Saver**

2. Choose the Screen Saver tab

Wake and Sleep Options

You can set your Mac to wake up at certain times of the day and go to sleep at night. You can also set up a time for the Mac to boot up and switch off.

1. Go to **Apple Menu > System preferences > Energy Saver**

2. Set the Computer and Display sleep times (when the computer goes to sleep the hard drive spins down)

3. If you want specific start up and shut down times click **Schedule...**

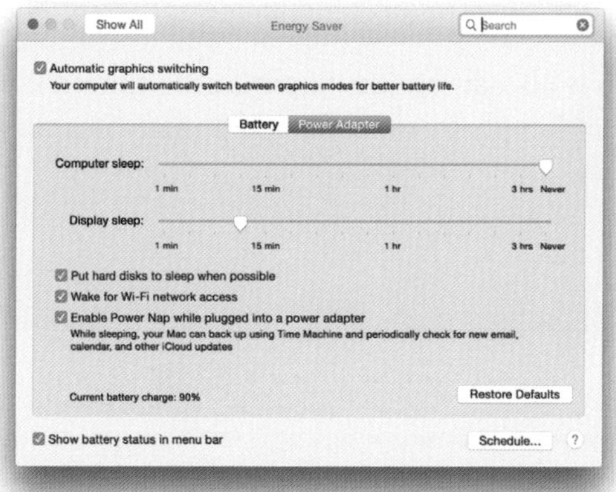

Macs tend to run their internal maintenance programs overnight so don't switch your Mac off every night.

Power Nap

This is a feature in Yosemite which, when enabled, allows system updates, and also updates email, notes and reminders even if your Mac is asleep. It will also still perform time machine backups (see pages 192-193)!

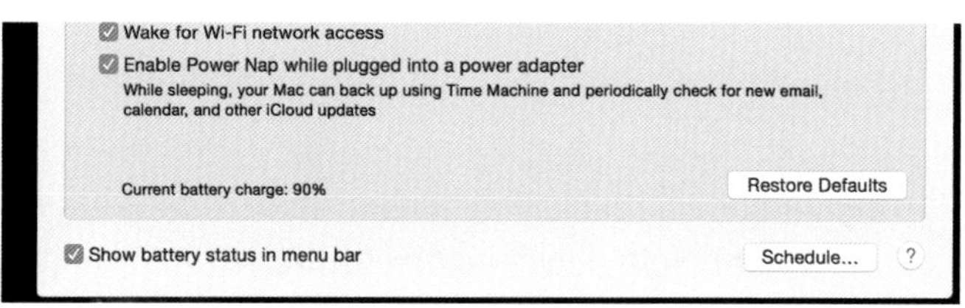

Change the Clock Display

1. Go to **Apple Menu > System Preferences**
2. Select **Date & Time**
3. You can choose whether to show the time and date in the menu bar by checking the box
4. You have the options of either a **digital** or **analog** clock, as well as showing the time with seconds
5. You can also use a **24-hour** or **12-hour** clock depending on your taste
6. There is also an option to announce the time on the hour although I cannot imagine many people using that option!

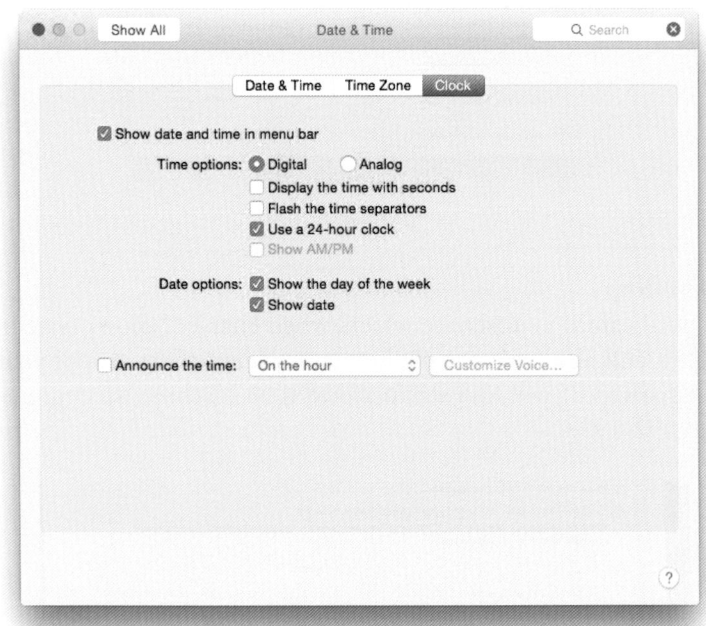

Set Your Time Zone

Setting the time zone is a useful function since you will need this for Calendar and other apps.

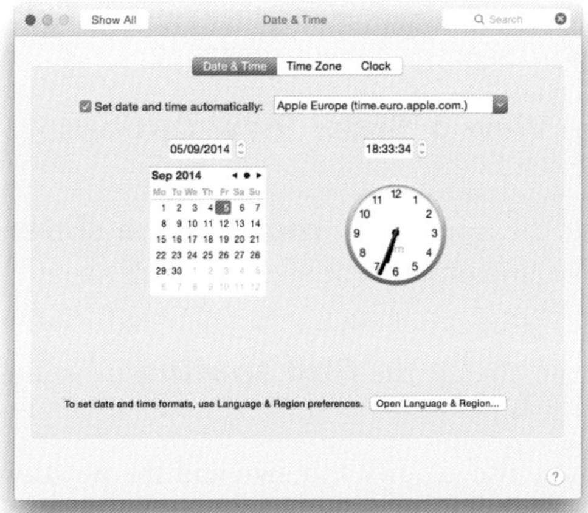

Set the time zone for your Mac or the Calendar app or many other apps will behave oddly.

1. Make sure the box is checked for **Set time zone automatically using current location**

2. A pin should drop on the world map showing your location

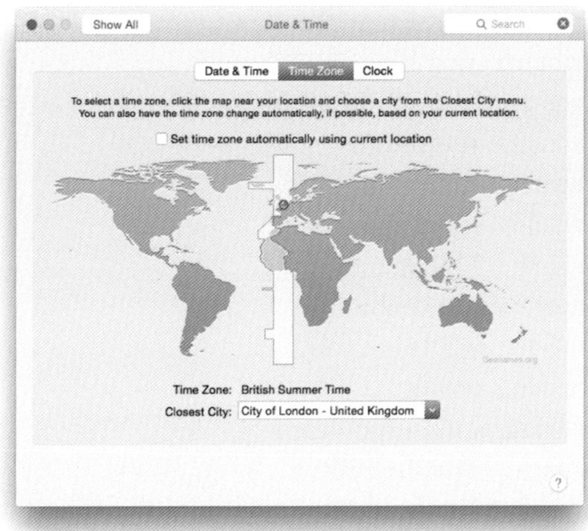

Change Your Icon Sizes

You can change the size of the icons representing folders, documents, and apps to suit your requirements. Some people like very small icons in folders or on the desktop, while other people like the icons to be large so they are easier to see.

Icons can be resized to (almost) any size you want, from the microscopic to gigantic!

To change icon size

1. Go to **View > Show View Options**

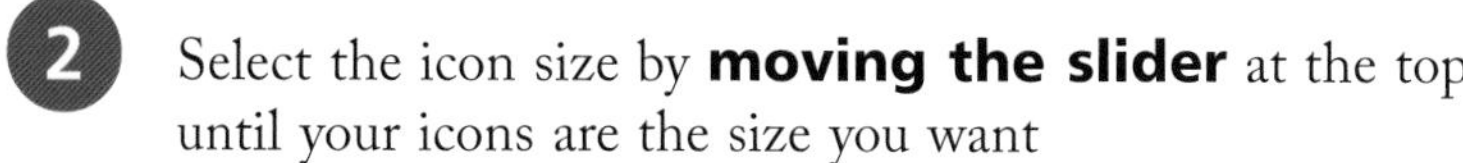

2. Select the icon size by **moving the slider** at the top until your icons are the size you want
3. You can change the **Grid spacing** by using the slider
4. You can also modify text size and the position of the labels to either Bottom or Right

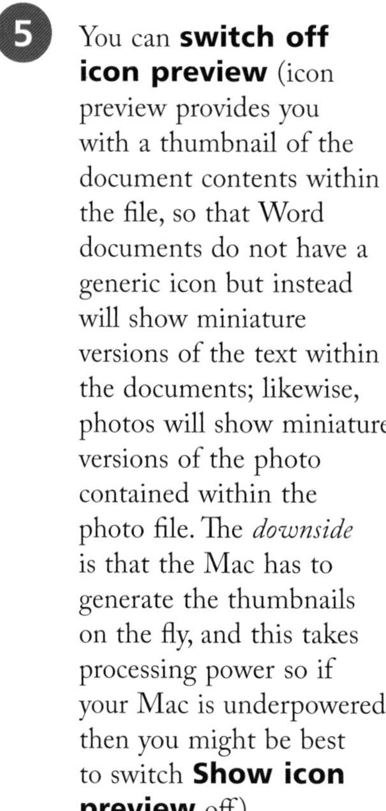

5. You can **switch off icon preview** (icon preview provides you with a thumbnail of the document contents within the file, so that Word documents do not have a generic icon but instead will show miniature versions of the text within the documents; likewise, photos will show miniature versions of the photo contained within the photo file. The *downside* is that the Mac has to generate the thumbnails on the fly, and this takes processing power so if your Mac is underpowered then you might be best to switch **Show icon preview** off)

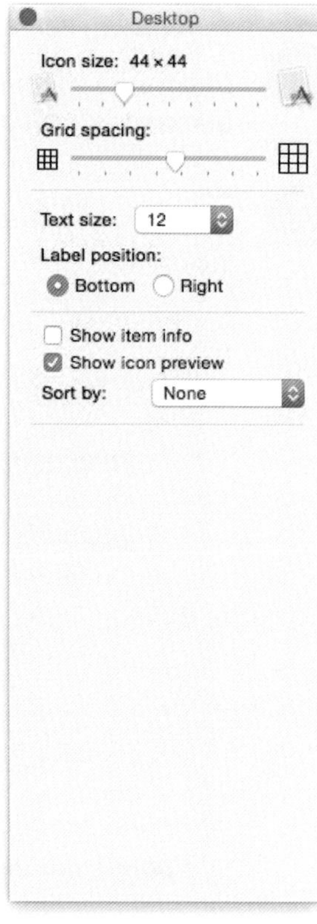

The Dock Options

The Dock has several options.

1. You can modify the size of the apps on the dock from very small to very large

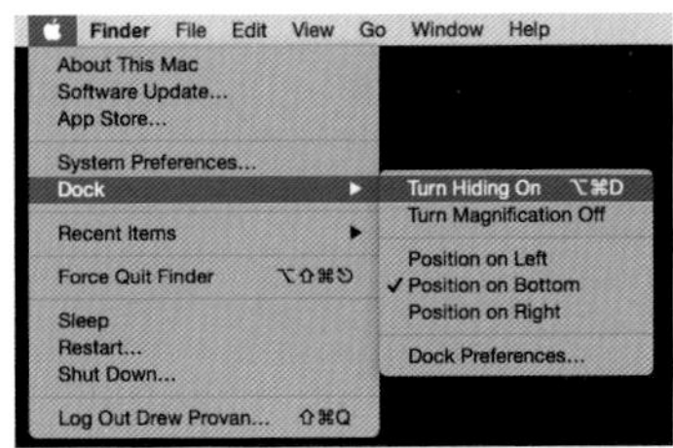

2. You can adjust the magnification which means that when you roll your mouse pointer over an icon it can magnify slightly or greatly depending on which you find more helpful

3. The Dock can also remain in its default position, i.e. Bottom of the screen, but if you prefer, you can move it to the left or the right

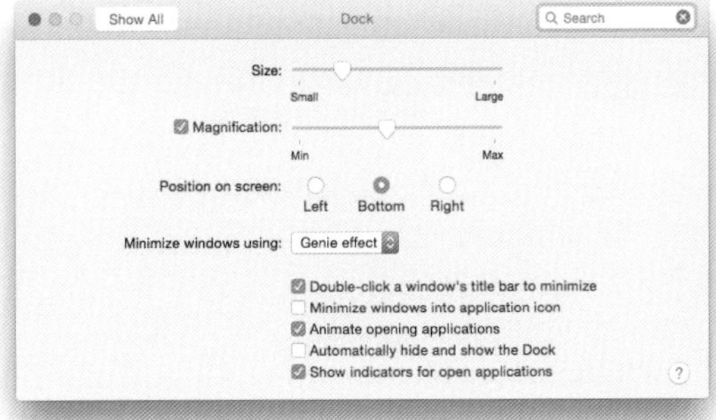

The fast way to resize your Dock icons is to drag the bar on the Dock left or right.

Resize your Dock fast!

Drag the divider bar to the *left* to make icons smaller or *right* to make them larger (no need to open System Preferences).

Add Folders to the Sidebar

The sidebar has three main sections:

1. **Favorites**
2. **Shared** – networked drives
3. **Devices** – disk drives both real, and virtual from disk images

How to make best use of the sidebar

If you are working on a project which has documents in a folder, rather than navigating your way to that folder each time to use a document, it is simpler to drag the folder onto the sidebar Favorites section.

To access the folder and its contents, simply click once on the folder and its contents will be displayed in the right pane.

Add folders you access frequently to the sidebar. You don't need to hunt for them again!

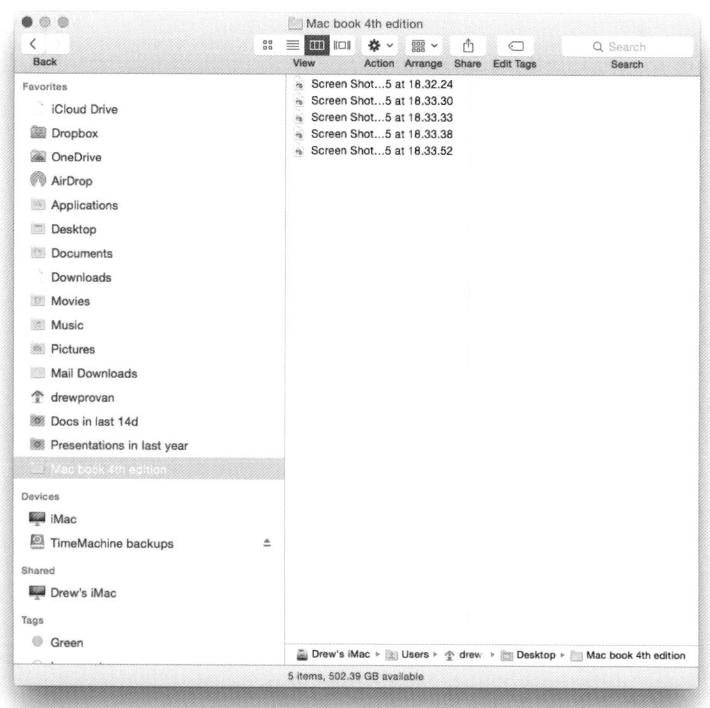

Set the Screen Corners

The four corners of your screen can be used as shortcuts for various functions. In the figure shown, the bottom left corner activates Mission Control, the right bottom corner puts the display to sleep. Other configurable functions for the hot corners include:

1. **Start Screen Saver**
2. **Disable Screen Saver**
3. **Application Windows**
4. **Desktop**
5. **Dashboard**
6. **Launchpad**

You can set up any corner to do any of these functions.

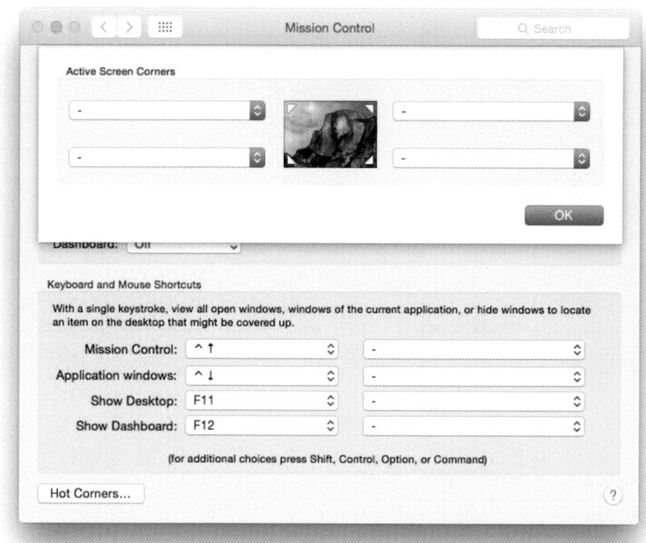

Spend time setting up your screen corners. Once configured they are real timesavers!

Mouse and Trackpad Settings

The mouse and trackpad are highly configurable. You can change the tracking speed of the mouse or the trackpad. You can also modify the gestures functions as well as scrolling direction.

The trackpad and mouse can be configured and adjusted to your specific requirements. Spend time playing around with the various settings.

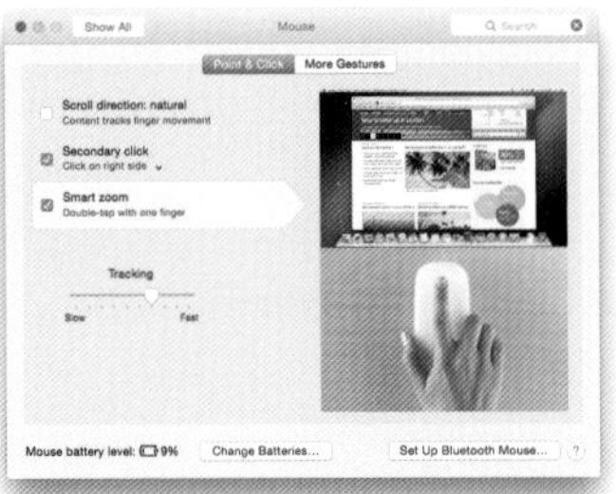

The Point & Click section lets you set up the right side of the mouse as right-click

If you are left handed you can set up the left side as the "right" click

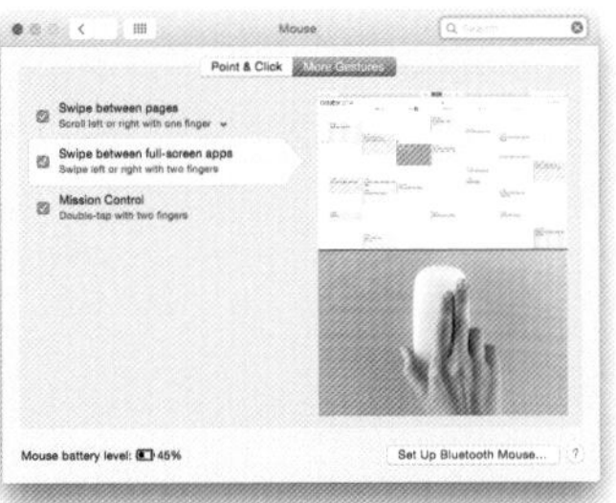

This option lets you switch on/off the two-finger swipe gesture which works with photos and other apps

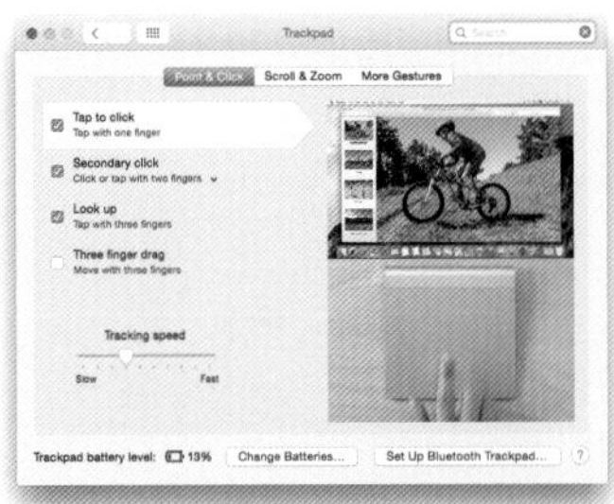

This trackpad option controls the Look up gesture

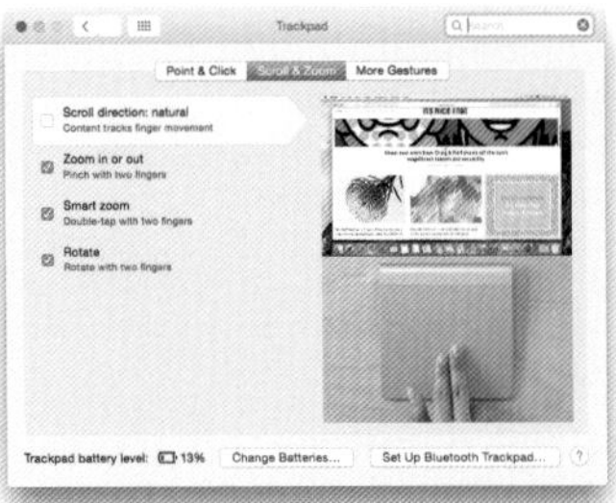

You can zoom in/out of documents and photos using two fingers on the trackpad, much like other touchscreen devices (iPhone, iPad, and iPod Touch)

Empty Trash Without Warning

If you place files in the Trash and then go to **File > Empty Trash** a warning will come up asking if you really intend to empty the contents of the trash. You can click Empty Trash each time or you can configure the trash so that it empties *without* giving you the usual warning.

Be careful, though, because you will now have to be 100% certain you do want to empty the Trash or you will lose work!

To disable the warning before entering the Trash

1. Go to **Finder > Finder preferences**
2. Select the **Advanced** tab
3. **Uncheck** the **Show warning before emptying the trash** checkbox

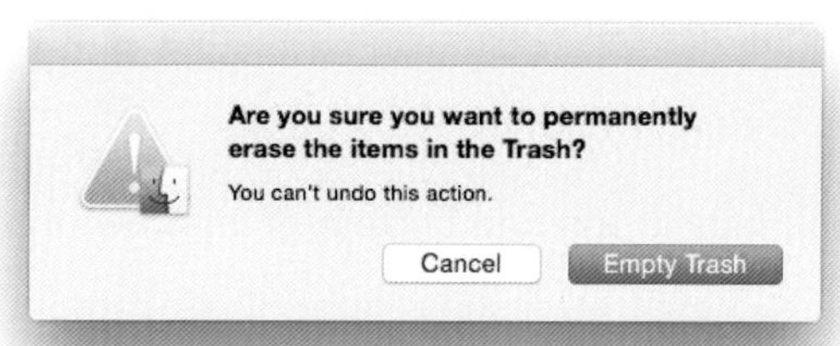

For fast Trash emptying disable the Show Warning message.

Pimp Your Windows!

You can change most of the elements of the Mac windows:

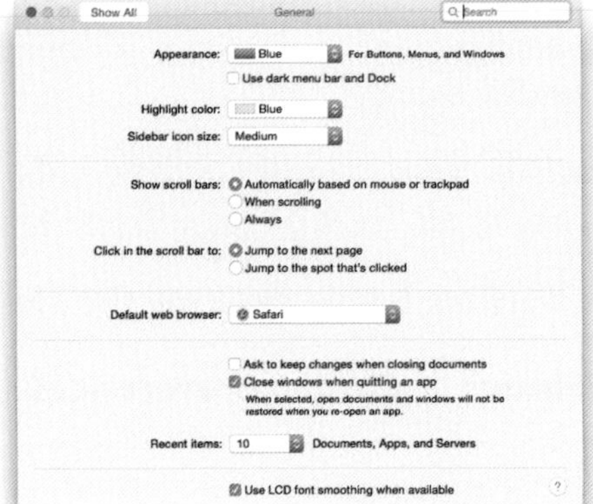

You can configure the scroll bars to be visible permanently.

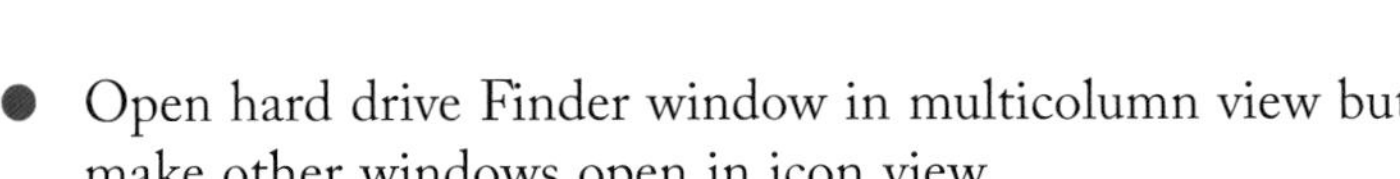

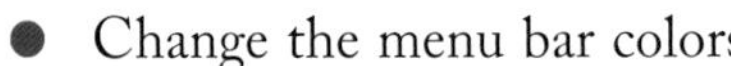

- Open hard drive Finder window in multicolumn view but make other windows open in icon view
- Change the menu bar colors
- Change the highlight color
- Make scroll bars always visible
- Have scroll bars at top and bottom of window or together
- Minimize windows by double-clicking their title bar
- Rearrange the order of the sidebar items
- Customize the toolbar

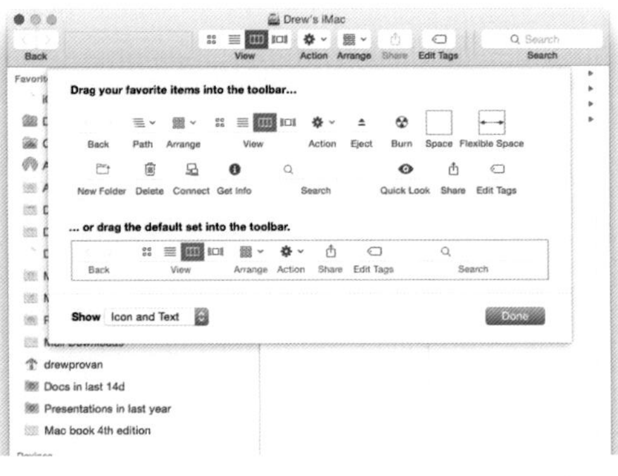

Customize Keyboard Shortcuts

There are many keyboard shortcuts. Lots of these are common to all apps, e.g. ⌘ + C (copy), ⌘ + P (print), ⌘ + V (paste), ⌘ + X (cut), ⌘ + Z (undo), etc. (see page 158). You can easily make your own shortcuts:

1. Go to **Apple menu > System preferences > Keyboard**

2. Select **Keyboard Shortcuts**

3. You can modify as many of these as you like

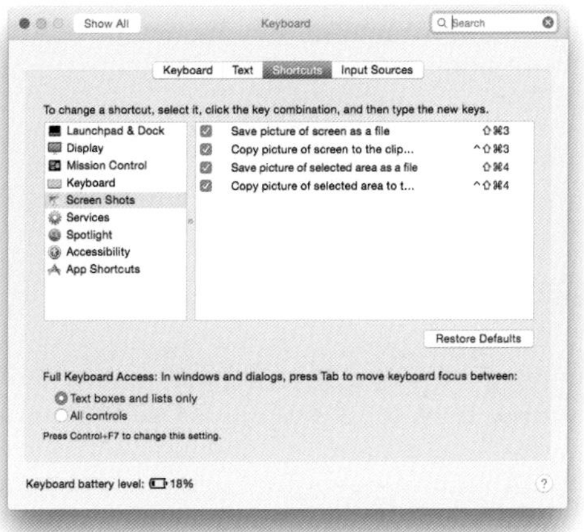

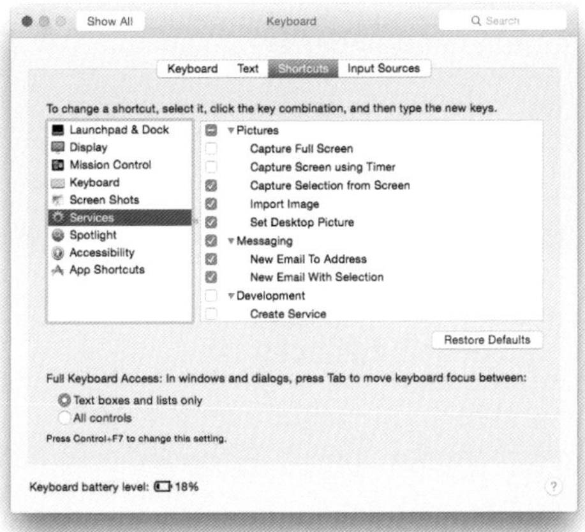

Change the Alert Sounds

The alert sounds are those made when there is a problem or tasks have completed. You can find these options under:

1. **Apple menu > System preferences > Sound**
2. Select **Sound Effects**
3. Play around with the various alert sounds until you're happy with these. In general, the default sounds are fine and there is little reason to change them

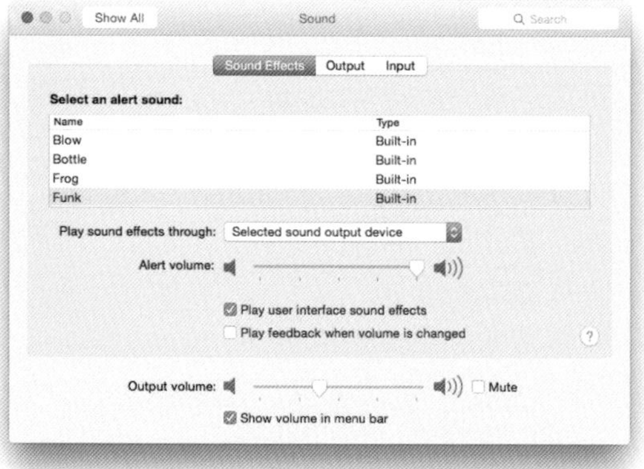

Can I add my own alert sounds?

Absolutely – it's easy! The file must be in AIFF format.

1. Go to **~/Library/Sounds**
2. Drag your AIFF file to the Sounds folder
3. Go to **System Preferences > Sound**
4. Click the **Sound Effects** tab
5. Your sound should appear in the alert sound list – select it to use it

12 Installing Software

You will want to add more apps to your Mac, and at times you will want to delete unused apps. This section describes the installation and removal of apps from the Mac.

Installing Apps is Easy!

There are several ways of getting new programs (apps, software) onto your Mac:

From an installer CD or DVD

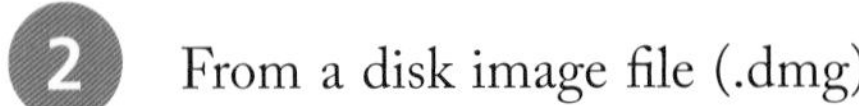
From a disk image file (.dmg)

The App Store (see Chapter 15)

Drag-and-drop onto the Applications folder

You should not directly copy apps from one Mac to another. You should always install properly.

What happens when you install software?

Sometimes when you drag a program onto a USB disk from one Mac to copy onto another the program won't run on the second Mac. This is because the original installer placed files in numerous locations all over your Mac in various folders, in the Library folder and elsewhere. When you drag your program from the Applications folder on one Mac onto the USB drive you do *not* copy across all the supplementary files required to run the program and so, on the second Mac the program would not run because it is missing some key pieces of information required to run the app. Theoretically, you could find the various components of the program on the hard drive if you knew which files are installed and where they are located but this is not practical. For that reason it is never a particularly good idea to copy programs from one computer to another simply by dragging the program across.

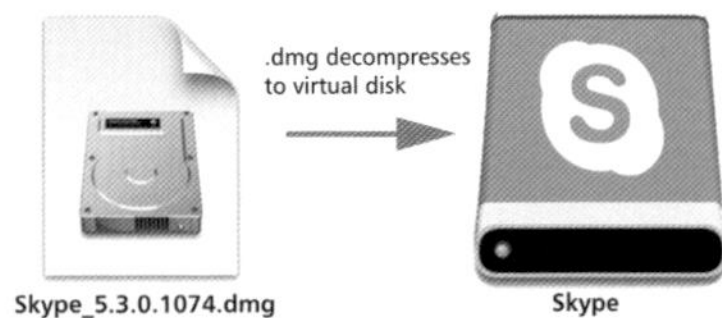

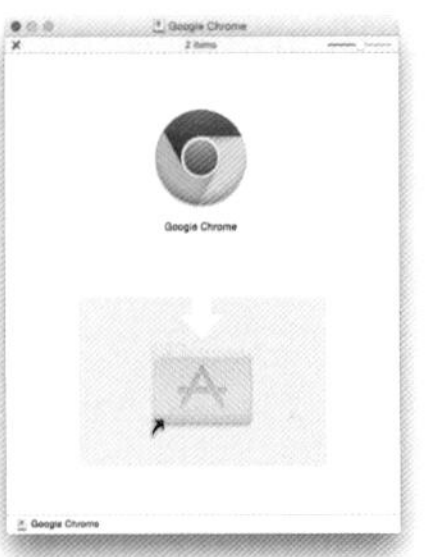

Installing From a .dmg File

Many apps are installed from disk image files (.dmg). These are generally downloaded from the Internet and once downloaded they appear on the desktop after they decompress, much like a physical drive connected to your Mac, but obviously they are not. Instead they are "virtual" drives.

How to identify the .dmg file?

The .dmg file has a white document icon with an image of the disk in the middle and if you look at the name of the file it will end with .dmg.

To install software from this type of image file

1. You need to **double-click the dmg**
2. Then a temporary virtual disk will mount on your desktop as if this were a disk drive plugged into your Mac
3. **Open the disk image** (white drive icon)
4. Generally, to install the software you have to **double-click an installer file** within this virtual disk but sometimes you will see instructions telling you to **drag the application to your Applications folder** (this does *not* mean that there was only one file for this program. Instead, when you first run the program it will then place lots of other files to the scattered locations mentioned earlier)

Once an app has been installed you can drag the installer (.dmg files and the virtual disk) to the Trash.

What do you do with .dmg and the virtual disk once the program has been installed?

After you have installed your software, you can drag both the disk image file and the white disk icon to the Trash.

Put an App onto the Dock

After installing a new app you can find it by

1. Going to the **Applications folder** and finding it there
2. Using **Launchpad** (you can find this on the Dock)
3. Typing ⌘ **+ Spacebar** and searching for the app by name
4. If you have used the program recently, you can go to the **Apple menu > Recent Items** and look for the app there

To add an app to the Dock drag it from the Applications folder to the Dock.

If you intend to use an app regularly why not put it into the Dock so you don't have to search for it?

How to place an app on the Dock

1. **Find the app** in the Applications folder
2. Click the app, and hold down the mouse button
3. **Drag the app to the Dock**
4. Move it to the exact location sideways on the Dock until you're happy with its position

To remove an app from the Dock simply drag it upwards off the Dock.

Remove an app from the Dock

1. Simply click and hold the pointer on the app and **drag it upwards off the Dock**
2. You will see and hear a puff of smoke

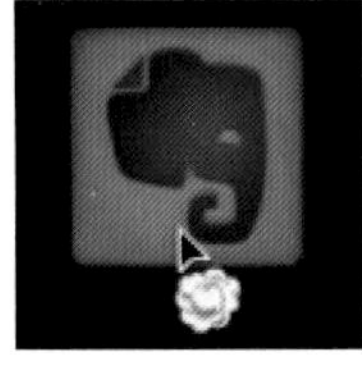

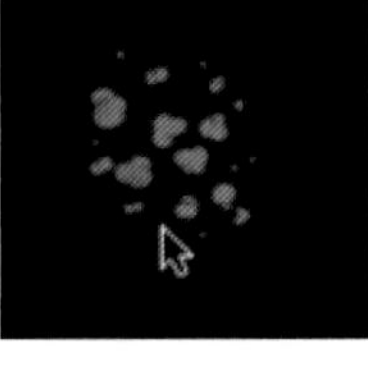

Removing Preference Files

Sometimes a program may misbehave, start crashing, or otherwise act erratically. Preference files store various bits of information such as page size, etc. and are required in order to run the program, but occasionally the preference files become corrupt and they cause the app to misbehave.

One way of sorting software problems is to remove the preference file from your Home Library.

To remove a preference file for Photoshop, for example

1. Go to your **Home Folder** (the one that looks like a little house and has your name on it)
2. Then locate **~/Library/Preferences**
3. Scroll down the list of preferences until you find, in this case: **com.adobe/Photoshop.plist**
4. **Drag this file to trash**
5. **Reopen Photoshop** and see if the problem has now resolved

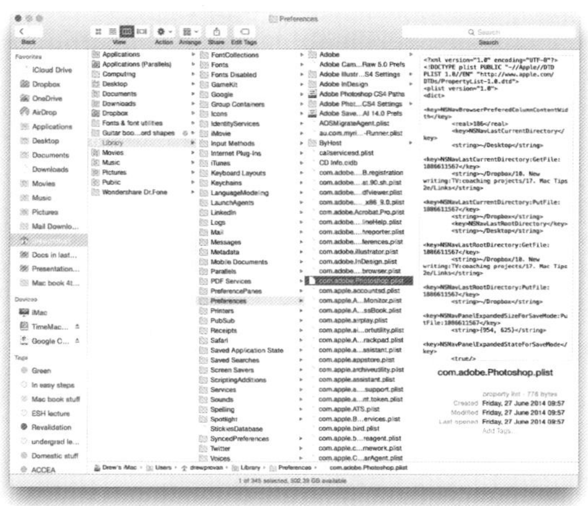

.plist files can be trashed if programs misbehave.

How to Uninstall Apps

PCs have uninstallers, e.g. the Windows Add/Remove Program Control Panel. Unfortunately, Macs don't have the same method for removing software.

Dragging an app to the Trash does not fully uninstall it – various files are left behind.

To remove apps

1. **Locate the app** in the Applications folder

2. **Drag the app to the Trash**

3. **Empty trash**

This is pretty simple but does not remove all the other supplementary files scattered around the hard drive when you installed the program, e.g. the preferences file and other files.

Although the Mac does not come with an uninstaller there are third-party programs which will uninstall all components of the program, so you can remove the program completely leaving no traces of files the installer has placed on your hard drive.

Examples of uninstallers

AppCleaner (**appcleaner.en.softtonic.com/Mac**) – free

AppDelete (**reggieashworth.com**) – $7.99

AppZapper (**appzapper.com**) – $12.95

(Note - prices correct at time of printing)

Use an uninstaller app to remove all the little files the original installer placed on your hard drive.

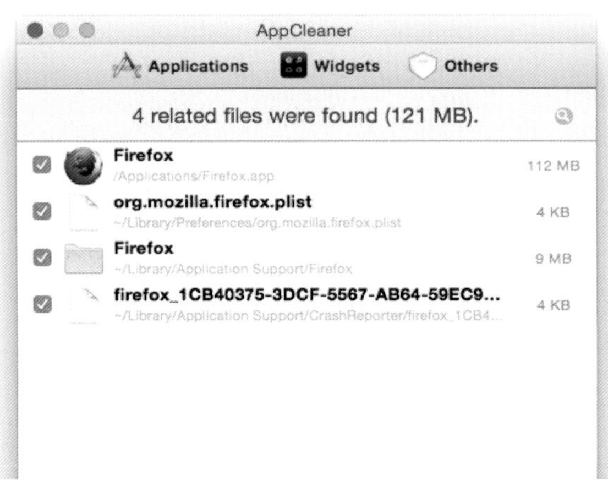

13 Switch from PC to Mac

Many people are switching to the Mac from Windows, largely driven by devices such as the iPhone, iPad and iPod Touch. The transition from PC to Mac is easy, and here we will look at the issues that may confuse users switching from the world of Windows.

Mac Desktop and Windows

There are some differences between the window layouts on PCs and Macs but these are pretty minor and you will soon get used to the Mac window layout. The desktop on both platforms is also fairly similar with the Task Bar on the PC being replaced by the Dock on the Mac.

The figures below show the main items on a basic Mac window and the Mac desktop.

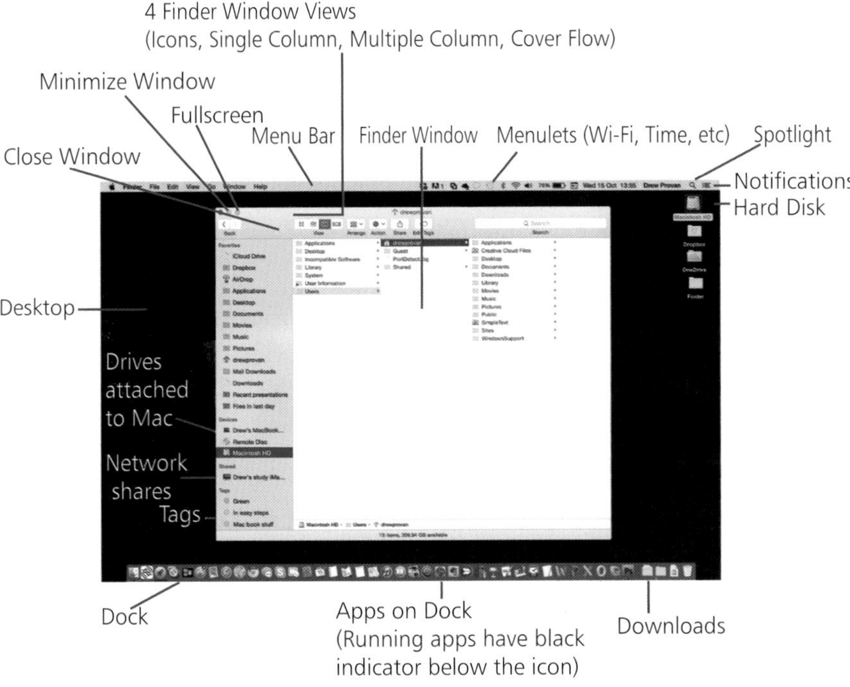

If you don't see a menu when you right-click on the desktop you probably haven't configured the right-click! See opposite page.

What you get when you right-click on the desktop

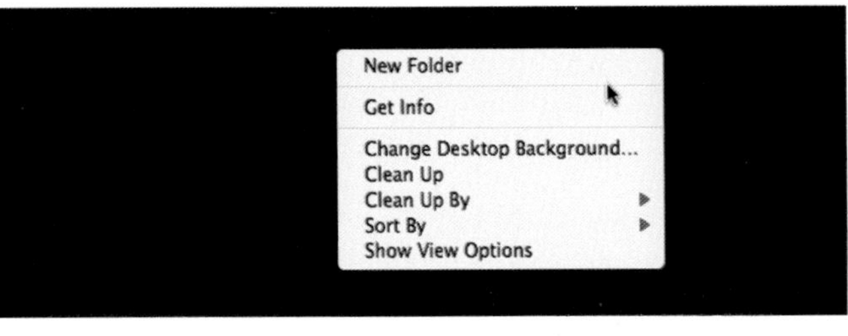

Single-Click Mouse?

Macs were sold originally with a one-button mouse which made right-clicking difficult. The Mac mouse is now a two-button mouse although it would appear when you first start using it to be only one button with no right-click.

Although the Magic Mouse does not appear to have distinct left and right sides, if you use your index finger on the left side this is a left-click and if you click your middle finger on the right side this constitutes a right-click.

To configure the mouse for right & left click

1. Go to **Apple Menu > System Preferences Mouse Point & Click**

2. You can configure the secondary click to be either right side or left side using the dropdown option

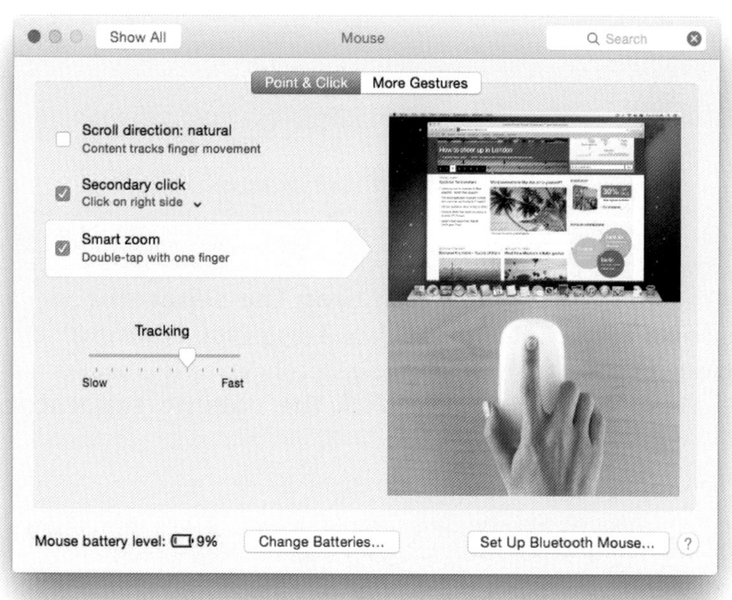

Where's Windows Explorer?

Windows Explorer is the program used on Windows computers to browse folders and their contents. The equivalent on the Mac is the Finder which is found on the Dock at the extreme left side. You can also use the Finder by typing **⌘ + F**.

Clicking the Finder will bring up a Finder window showing the drives, folders, and files. What you see will depend on how you have set up your Finder windows, and can be icons, single column or multicolumn view. The multicolumn view is probably the most useful since you can see the hierarchical structure of your folders on any attached drive.

The Finder is the Mac equivalent of Windows Explorer.

Resizing the columns

To **resize** a column **click and drag the separator** line. To **resize ALL columns** click and drag while **holding down the Option** key. To resize a column so it is as wide as the widest file name **double-click the column separator**.

The Start Menu

There is no Start Menu on the Mac and the nearest equivalent would be the Dock onto which you can drag your favorite apps.

When you start using a Mac there will already be some apps on the Dock, such as Finder, Mail, Safari, DVD Player, iMovie, and several others. But as you install more apps yourself you will probably want to drag some of these to the Dock.

On a PC you can shut the computer down from the Start Menu and on the Mac you can press the Power Button and you will be asked *"Are you sure you want to shut down your computer now?"*.

Alternatively, from the Apple Menu choose

- **Apple Menu > Sleep**
- **Apple Menu > Restart...**
- **Apple Menu > Shut Down...**

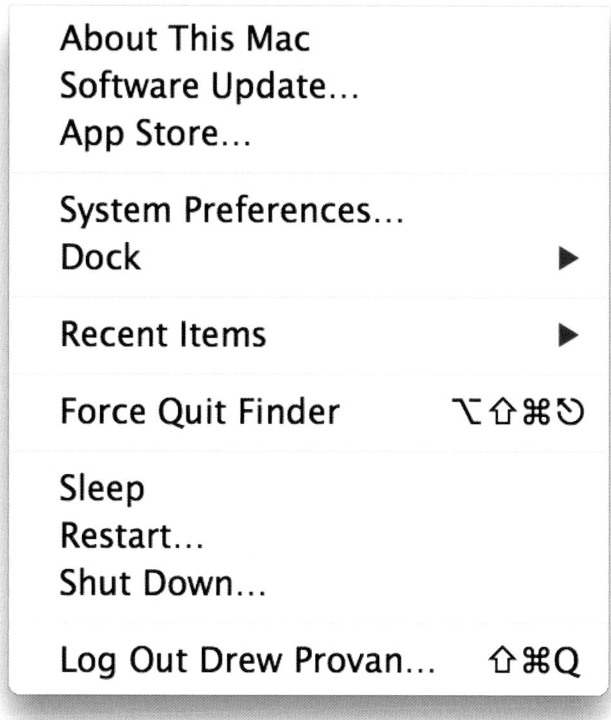

Keyboard Shortcuts

Keyboard shortcuts save huge amounts of time. If you know some PC shortcuts you will be relieved to hear that they are similar on the Mac, mainly replacing the Control key with Command (⌘) key.

PC	Shift	Control	Alt	WinKey	Backspace
Mac	Shift	Control	Option	Command	Delete
Symbol	⇧	^	⌥	⌘	⌦

Action	PC	Mac
Copy	Control + C	⌘ + C
Paste	Control + V	⌘ + V
Cut	Control + X	⌘ + X
Undo	Control + Z	⌘ + Z
Print	Control + P	⌘ + P
Screen capture	PrntScrn	⌘ + ⇧ + 3
Capture active window		⌘ + ⇧ + 4
Close window	Control + W	⌘ + W
Copy file/folder	Control + Drag	^ + Drag
Create alias	Right-click and create shortcut	Right-click and create alias OR ⌘ + L
Find	Control + F	⌘ + F
Get item info	Alt + Enter	⌘ + I
Max window	Control + F10	None
Min window	Windows + M	⌘ + M
New folder	Control + N	⌘ + ⇧ + N
Open file	Control + O	⌘ + O
Quit app	Alt + F4	⌘ + Q
Save file	Control + S	⌘ + S
Select all	Control + A	⌘ + A
Send item to trash	Delete	⌘ + Delete
Toggle through apps	Alt + Tab	⌘ + Tab
Type special chars	Alt + Key	⌥ + Key
Force quit app	Control + Alt + Del	⌘ + ⌥ + Esc

Here's a fantastic tip hardly anyone knows! To find a file by name only (i.e., excluding all the text within the file itself) use Shift + Control + Cmd + F).

Control Panel

Control Panel on the PC is used to set up preferences for networking, printers, sharing, user accounts, screen display, sound, and many other functions. These same functions exist on the Mac but they are called **System Preferences** and if you are comfortable using Control Panel on the PC then you will almost certainly have no problem with system preferences on the Mac.

Search for System Preference by name

1. Go to **Apple Menu > System Preferences**
2. Type the name of the System Preference you are looking for in the **search box** (top right)

Search for System Preference by function

Suppose you want to know which System Preference controls the Mac sleep function?

1. Type *sleep* into the search box
2. The System Preferences that control Mac sleep are highlighted while the others are dimmed
3. You also have other options shown below the search box

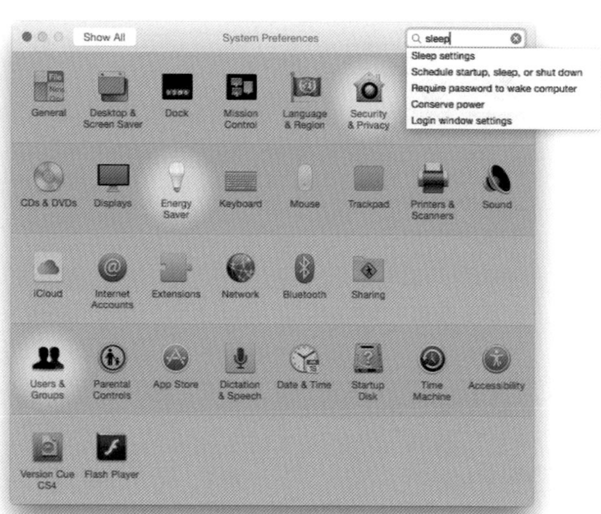

To help find a System Preference associated with a specific function, type the function into the search box. The relevant System Preference(s) will be highlighted.

Network Settings

Networking Macs is very straightforward and arguably much easier than networking PCs. In general, Macs on the same network see each other with no problem. They also see peripheral devices attached to other Macs such as printers or drives, with minimal fuss.

Network settings are covered in Chapter Nine.

Connect to server

1. If you know the IP address of the server, you can connect by choosing **Go > Connect to Server...**

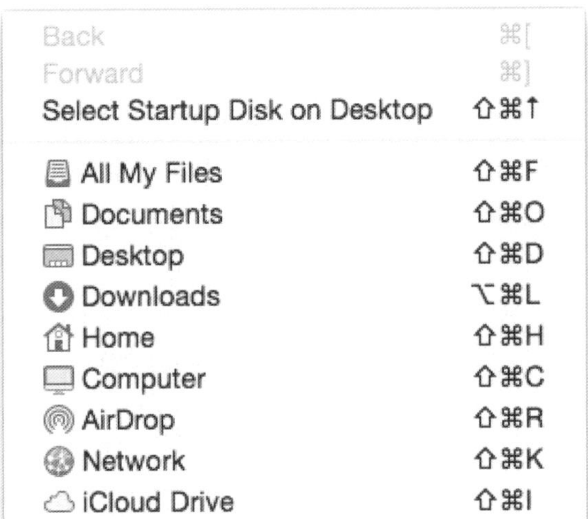

2. **Enter the IP address** in the address box

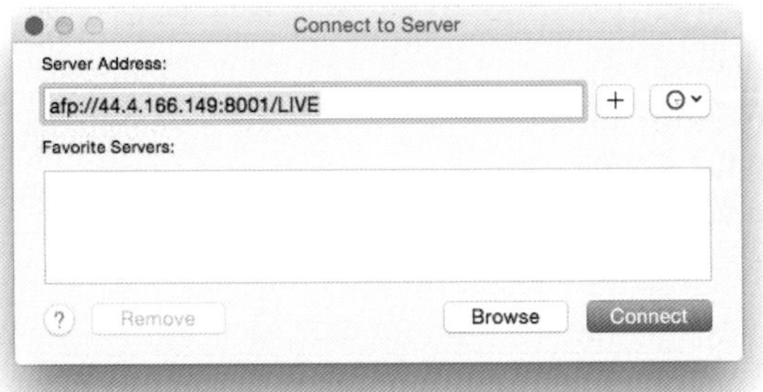

3. Hit **Return**

Printers & Scanners

Adding printers to a Mac is extremely easy. OS X comes with inbuilt printer drivers for most printers around.

To add a printer

1. **Plug the printer into the Mac**

2. Go to **Apple Menu > System Preferences > Printers & Scanners**

3. Click the **+** to add a new printer

4. The Mac searches the hard drive for the printer driver, after which time your printer will appear in the left pane

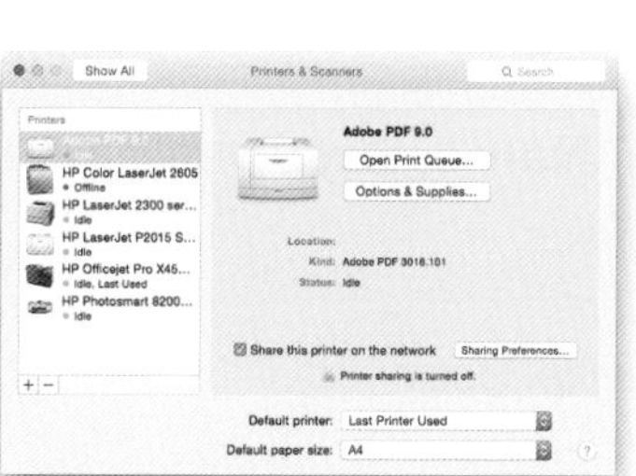

5. You can then **close** the Printers & Scanners window

If a document fails to print to a wireless (or wired) printer, try deleting the printer and re-installing it.

To check printer RAM and other functions

1. Go to **Apple Menu > System Preferences > Printers & Scanners > Open Print Queue... >Printer Settings > Options**

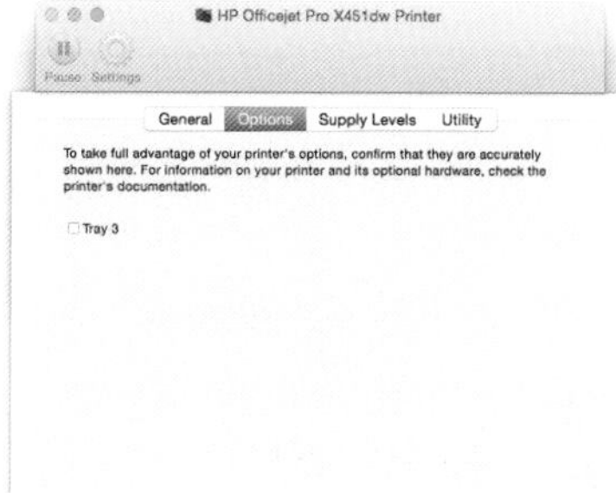

User Accounts

User Accounts on the PC is replaced by **Users & Groups** on the Mac.

Setting up a new account

1. Go to **Apple Menu > System Preferences > Users & Groups**
2. Click **padlock** and enter **password** to make changes
3. Click the **+** to add a new account
4. Decide on the **account type** (Administrator/Standard/Managed with Parental Controls/Sharing Only) – Administrators have full rights to install and delete apps. If unsure set up as Standard
5. Enter **Full Name, Account Name, Password and Hint**
6. Click **Create User**

Login options

1. You can allow **Automatic login** (no password required) or switch this off
2. On shared computers it is better to switch **OFF** automatic login to prevent people having access to your files

Do not disable Automatic login if more than one person will be using the Mac.

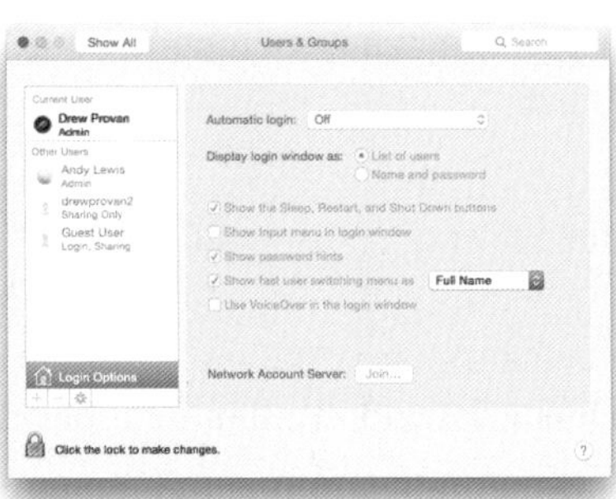

Migrate Your PC Files to Mac

There are several ways to get your PC documents onto the Mac. Obviously PC *programs* will not run on the Mac so you are mainly looking to copy across pictures, music, Microsoft Office documents, and others to the Mac.

Using removable media

1. The easiest way is to use a USB stick: plug it into the PC, navigate to My Documents and drag this folder to the USB stick
2. Unplug the USB stick from the PC and plug it into the Mac
3. Copy pictures to Pictures folder on the Mac, music to Music folder, and so on

The network option

You can network PC and Mac wired (Ethernet) or wirelessly:

1. On the Mac select **Go > Connect to Server**
2. Type in your PC's network address using the format *smb://DNSname/ShareName* or *smb://IPaddress/ShareName*
3. Click **Connect** and follow the on-screen instructions
4. Once the PC appears on the Mac **drag and drop** the PC files onto the Mac desktop
5. You can also mount the PC on the Mac desktop wirelessly and drag and drop files that way

If you are running Windows on your Mac (see page 164)
If you have installed Boot Camp and Windows 7 or 8 (or VMWare Fusion or Parallels Desktop) run the Windows Easy Transfer Wizard. See **www.vmware.com/Fusion, http://www.parallels.com** and Apple's help pages: **http://www.apple.com/support/switch101**

Run Windows on the Mac

Since Macs have Intel processors you can run Microsoft Windows using two different methods:

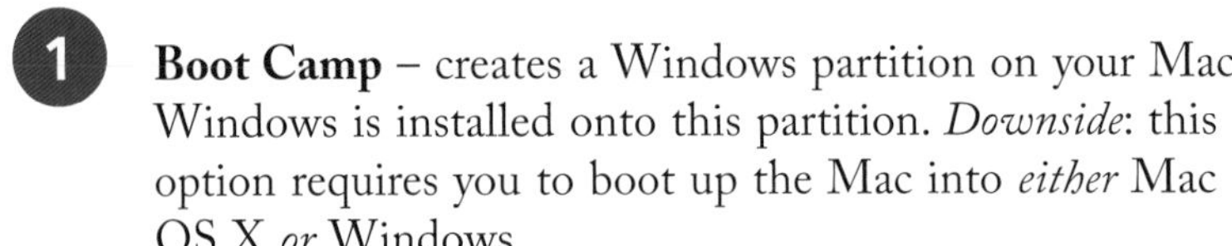

1. **Boot Camp** – creates a Windows partition on your Mac. Windows is installed onto this partition. *Downside*: this option requires you to boot up the Mac into *either* Mac OS X *or* Windows

2. **Virtualization** – using VMWare Fusion or Parallels Desktop. Creates a Windows partition on your Mac onto which you install Windows. When running OS X you can boot up Windows and have the Windows desktop running *on top* of the Mac desktop with sharing of files, folders and drives between Mac and Windows

The Boot Camp option means you can ONLY boot into one system at a time, i.e. Windows OR Mac. If you want to run them side-by-side use Parallels Desktop or VMWare Fusion.

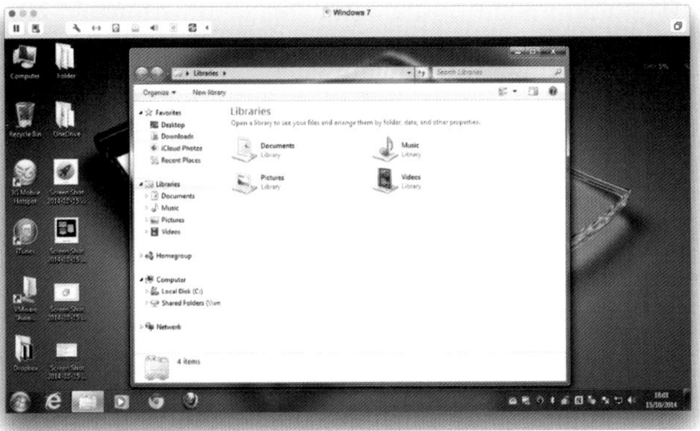

Boot Camp installation

1. Go to **Utilities > Boot Camp Installer**

2. Run the installer, allocating sufficient disk space for Windows

3. Insert your Windows installation disk and follow the on-screen instructions

VMWare Fusion and Parallels

These come with installer DVDs. Follow the on-screen instructions or visit the manufacturers' websites.

14 Burn CDs and DVDs

Although USB drives are getting cheaper we still need to burn files onto CD and DVD occasionally. This chapter walks you through the various choices available for burning different media onto CD and DVD.

Burning Music to CD

Burning is the term used for copying files onto CDs or DVDs. You can copy files onto these disks using a variety of methods, e.g. using the Mac's inbuilt burning software or using third-party apps such as Toast Titanium.

Making your own music CDs

1. **Insert a blank CD-R** into the optical drive

2. When you see the message "*You inserted a blank CD. Choose an action from the pop-up menu or click ignore.*" **Click OK**

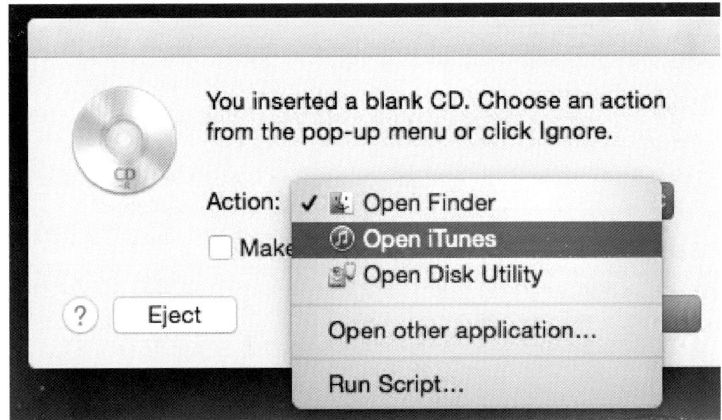

3. **Open iTunes**

4. **Make a new playlist** (File > New Playlist)

5. **Select the tracks** you want to copy onto the CD

6. **Drag the tracks onto the new playlist** (give the new playlist a title)

7. **Right-click on the new playlist** and select **Burn Playlist to Disc**

8. Or go to **File > Burn Playlist to Disc**
9. iTunes will burn the tracks onto the CD
10. Once finished you can eject the CD

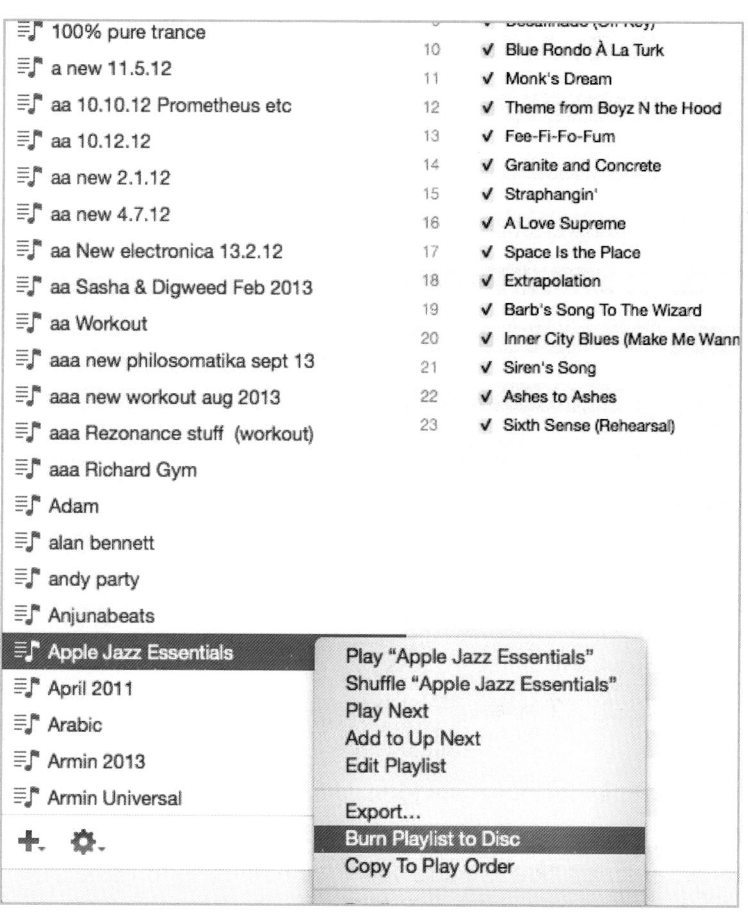

Burn Photos onto CD/DVD

You can burn photos from iPhoto either as photo files or as slideshows.

Copy photos onto CD/DVD

1. **Insert CD/DVD** into the optical drive
2. **Open iPhoto**
3. **Select the album** you want to copy
4. Click **File > Export**

Besides burning photos to DVD there are several other ways to share your pics – you can share them on social media sites, such as Facebook and Twitter, or order prints.

Copy Files and Folders onto CD/DVD

You can copy files and folders onto CDs or DVDs easily.

1. **Insert a blank CD/DVD** (can be -R or -RW) into the optical drive

2. At the message "*You inserted a blank CD. Choose an action from the pop-up menu or click ignore.*" **Click OK**

3. You will see Untitled CD on the desktop

4. Copy your files/folders onto the CD by **Option-dragging** the files or folders (if you only drag the file you will simply copy an *alias* onto the CD and *not* the files/folders)

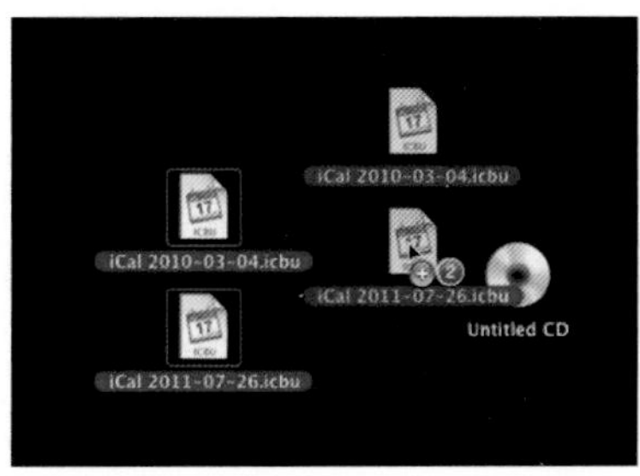

5. After you see the files being copied onto the CD or DVD, right-click the CD icon and choose **Burn "Untitled CD"...**

6. Once burned, you can eject the CD

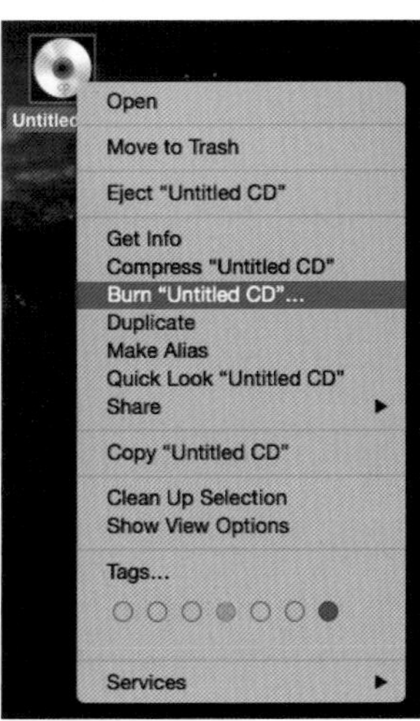

Burn CD/DVD with Disk Utility

You can also copy files onto CDs or DVDs using the Mac app Disk Utility (in the Utilities folder **Go > Utilities**).

1. **Open Disk Utility**

2. Select **New Image**

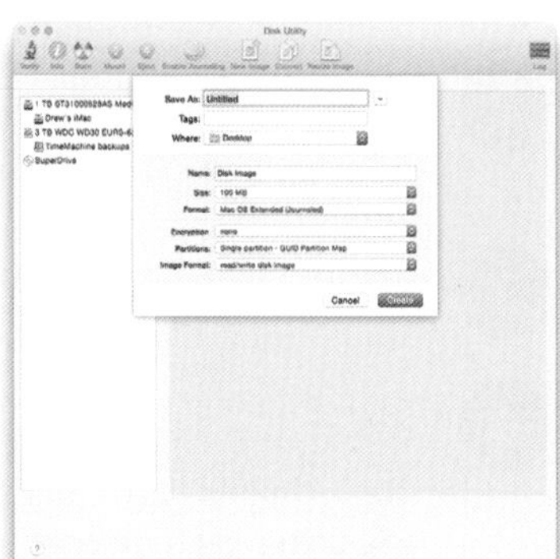

3. Give it a name

4. Disk Utility will create a .dmg file on the desktop and will also create a virtual drive called *Disk Image* on the desktop

5. **Drag your files or folders to Disk Image**

6. You will see them copy across

7. **Right-click Disk Image** and select **Burn "Disk Image" to Disc...**

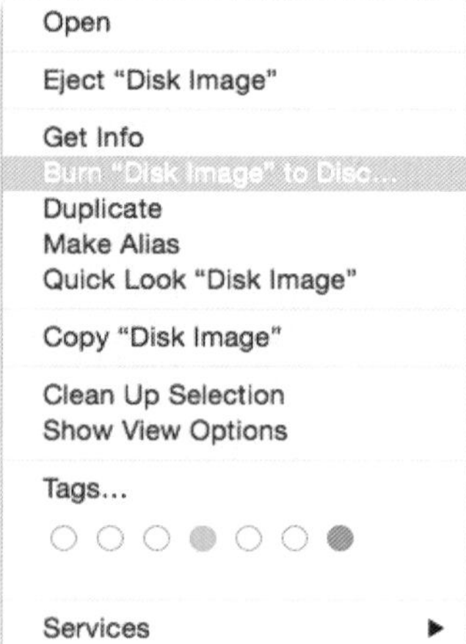

8. **Eject the CD/DVD** once burned

9. To see the files, insert the CD/DVD into the optical drive

15 App Store & iBooks

The App Store *is a huge repository of apps covering all categories. Here we look at how to find, purchase and install apps from* The App Store. *With the addition of iBooks to Mac OS X you can now buy and read books on your Mac just as you can on iOS devices.*

What is the App Store?

The App Store on the Mac mirrors the App Store seen on iOS devices (iPhone, iPad, iPod). Rather than buying software in a shop or from a website, this app lets you browse thousands of software titles and when you find the one you want you simply click to download.

Updates are easy

Because of the Updates tab, you can easily see when there is a new version of your app. It's a simple matter of clicking to update the software.

You cannot use the App Store unless you have set up an iTunes account.

Basic layout of the App Store

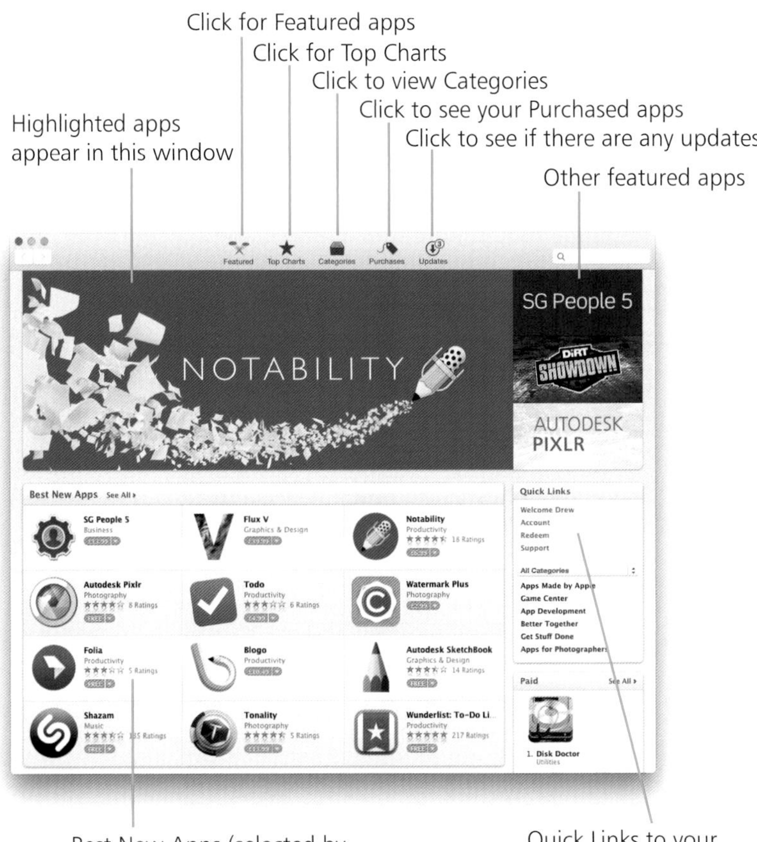

The App Store will update your apps in the background if you go to the App Store System Preference and select that option.

Top Charts

Apps that are selling well appear in the Top Charts. Generally, they have received good user reviews (always read the reviews for any app – it prevents you from buying something which has bugs, crashes or is substandard).

There are thousands of apps and not all are worth buying.

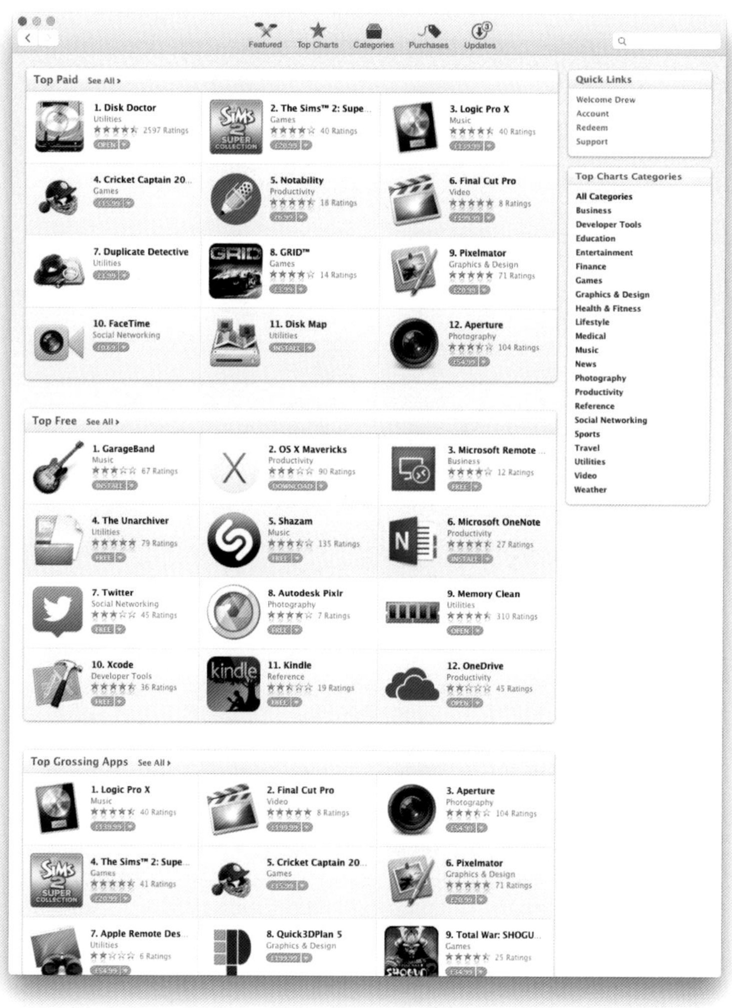

Always read the software reviews. Just because an app is available to purchase does not guarantee its quality! New apps are checked by Apple so you don't need to worry about them containing viruses.

Categories

With so many apps, it can be a nightmare trying to find what you are looking for. Sometimes it's a good idea just to start by category. For example, if you are interested in sport, working out, and fitness try clicking the Fitness category and browsing there.

But beware, there are many apps in each category so it may still take a long time to find exactly what you want.

Once you select a category you can browse the top Paid and Free apps, and explore other features.

Purchased

Are you spending too much? Which apps have you bought? It's easy to see what purchases you have already made by clicking the Purchased tab.

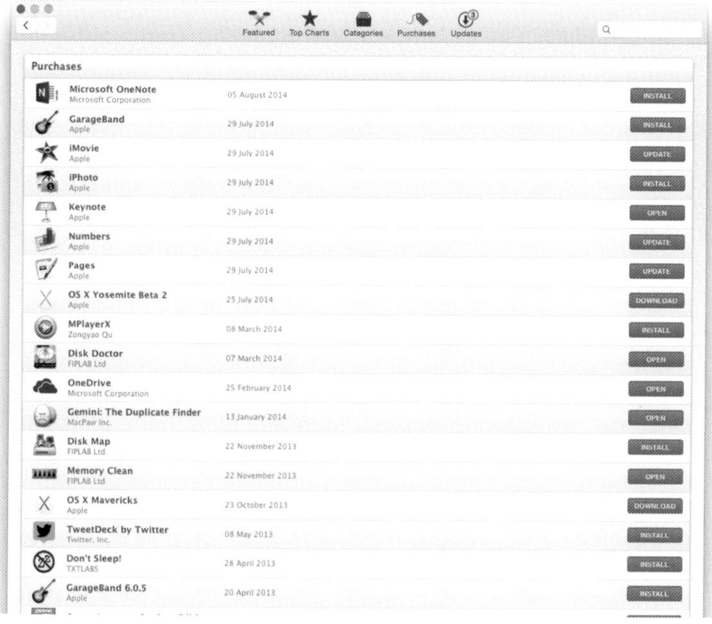

You can review your purchases by clicking the Purchased tab.

Information about a purchased app

Click on the title of an app to get more information, details about the developer, etc.

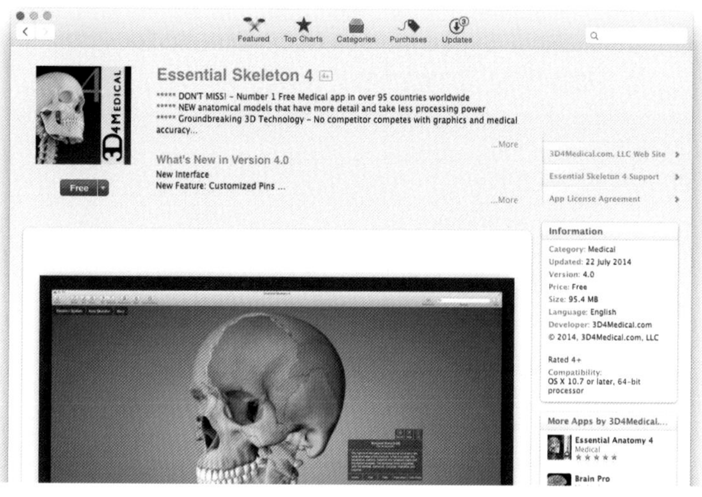

Updates

Once you have bought and installed an app, the developers will from time to time post updates, fixing the software or adding new features. You can see what updates are available by clicking the Updates tab.

Interestingly, it looks as though the App Store does not recognize apps you have bought outside the App Store (for instance, on CD, DVD or ones you've downloaded elsewhere) so you will probably have to update those the conventional way (launch the app and check Updates).

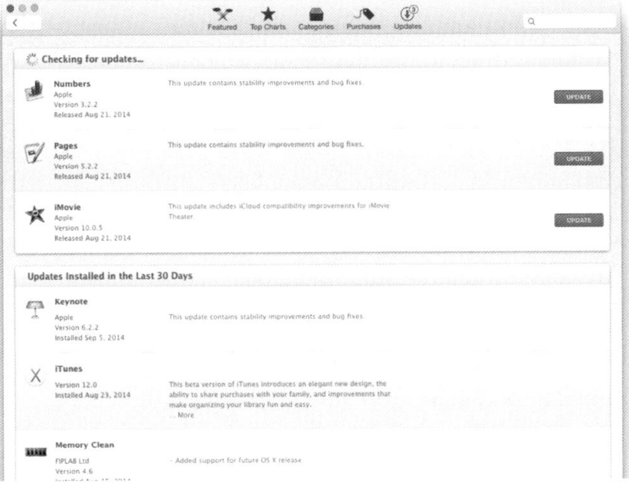

Check for Unfinished downloads

1 Go to **App Store > Store > Check for Unfinished Downloads...**

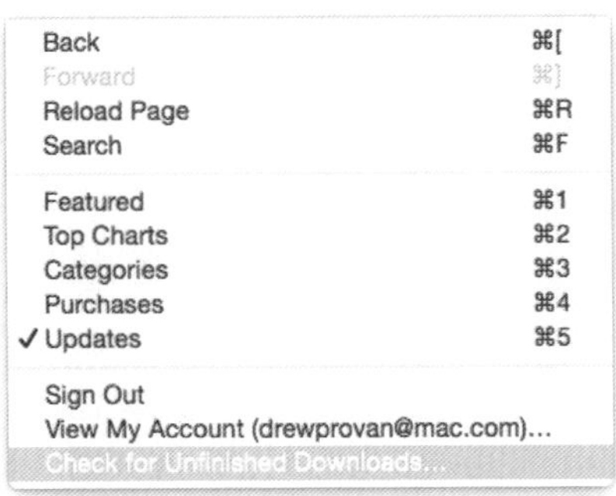

How to Buy an App

You will need to be signed in to the App Store before you can buy anything. The App Store uses your iTunes account details. Sign in using your usual name and password.

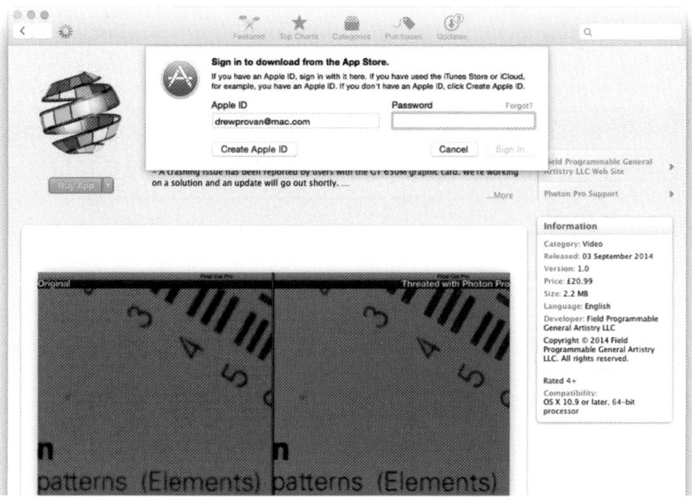

How to buy an app

1. **Find the app** you want
2. **Click the price** (or Free, if it's free)
3. The app will download

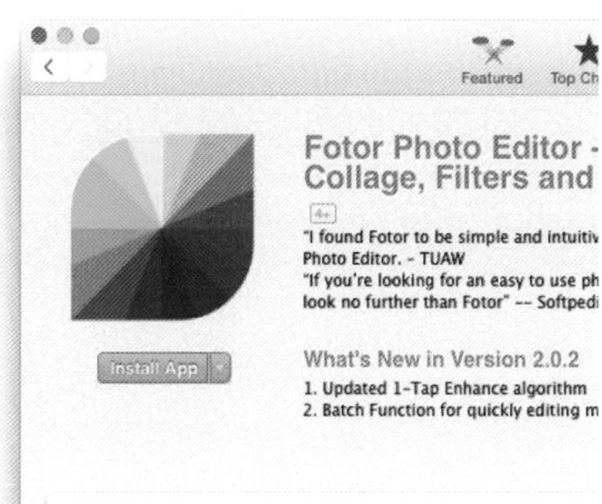

You still need an iTunes account even if the app you want to download is free.

Tell a Friend

If you see a great app and want to alert a friend, there's a Tell a Friend button.

1. Click the dropdown next to the price
2. Select **Tell a Friend**
3. This will open Mail and the link will be in the message

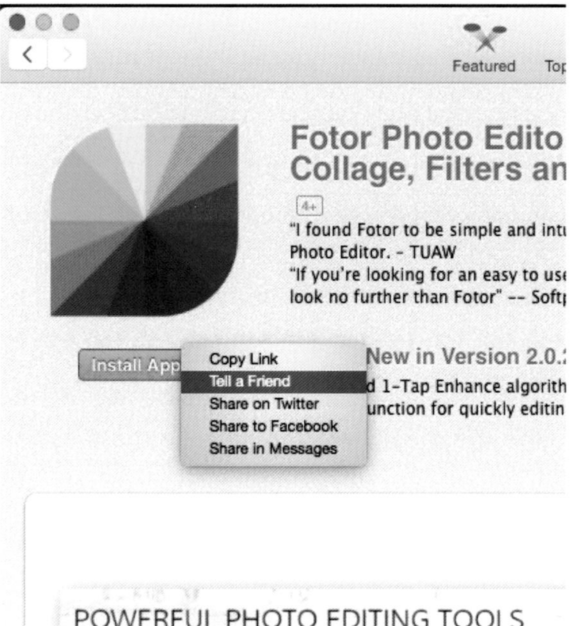

Sharing

You can also share information about apps on:

- Twitter
- Facebook
- Messages

iBooks

iBooks on the Mac is very similar to iPhone, iPad and iPod Touch. Once you open the app and log in using your iTunes password you can read your previously-purchased books and buy more from the iBooks Store.

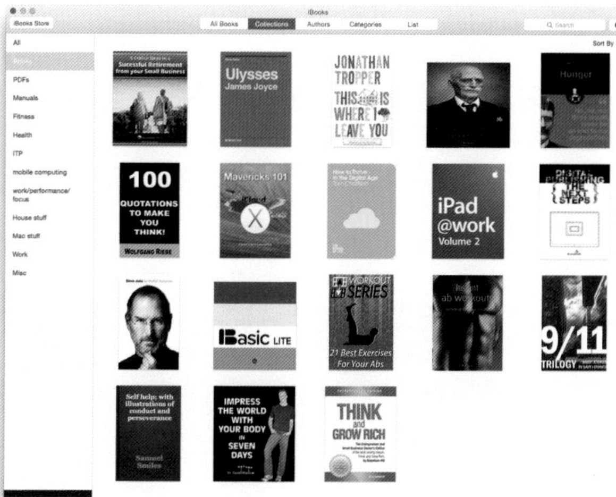

This view shows your books.

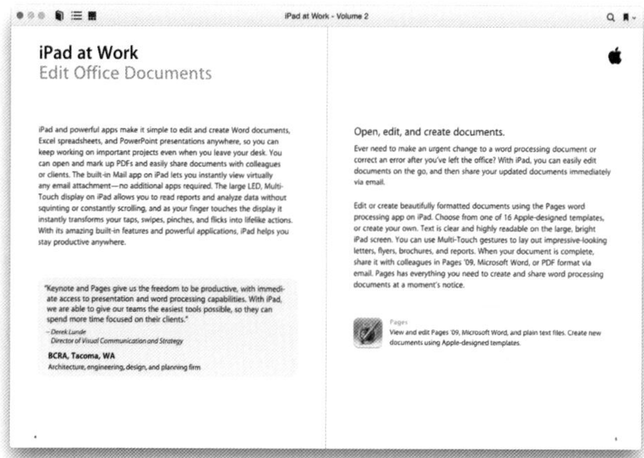

Opening a book gives a view similar to that seen on an iOS device.

Searching for Apps

You can search for specific apps or categories using the search box.

1. Enter the search term

2. Hit **Return**

If you can't find an app easily on the app store, try doing a Google search and see what other people are recommending.

16 Keep Things in Sync

With our data such as calendars, contacts and documents held on so many different devices these days it is useful to be able to keep these in sync. Here we will look at options for syncing all your important information.

Keeping Email in Sync

It is very useful to be able to see all your emails on all your devices – Mac, PC, iPhone, iPad, and other devices. It is far more useful than having to use one particular device to view your mail. This is very easy to achieve if you use any email service that allows you to set up your email as IMAP (Internet Message Access Protocol) as opposed to the older POP3 type account.

IMAP email is more useful if you intend to view your emails using more than one computer, or iPad, iPhone, etc.

Why is IMAP so useful?

It lets your email program see your emails on a server. The emails do not reside on your Mac so you can view all folders and emails using any device since no device actually holds the email.

Which services use IMAP?

There are several but the two commonly used are

- iCloud
- Google Mail

Set up an IMAP account

This is covered in Chapter Four.

The biggest advantage?

All your emails are synced and all devices can see identical emails and attachments.

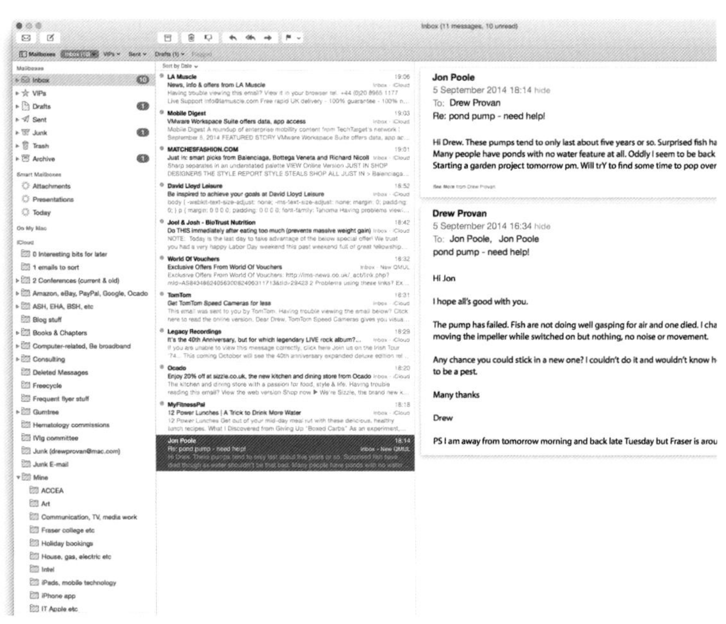

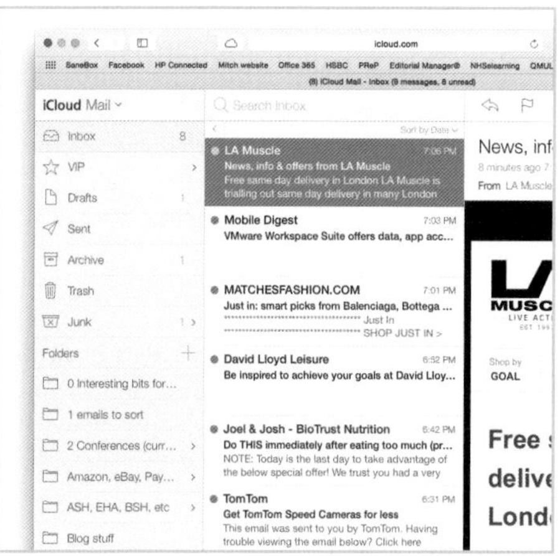

The same IMAP folders on iCloud using the Safari browser...

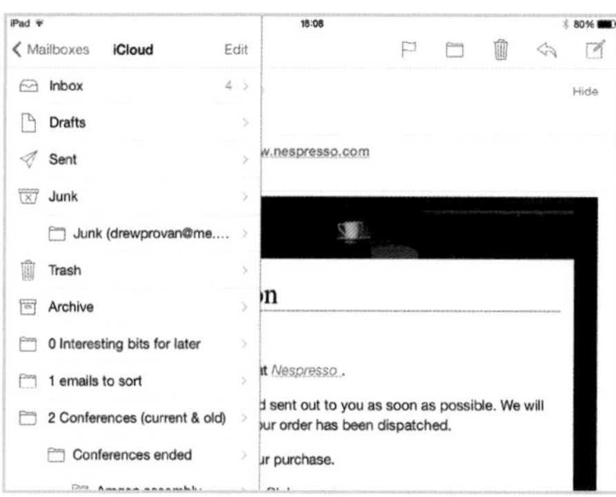

And viewed on an iPad...

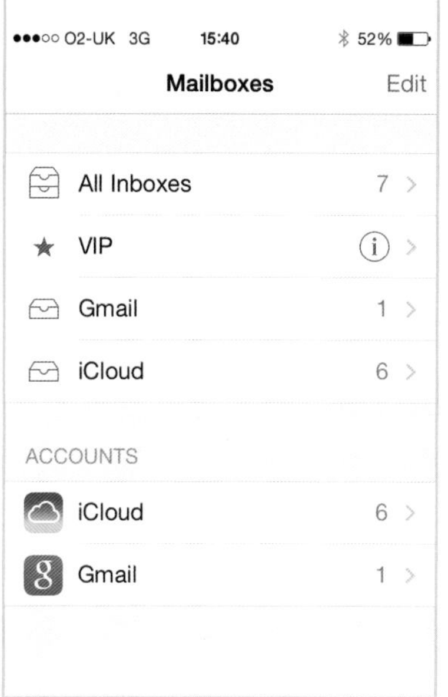

And finally, on the iPhone

Calendar Syncing

If you use Calendar on your Mac you may also want to access Calendar using your iPhone, iPod Touch, or iPad. You may also view Calendar on multiple Macs or even using a PC (e.g. by logging into iCloud on the PC using a browser).

Best apps for keeping calendars in sync

- iCloud
- Google Calendar

Wireless syncing is much more convenient than the wired method.

Both of these are web-based. If you add an event to Calendar on your Mac the event will sync via the cloud to the iCloud server and be "pushed" to other devices such as an iPhone if you have set up an iCloud account on the iPhone.

Using iCloud to sync Calendar events

1. Open the iCloud System Preference
2. Make sure Calendars is checked in order to sync Calendar data from Mac or PC to mobile device (iPhone, iPad, or iPod Touch)

Google Calendar

Google Calendar can be viewed on any PC or Mac so you can see all your appointments even if you're away from your own Mac. Calendar can be configured to sync with Google calendar.

It is easy to add your Google Calendar to Calendar.

Setting up Calendar sync with Google Calendar

1. Open Calendar
2. Go to **Calendar Preferences > Accounts**
3. Add the **+ to add a new account** and choose **Google** from the options on the right
4. Enter your **name and password** to configure the account

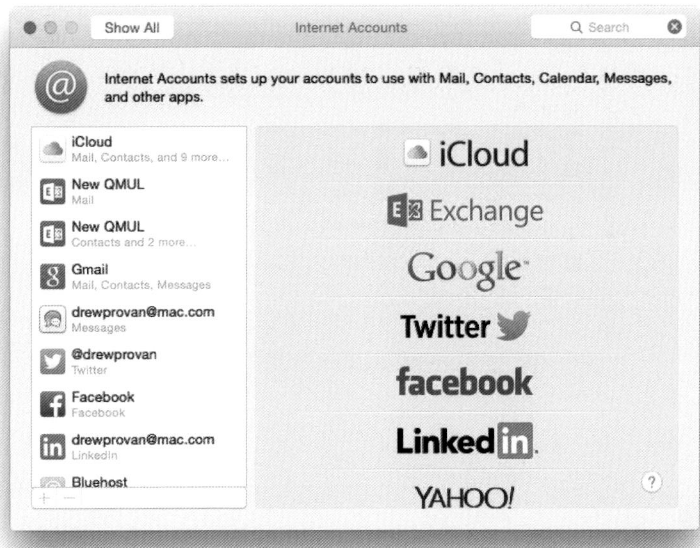

Syncing Contacts

It is useful to have the same set of contacts on all your Macs and mobile devices. This is easy to set up using:

- iCloud
- Google Contacts (log in to Google Mail to view Contacts)
- Configure iCloud to sync contacts from the Contacts app

Apple Contacts makes it simple to import all your Google Contacts.

Syncing Google contacts in Contacts

1. **Launch Contacts**
2. Click on the **Contacts menu > Preferences**
3. Click on the **Accounts** tab

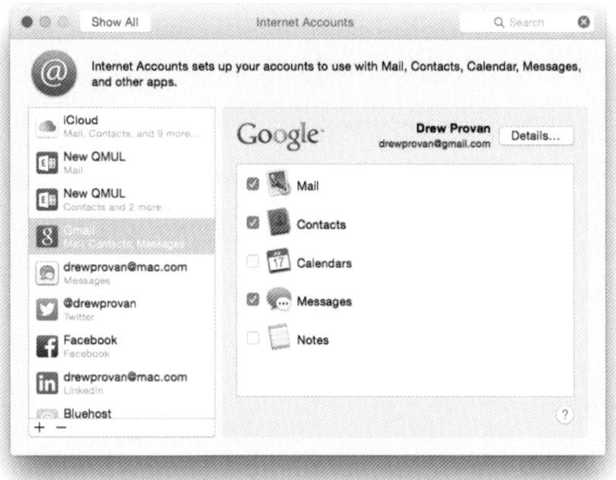

4. Select your Google account under the accounts on the left
5. Check the checkbox accompanying **Enable this account**

Keep Your Notes in Sync

Mobile devices such as iPad and iPhone have a Notes program. The Notes app is also included in Yosemite so you can add, delete and edit Notes on all your devices and they will remain in sync.

Setting up the Notes sync

1. Go to **System Preferences > iCloud**
2. Check the Notes box
3. Do the same on your other devices (other Macs, PCs, iPhones, etc.)

4. Now your Notes will be synced across all devices and pushed to the devices from iCloud

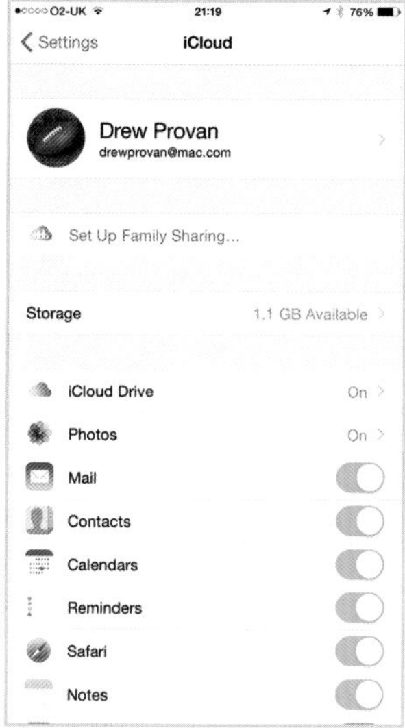

Above shows Notes ON in the iCloud configuration screen on the iPhone

Keeping Safari in Sync

It is great having Safari bookmarks synchronized on all devices and your Mac. This is very easy to set up:

Using iCloud

1. Go to **Apple Menu > System Preferences > iCloud**
2. Make sure **Bookmarks** is **ticked**

iCloud Keychain

This feature of OS X Yosemite allows you to sync usernames, passwords and credit card information across all your devices.

To set up iCloud Keychain across your devices

1. Go to **Settings > iCloud** on your iPhone or iPad
2. Make sure iCloud Keychain is **ON**
3. On your Mac open the **iCloud System Preference**
4. Make sure Keychain is **ON**

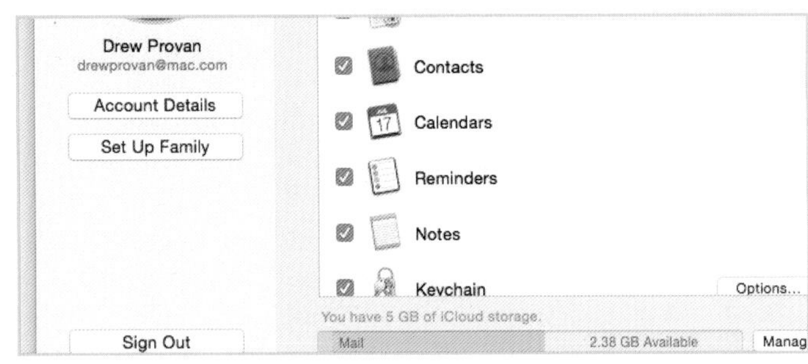

iCloud Keychain only works with Macs and iOS devices at the time of writing. Although you can download the Windows iCloud Control Panel you cannot use it to sync data across devices.

17 Back up Your Files!

No-one likes doing backups but if your computer dies you could lose a serious amount of hard work. Here we look at various backup strategies to help recover your work if you suddenly have a hard drive failure.

Simple Copy Methods

The simplest method of backing up is to drag folders or files to a separate disk. If your Mac has an external USB drive plugged in you could copy your important files from the internal drive to the external USB drive.

Drag and drop backup is not ideal – you are likely to forget to do it!

Pros

- Quick
- Easy
- Cheap

Cons

- You need to remember to do it
- If you leave the drive plugged in and your Mac is stolen, you lose all your work!
- USB drives can fail without any warning

How to do it

1. Make sure you can see the backup drive on the desktop
2. **Locate the files** you wish to back up
3. **Click and drag** these to the backup disk

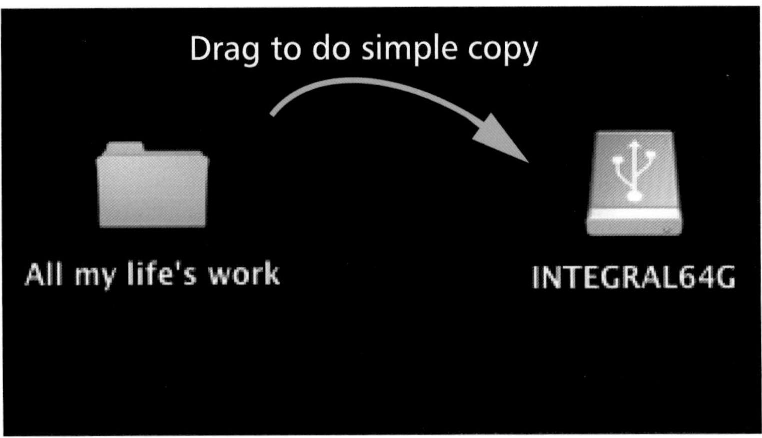

Keep Files on the Cloud

Rather than copy folders and files to a physical hard drive attached to your Mac, you could use a cloud service. There are several services available including:

- iCloud
- Dropbox
- Microsoft OneDrive

Pros

- Files are kept away from your home and your Mac so if the house burns down you could retrieve your work easily
- Easy-to-use

Cons

- You need to remember to do it
- Expensive if you need lots of storage space

How to use Dropbox

1. **Open account** (dropbox.com)
2. **Copy files to the Dropbox folder** on your Mac
3. These files will automatically sync to the Dropbox cloud
4. You can **access all your files** using any PC or Mac by logging into your Dropbox account

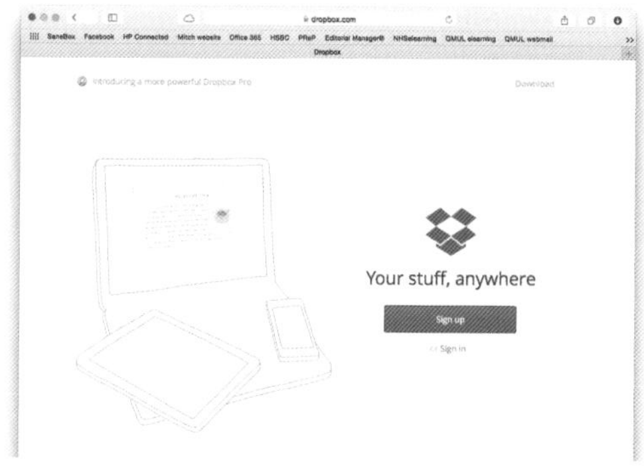

iCloud Drive is built into Yosemite. All users are provided with 5GB free cloud storage by Apple. Like Dropbox and other cloud storage providers, you can store any type of file on your iCloud Drive.

Keeping your documents on a cloud means you can retrieve them using any computer in any location.

Time Machine Backups

Time Machine comes built-in with OS X and provides an automated backup solution (encrypted if you want to be extra safe), backing up your Mac to an external drive. After the initial backup of your entire drive it will back up your work every hour, backing up only those files you have changed. In the event of a disaster or accidental deletion of a file you can go back in time and salvage the file and bring it back.

Don't skimp on your Time Machine backup drive. Buy a large one, at least 1 Terabyte (TB).

Configure Time Machine

1. **Connect an external drive** to your Mac
2. You will usually be asked "*Do you want to use* diskname *to backup with Time Machine?*"
3. Click **Use as Backup Disk**
4. Time Machine will then format the drive ready for use
5. Time Machine will then perform an initial backup of your entire drive (this may take some hours depending on how much data you have on your hard disk)
6. After the initial backup Time Machine will perform hourly backups, backing up all the files which have changed

Should you back up everything?

The lazy way to do it is to let Time Machine back up everything but it is better to exclude some files from the backups, e.g. System, Applications folder.

Set up an exclusion list

1. **Open Time Machine preferences**
2. Click **Options...**
3. Click on the **+** symbol to add files or folders to the exclusion list

This is the basic Time Machine System Preference. You can **Select Disk...** to choose which drive you use for backups. **Options...** lets you exclude certain files from the backup.

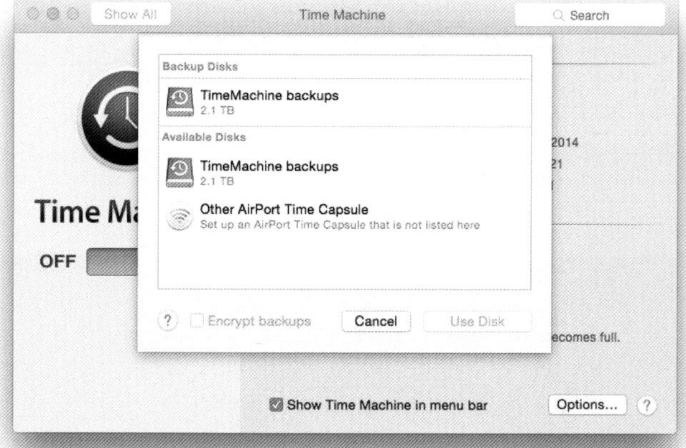

Options: you can see that some items have been excluded from the Time Machine backups. These include the user library (**~/Library**), **System files**, **Applications** and some other hard drives.

You can now encrypt your Time Machine backups for added security.

Encrypting a Time Machine backup involves using a security password chosen by you so data can only be accessed with this password. Go to **Time Machine Preferences > Select Backup Disk** and tick the **Encrypt backups** option.

Restore Files with Time Machine

If you accidentally delete a file or folder you can bring it back as follows:

1. Make sure the Time Machine backup drive is connected to your Mac
2. **Open Time Machine** (click its icon on Dock)
3. **Use the timeline on the right** side of your screen to step back in time and locate the file you want to retrieve. *Note*: you will need to remember which folder contains the file you deleted. If the file was on the desktop then make sure you are browsing the desktop files in Time Machine
4. Once you see the file **click once**
5. Click **Restore**
6. The file will be copied to the correct place, i.e. to the folder which contained the deleted file or folder
7. Time Machine will then exit and you'll be returned to the current time

To restore a file using Time Machine you need to know its location (which folder was it in?) otherwise it is going to be very difficult to locate it once Time Machine is launched.

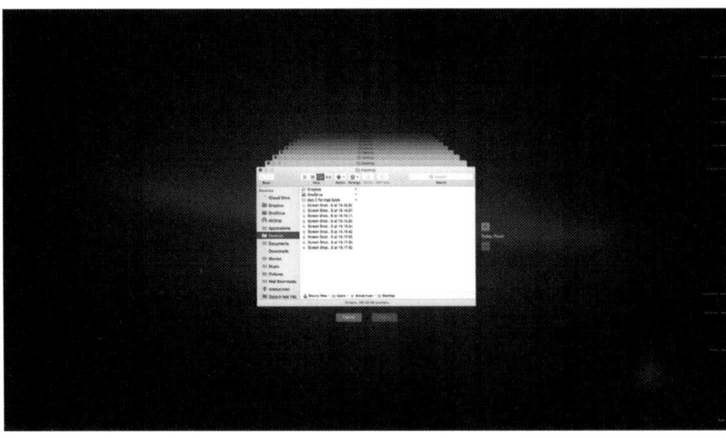

Scheduled Backups

There are third-party apps for carrying out scheduled backups. This is useful if you carry around your work on a USB stick. If you lost a USB stick your work would be lost. ChronoSync is a paid app that lets you carry out scheduled backups, e.g. daily or weekly, or each time you plug the USB stick into the Mac it will automatically copy the files which have changed on the USB stick back to the Mac.

- The synchronization can be one way, e.g. USB to Mac or two-way
- The two-way sync keeps the USB stick and the Mac files completely in sync with each other

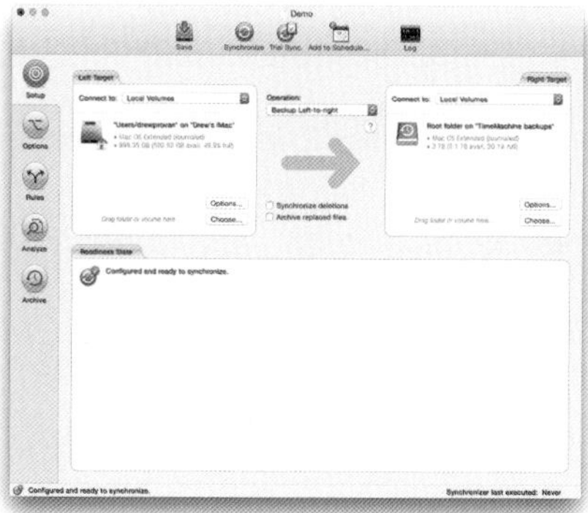

The above screenshot shows a one-way ChronoSync sync. From the image below you can see that the app has many user options

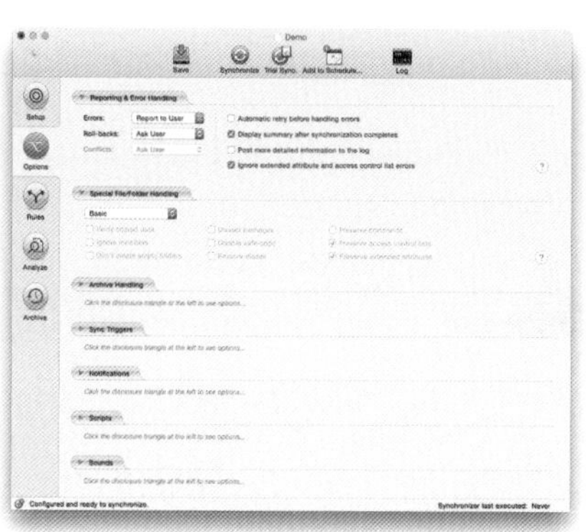

Scheduled backups mean you don't have to remember to perform the backup. The whole thing is automated.

Cloning Your Drive

Time Machine is good at backing up your drive contents but it is useful to have an *exact replica* of your hard drive which is bootable (by bootable, we mean the drive can be used to boot up your Mac if your main hard drive was to fail).

If your main drive fails you can use the cloned drive to start up your Mac, since the bootable cloned drive will have identical folders and files to the main drive and once the bootable drive is running you can then troubleshoot the main (failed) drive.

A cloned hard drive can be used to boot up your Mac and help you salvage the main hard drive if problems occur.

Options

- Carbon Copy Cloner (**bombich.com**) – US $39.99
- SuperDuper (**shirt-pocket.com/superduper**) – US $27.95

Note - prices correct at the time of printing

Using Carbon Copy Cloner

1. Launch Carbon Copy Cloner
2. Select **Source** (the drive you want to copy)
3. Select **Destination** (will become the carbon copy)
4. Click **Schedule this task...**
5. Choose an option such as Weekly (mine is scheduled for Sunday evenings)
6. Click **Clone**
7. The drive will be cloned

Note: the Destination drive should be larger than the Source drive or it will not be able to copy the contents to the clone.

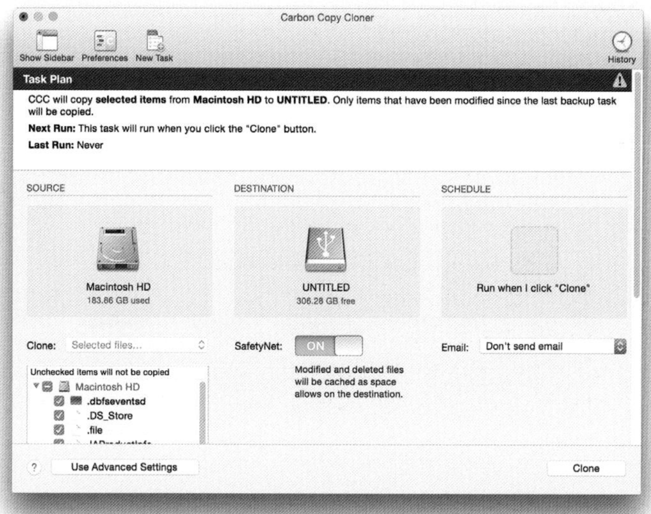

This is the main Carbon Copy Cloner interface. You select the drive to be cloned on the left and the destination (clone) on the right.

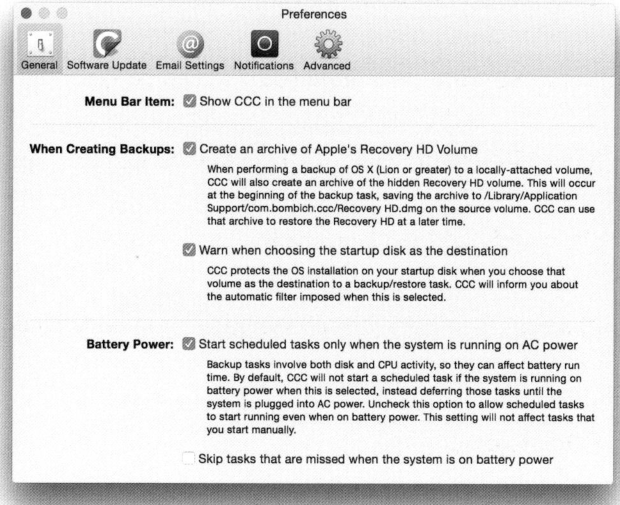

There are many user options available to customize the cloning process.

SuperDuper

This works very much like Carbon Copy Cloner, possibly with a simpler interface.

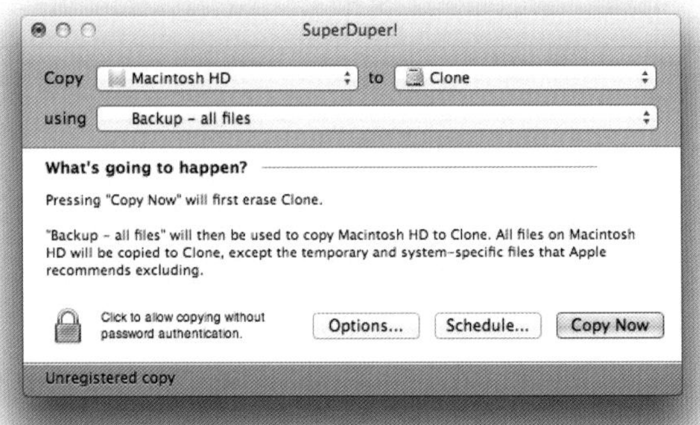

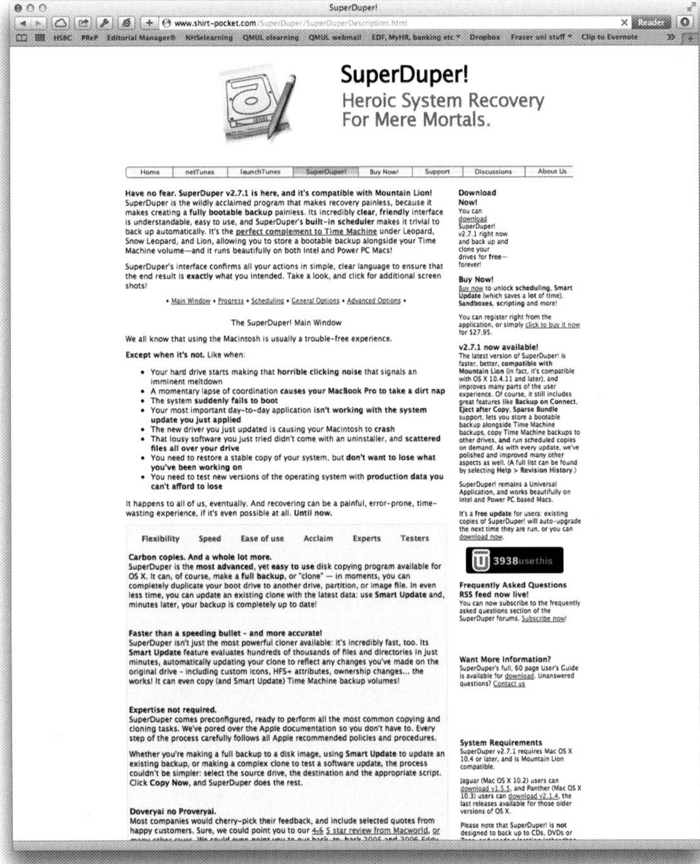

18 Tips & Tricks

In addition to altering settings in the System Preferences there are loads of other tricks to get more out of your Mac.

Keyboard Tricks

Typing special characters

If you need to type accented or other foreign characters there are two ways of getting these:

1. Go to **Menu Bar > Show Character Viewer**
2. Choose **Latin** and then find the character you want

Foreign characters are now built in to OS X. Hold down the appropriate key and choose the accented character you need.

Second method

1. You can hold down some keys and special characters will pop up (much like the iPhone and iPad)
2. These keys are **e y u i o a s l z c n**

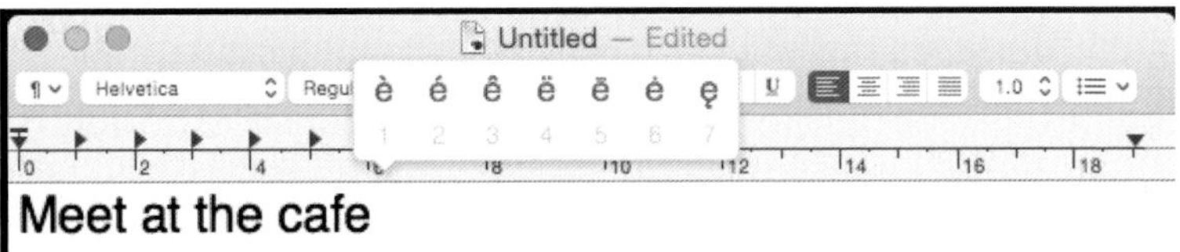

Take snapshot of the screen or window

- To take a snapshot of the whole **desktop** type **⌘ + ⇧ + 3**
- To take a snapshot of a **selected area** type **⌘ + ⇧ + 4**
- To take a snapshot of only one **active window** type **⌘ + ⇧ + 4 + spacebar**

Commercial apps for taking screen snapshots

http://www.ambrosiasw.com/utilities/snapzprox/

Organizing System Preferences

If you go to Apple Menu > System Preferences you will see a series of icons. Apple has arranged these for you but you can change the order. You can even remove them so they are hidden:

1. Go to **Apple Menu > System Preferences**

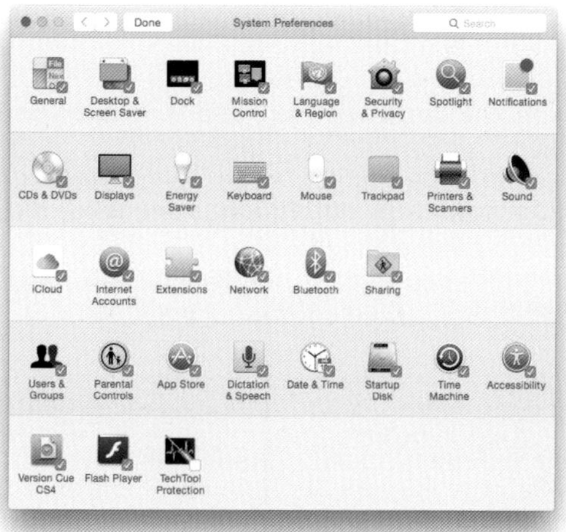

2. Go to menu bar **View > Customize**

3. The icons will have an **X** beside them – click to hide the icon

4. You can also Organize by **Category** or make them **Alphabetical**

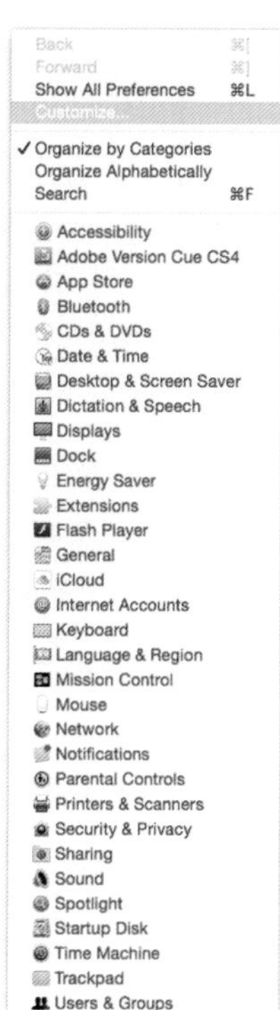

Compare Documents Quickly

Sometimes you can have two documents that look identical – but are they? You could open them both and check the differences but a quicker way is to:

1. **Click once on both documents** (to select them)
2. Type **⌘ + I** (provides Information, hence the "I")
3. Look at the document size and date last opened
4. You can now work out which is the most recent

Use the **⌘ + I** shortcut to get information about a document.

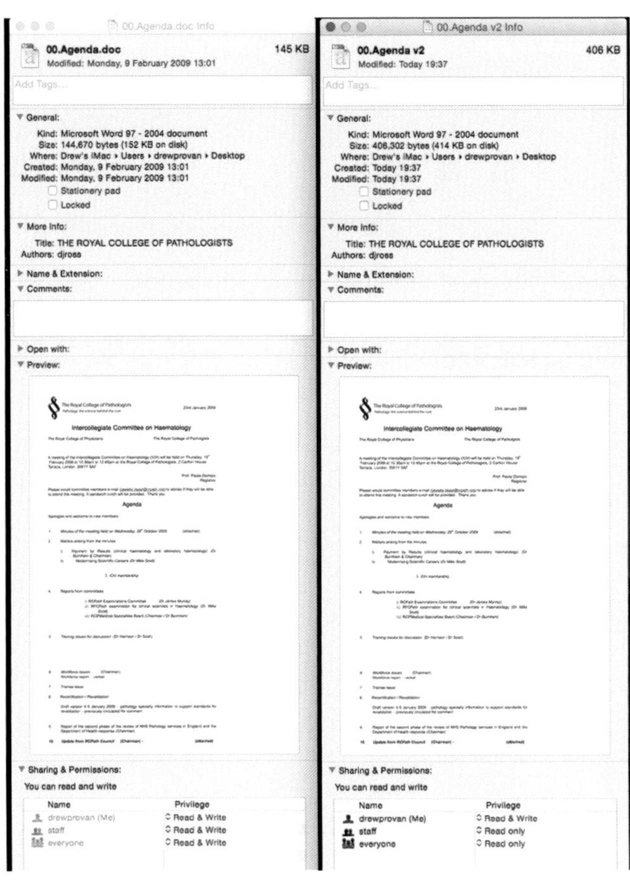

Although they look similar in terms of date and time, the document on the left is only 25 KB while the other has had an image embedded and is much larger at 918 KB.

How Much Disk Space is Left?

As you add videos, documents, and programs to your hard drive it will fill up, until eventually there is no more space left.

How can you see how much you have used?

There are two ways

1. Go to your Mac HD icon
2. Click once then type ⌘ **+ I**
3. Look at **Capacity, Available**, and **Used**

The other method

1. Go to **Apple Menu**
2. Select **About this Mac > Storage**
3. You will see a diagram which will reveal how much disk space has been used and how much is free

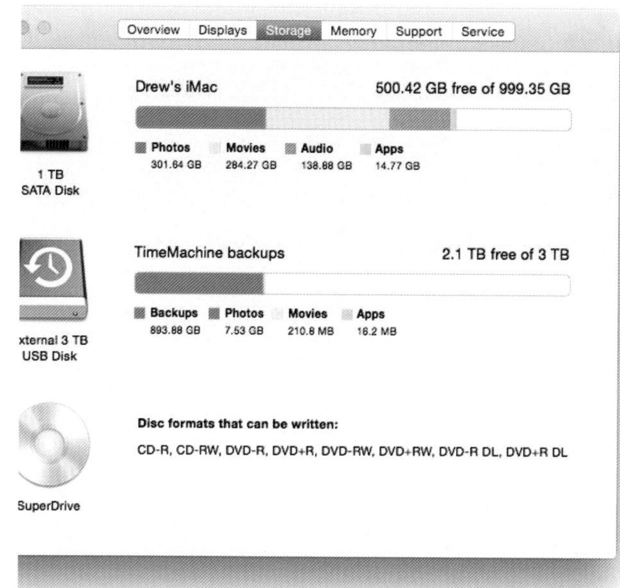

Keep an eye on how full your hard drive is becoming. You may be able to prevent your Mac slowing down by keeping enough free space on the main hard drive.

Extract Pictures from PDFs

You can grab pictures from PDFs, web pages and other documents easily.

PDF files

1. Open the PDF file

2. Make sure the picture is as large as you can make it, i.e. it fills the screen

3. Take screen snapshot ⌘ + ⇧ + 4

For web pages

1. You can **right-click the image** on a web page

2. Then select **Download** linked files as... (choose destination)

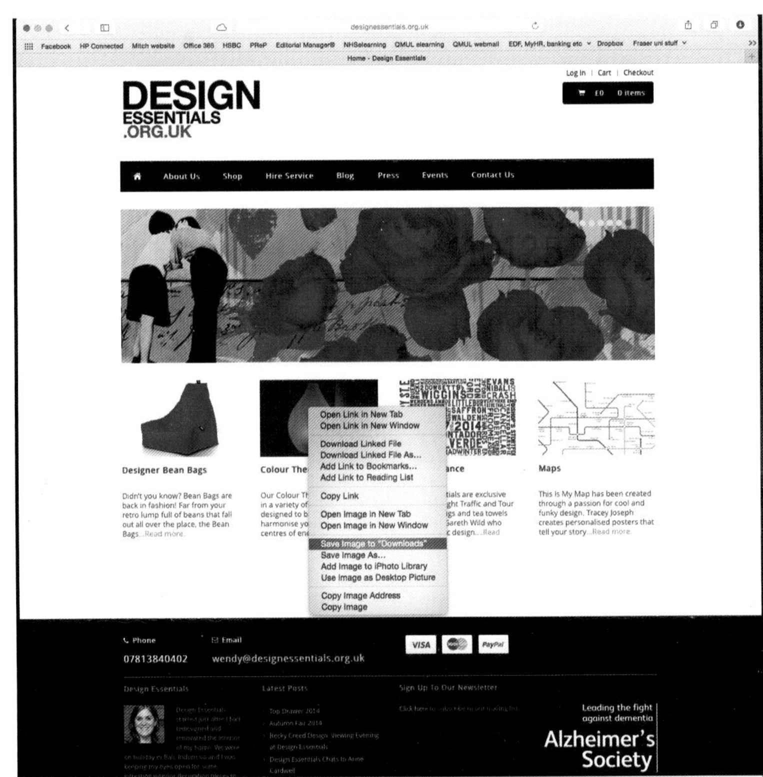

Where are the Scroll Bars?

By default you will notice that the scroll bars have vanished until you start to scroll, then they appear.

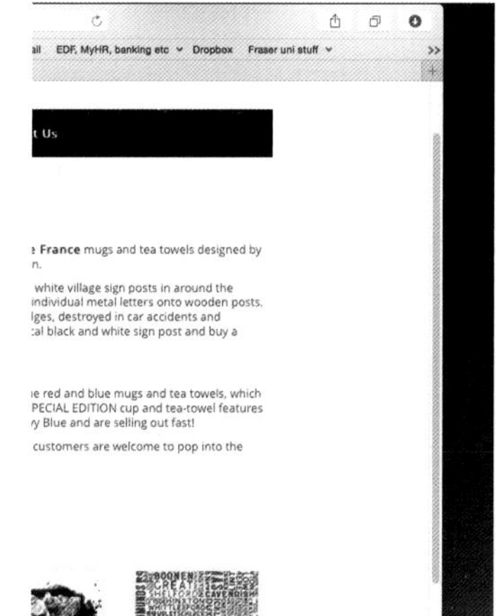

Do you want to see them all the time?

1. Go to **Apple Menu > System Preferences**
2. Select **General**
3. Choose **Show Scroll Bars: Always**

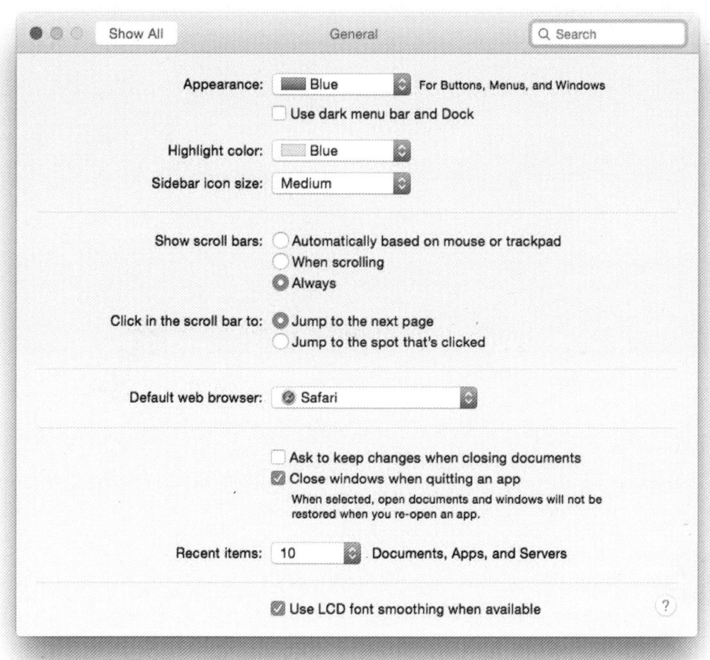

Make scroll bars permanent by selecting this in the General System Preferences file.

Application Switcher

How do you switch between apps quickly? You could click the app's icon on the desktop but there is a way to see what's running, bring an app to the front, and even quit the app effortlessly using a couple of keystrokes.

1. Type ⌘ **+ Tab**
2. A bar will pop up on the screen showing all running apps
3. To select an app (make active and bring to the front), click it
4. To quit, hover the pointer over it to select it, and press ⌘ **+ Q**

Dim screen fast!

If someone walks in and you want to hide what's on your screen you can:

1. Move pointer to the Sleep corner (if you have set that up in **System Preferences > Desktop & Screen Saver > Screen Saver > Hot Corners...** (see page 141)
2. *Or even faster* – type **Ctrl + Shift + Eject**

The screen will go black (Sleep mode).

Make your screen instantly black by typing Ctrl + Shift + Eject!

Select the Default Browser

You may not want Safari as your default web browser each time you click a link to a web page.

How to select your default browser

1. **Open System Preferences**

2. **Select General >**

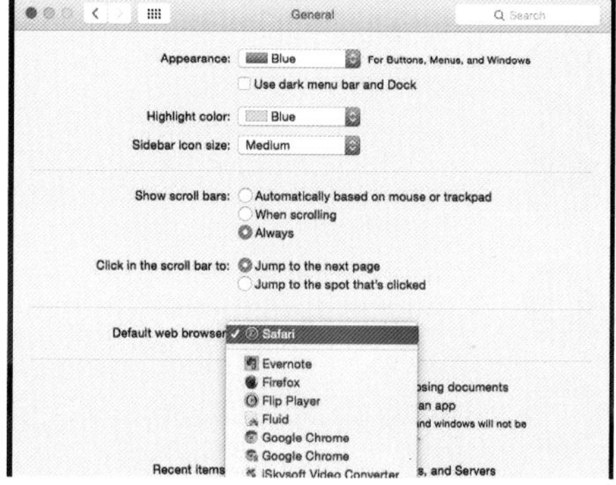

3. From the dropdown menu **choose** the one you want to be the default browser

Incidentally...

The same is true for email, if you want to use an email program other than Apple Mail you need to:

1. **Open Mail**

2. Go to **Preferences > General**

3. **Default email reader:** choose from the list

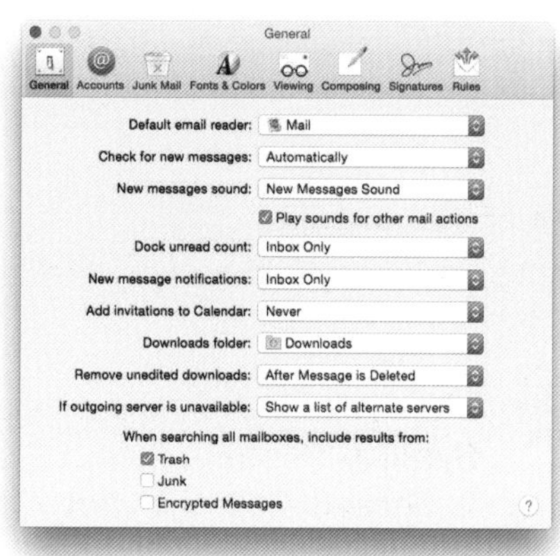

Sharing Map Locations

Mac OS X includes Maps, which is very similar to the iOS version. You can view as Standard maps, 2D, 3D and Satellite views. Locations can be shared or added to Bookmarks.

How to share map locations

1. Email
2. Messages
3. Twitter, Facebook, LinkedIn, Flickr, Vimeo and others
4. Contacts app
5. iOS devices by sending the location directly from the app

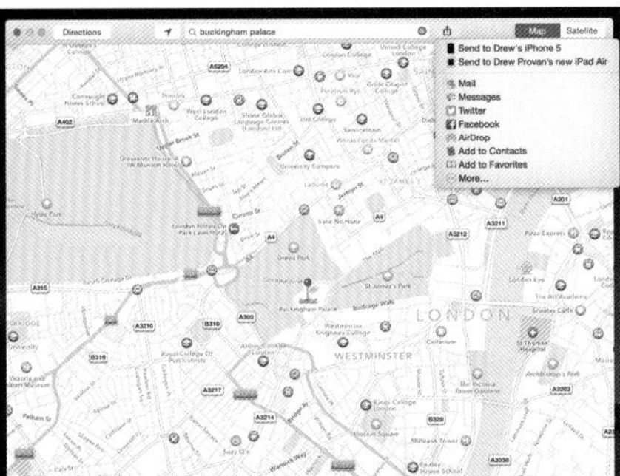

Location shown on Maps on the Mac. The dropdown Share menu shows how the location can be shared. This location was sent to the iPad (below).

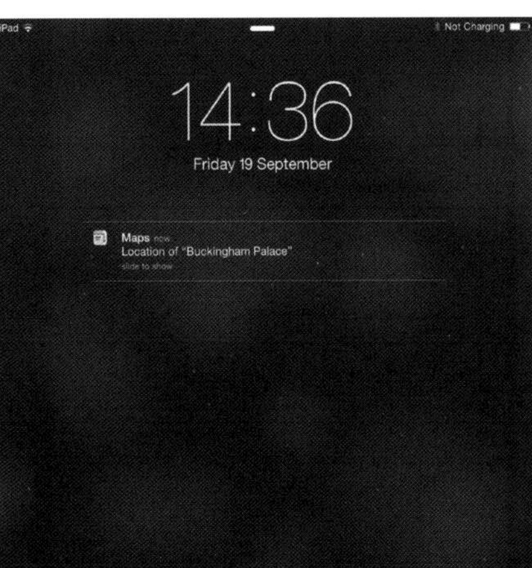

The location shows up as a notification on the iPad. Tapping on the notification takes you to the Maps app on the iPad.

Access Someone's Drop Box

If you want to give someone a file that is too large to email, one option is to log into their computer and drop the file into the user's Drop Box (not to be confused with Dropbox, the third-party app).

Accessing a user's Drop Box

1. **Go > Network**
2. Look under **Shared** for the User's Mac
3. Connect to it as a **Guest**
4. Click the user's **Mac**
5. Click on the user's **Public Folder**
6. You should then see **Drop Box**
7. **Drop your file** onto that (you cannot open the Drop Box)
8. The user can then navigate to his or her Drop Box and drag the file out

Drop Box is not the same as Dropbox. Drop Box is a folder on your Mac into which people can add files. Dropbox is a cloud service provided by **dropbox.com**

Change the Login Picture

The login screen is good, but you may want to change this. There's no System Preference for this so you need to do a bit of digging to find the picture file then replace it.

The login picture can be changed but be careful when removing the original file – keep a copy somewhere in case your efforts go badly wrong!

1. Find the original background file at */System/Library/Frameworks/AppKit.framework/Versions/C/Resources*
2. The file is called **NSTexturedFullScreenBackgroundColor.png**
3. **Back up the original file** (copy onto another drive, e.g. USB stick)
4. Choose the image file you want to use, and take it into Photoshop or other image editor program
5. The image file needs a **resolution of 72 pixels per inch**
6. Save your own image with the name **NSTexturedFullScreenBackgroundColor.png**
7. **Move it** to where the original image was
8. You will need to **Authenticate** using your password
9. **Reboot** to make sure it works

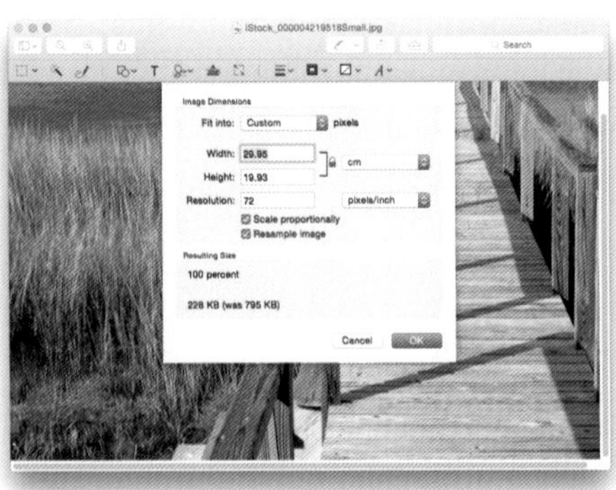

Undo Mistakes with Versions

Apple now provides Versions, a bit like Time Machine. If you are working on a document it will save various versions. If you want to go back to a previous version you can locate this using Versions.

To use Versions

1. As you are working on a document, save frequently

2. When you want to see earlier versions, go to **File > Revert To > Browse All Versions**

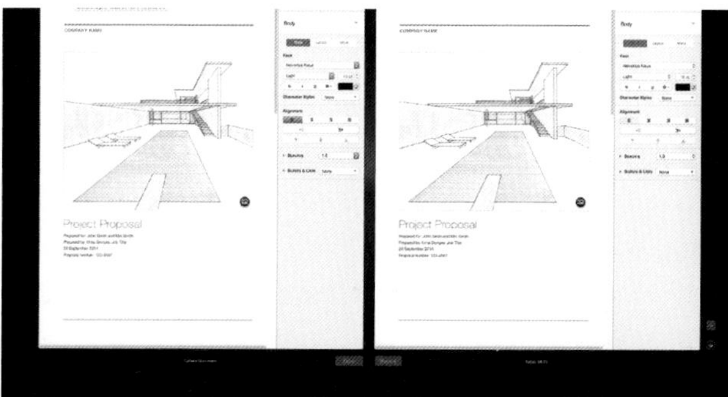

Restore the "Save As..." option

Apple removed Save As... when they introduced Versions. To restore this function:

1. Go to **System Preferences > Keyboard > Shortcuts > App Shortcuts**

2. Click the **+** icon

3. Type "**Save As...**" in the menu title and assign the keystrokes you wish to use (e.g., **Cmd + Shift + S**)

4. The Save As... option will now appear in all apps

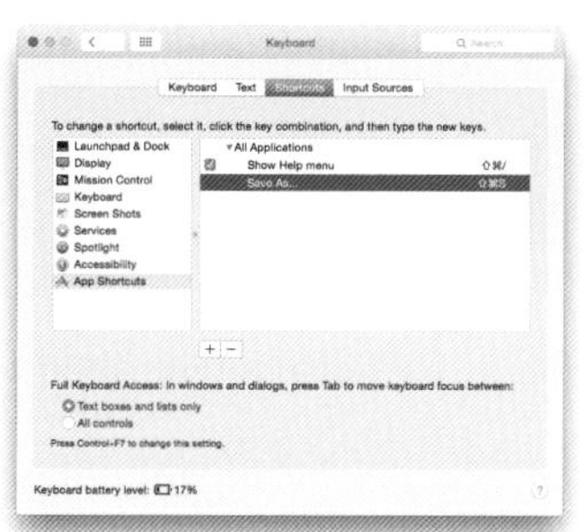

Versions makes it easy to go back to an earlier version of your document.

Make Mac Always Open With

When you double-click a photo it will usually open with Preview which is fine for most people. But you may prefer to have the photo opened with Adobe Photoshop instead.

To open a photo or image with Photoshop instead of Preview

1. **Click once on the image file** to select it
2. Right-click and choose **Open With**
3. Then scroll down the list until you see Adobe Photoshop

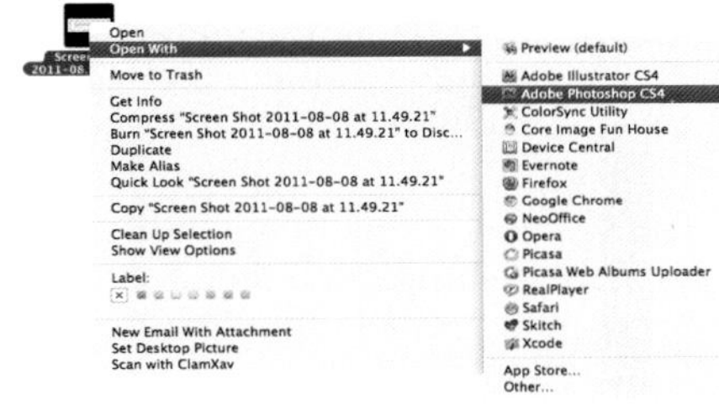

Hot tip

You can force the Mac to always open a specific file type using a specific program.

If you always want a specific program to open the document

You can tell the Mac to always open a photo or image with Photoshop by default, rather than Preview

1. **Click once on the photo** to select it
2. **Right-click** but hold down the **Option** (⌥) key until you see **Always Open With**

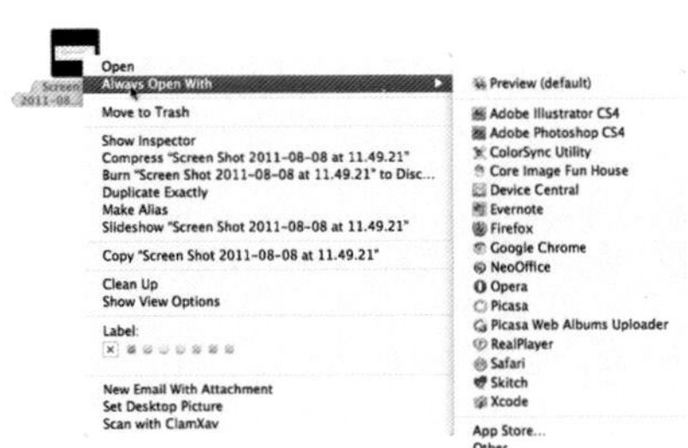

3. Now, whenever you double-click a photo it will open with Adobe Photoshop if you chose that option

19 Mac Maintenance

Macs run pretty smoothly even if you do no maintenance but it is a good idea to clear out unwanted files and do some basic housekeeping. This will keep your Mac running as fast as it was when brand new.

Repair Permissions

Mac OS X is based on Unix. This uses a permissions system for read/write access to files. Over time, permissions can become wrongly set or corrupt, and this will cause your Mac to behave erratically or slowly.

If you find your apps start to crash, fail to open, or behaving strangely it is worth repairing permissions.

Repair permissions regularly (e.g. weekly) to help prevent problems.

To repair permissions

1. On the menu bar select **Go > Utilities (Shift + Cmd + U)**
2. Select **Disk Utility**
3. **Launch Disk Utility**
4. Select your main hard drive and select **Repair Permissions**

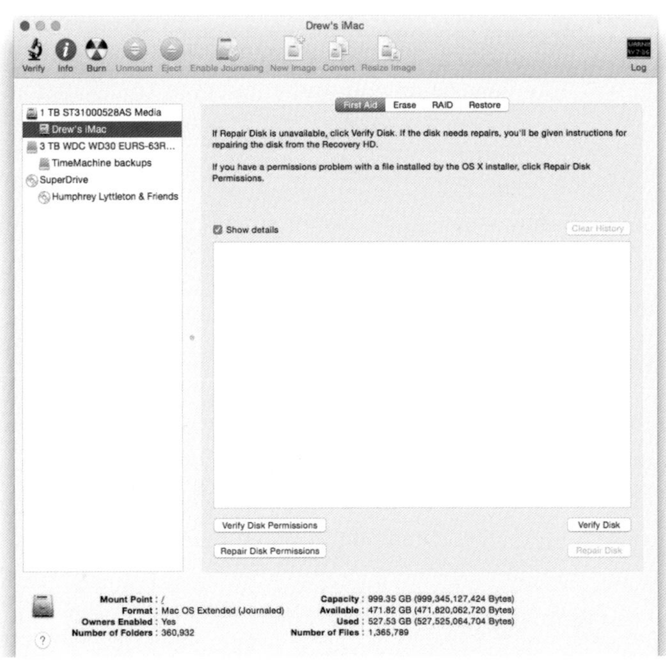

Maintenance Programs

Some basic maintenance of your Mac will keep it running smoothly and prevent any slowing down.

Inbuilt maintenance programs

1. On the menu bar select **Go > Utilities > Disk Utility**
2. Select your main hard drive
3. Select **First Aid**, **Verify Disk**, or **Repair Disk** if the drive appears to be having problems

Tech ToolPro 5

This is a heavyweight paid application. TechTool Pro 5 can check drives for faults, and it will also check your RAM, volume structures and perform many more functions. You can download the program from **www.micromat.com**

1. Launch TechTool Pro 5
2. You will see all the drives connected to your Mac
3. Select which tools you want to use

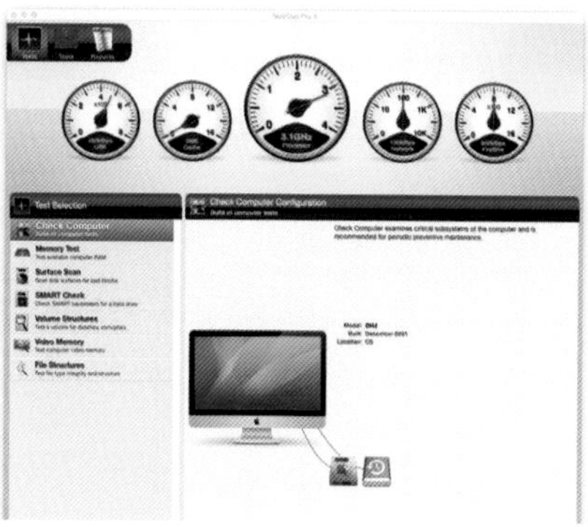

DiskWarrior

This is another powerful suite of tools that can scan your drives for errors and may be able to fix unmountable drives. You can download DiskWarrior from **www.alsoft.com/diskwarrior**

Make sure you back up any important data before you perform any of these functions in case there is a major crash – you could lose your files!

The OS X app Disk Utility is useful for performing basic maintenance.

Clear Your Desktop!

People with messy physical desktops at work tend to have messy desktops on their computers! Having loads of Word files and other documents strewn across your Mac desktop may make it slightly easier to find the documents you're working on, but this clutter means your Mac has to redraw and keep track of these files constantly. The net result is that your Mac will probably start to slow down.

File those docs!

1. Go to your **Home Folder > Documents**

2. Create some **New Folders** (⌘ + **N**)
3. **Name them**, e.g. Household, Personal, Work, etc.
4. **Make folders within folders**, e.g. Personal > Banking, Personal > Dental, etc.
5. **Drag the desktop files** to their appropriate folders
6. Aim to have no documents (or other files) on your desktop!

Keep the desktop clear of documents and folders!

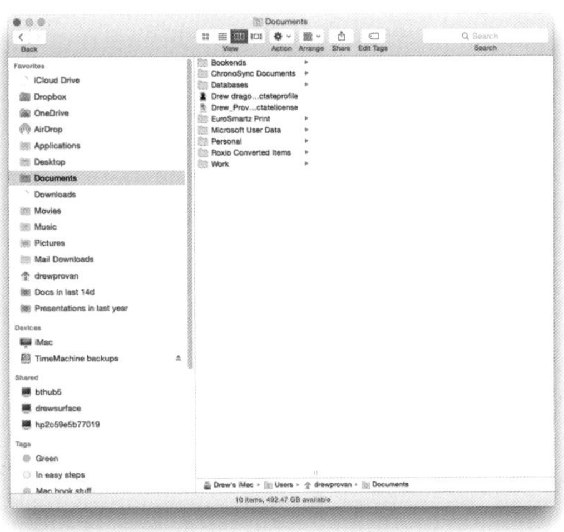

Reset Safari

Over time, Safari (and other browsers) will accumulate large amounts of cache data – text, images, sound files, etc. It is worth clearing:

- History
- Top Sites
- Web page preview images
- Downloads window
- Cookies

To reset Safari

1. Go to **Safari > History > Clear History**
2. Click **Clear History**

Remove cookies

1. Go to **Safari > Preferences > Privacy**
2. Select **Remove all Website Data...**
3. Your browser is now cleaned up!

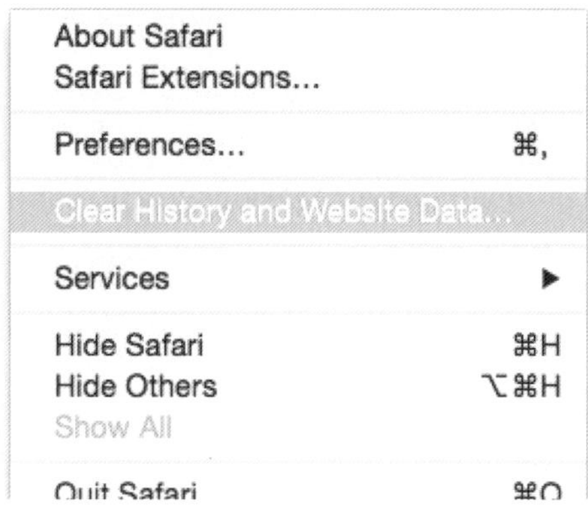

Websites collect information about you as you browse, using cookies. Reset Safari regularly and clear out the cookies!

Rebuild Spotlight Index

Spotlight (the search app) keeps a database of all your files, both their names and also text within the files. It is sensible to delete the Spotlight Index and force it to rebuild it from time to time. This makes finding files much easier since Spotlight is working from a fresh index.

1. Open **System Preferences > Spotlight**
2. Select **Privacy** tab
3. Drag your main hard drive onto this window
4. This deletes your current index (Spotlight thinks the entire hard drive is to be made private and therefore not indexed)
5. **Quit** System Preferences then **reopen**
6. Go to **System Preferences > Spotlight > Privacy**
7. Select your hard drive and click the – button to remove your hard drive
8. Spotlight will now re-index the entire hard drive since it is no longer private

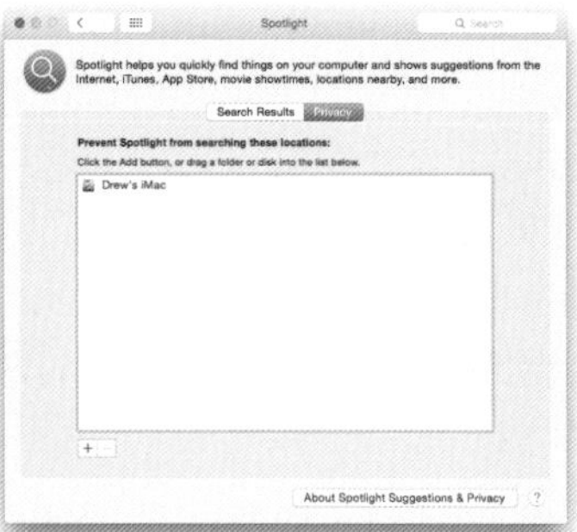

Rebuild Mail's Database

To ensure smooth running of Apple Mail it is useful to rebuild Mail's database from time to time. This makes Mail run faster, especially if you have a large number of saved emails.

1. **Select the account** you want to rebuild
2. **Select Inbox**
3. Select Mailbox on the menu bar and scroll to the bottom and select **Rebuild**
4. The mailbox will now be rebuilt
5. Do this with all the mailboxes you wish to rebuild

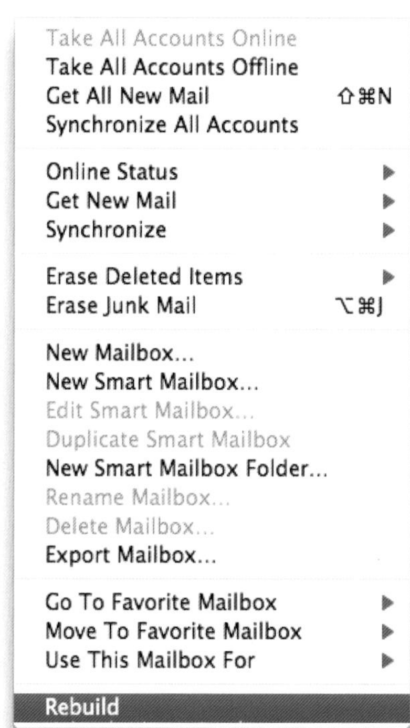

Mail can become sluggish if you have tons of emails. Rebuild your mailboxes periodically.

Alternative method

1. **Quit Mail**
2. Locate file **user/library/Mail/V2/MailData/Envelope Index**
3. **Make a copy** of this file and keep it somewhere safe – in case all goes wrong!
4. **Drag** user/library/Mail/V2/MailData/Envelope Index **to the Trash**
5. **Restart Mail**

Defragmenting Drives

There is much debate about whether you actually need to defragment the hard drive under OS X. When hard disks contain large amounts of data, big files are split (because of insufficient space to write the large file as a single file). Theoretically, computers may slow down if they have many fragmented files. Defragmentation of hard drives has been part of the PC world for many years and older Macs seemed to benefit from defragmentation too.

If your hard drive is relatively small, e.g. 320-500 GB, and you have little free space left then it probably is worth defragmenting.

Tools available

There are no inbuilt defragmentation tools with OS X. You need to use a third-party app, e.g. iDefrag 2. Download this from **www.coriolis-systems.com**

iDefrag 2 works with OS X Yosemite, although some features are not available at the time of writing this guide; the developer will have full compatibility soon.

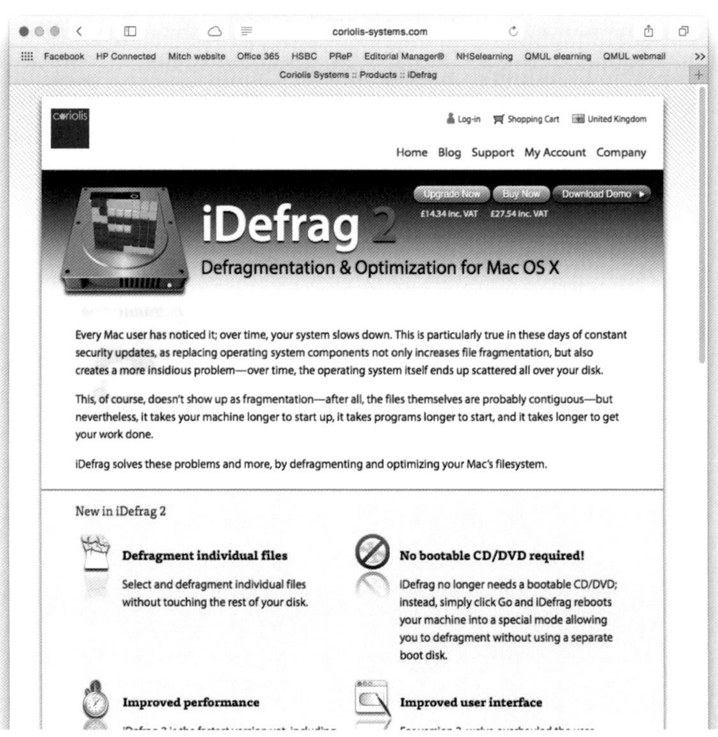

Remove Unneeded Login Items

Some programs will open when you first log in to your computer. However, you may not need all of these, and having these launch at login may slow your Mac down, especially if it is short of RAM or if you have a slightly older Mac. So it is a good idea to remove any unnecessary items that you will not be using when you first log in to your computer.

To remove login items

1. Go to **Apple Menu > System Preferences**
2. Open **Users & Groups**
3. Click the name of the **main admin account** (your account)
4. Click **Login Items**
5. Look through the list and decide what you want to remove – are there any apps that you do not use regularly?
6. **Click the check box** for the item you wish to remove and that item will be prevented from booting up at login

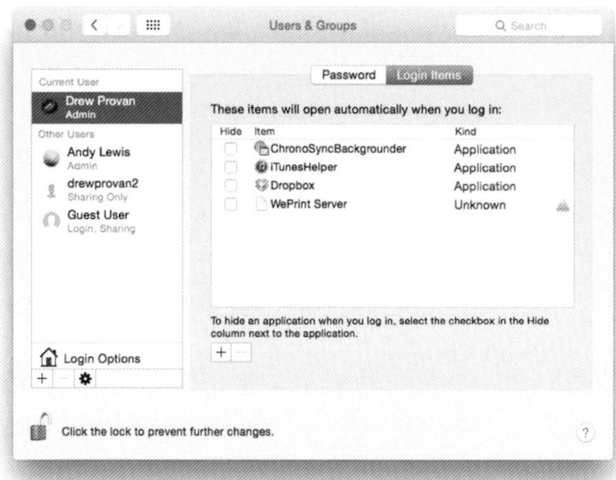

Any login items not needed? Get rid of them.

Don't Ignore Software Updates

Apple and other third-party developers release updates regularly for their software. For most apps you will be notified of an update when you launch the app.

1. Go to **Apple Menu > System Preferences > App Store**

2. You will then be taken to the **Updates** section of the App Store

3. See what updates are available and download

4. You can also go straight to the App Store for updates, rather than via the Apple Menu, which saves time

5. The App Store provides updates for purchased as well as OS X software

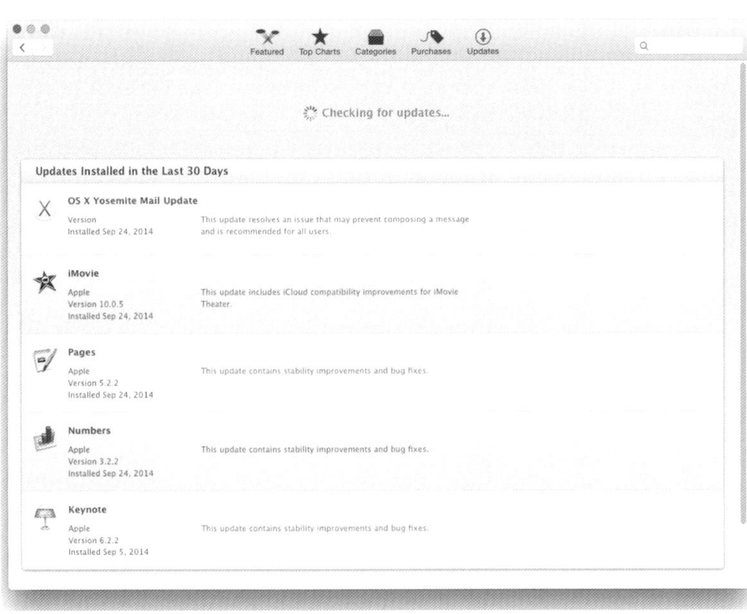

Software Updates provide security patches and updated software. Don't ignore it when it alerts you to the fact that updates are available.

Remove User Accounts

You may let other people use your computer and you may have given them their own user accounts.

If they are not regularly using your Mac, remove these accounts since this will free up space and possibly improve your Mac's speed. Overall it helps slim down your system.

1. Go to **Apple Menu > System Preferences > Users & Groups**
2. **Click the padlock icon** and enter your **password** to make changes
3. **Select the account** you wish to remove
4. **Click the – button** and the account will be removed along with the documents and settings associated with that account

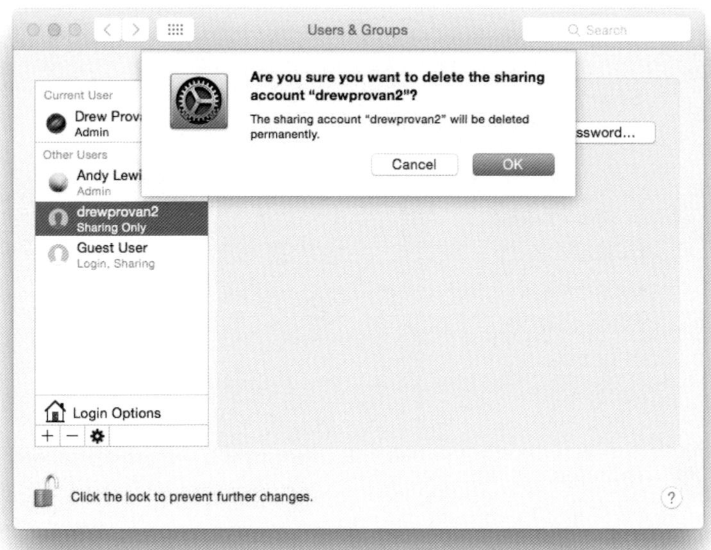

Scan for Viruses

The PC world is full of viruses. Luckily there are very few for the Mac at present but if you receive an email with an attachment containing a virus you can spread this if you email the attachment to someone else. It is therefore useful to detect and eliminate viruses as they come into your system.

Why spend money when you don't need to? ClamXav is enough for most people when it comes to antivirus software.

Antivirus software

There are several programs available, e.g. Virus Barrier (**www.intego.com**). But you may as well use free software, e.g. ClamXav (**www.clamxav.com**). This Open Source (and hence free) app is fine for most users. It uses very little resource, i.e. RAM.

Install ClamXav

1. **Download ClamXav** from **www.clamxav.com**
2. **Install**
3. **Run** program
4. **Update virus definitions** (click the update definitions button)
5. **Start Scan** and select the drive or the folder you wish to scan
6. If you choose to scan an entire hard drive this may take some time

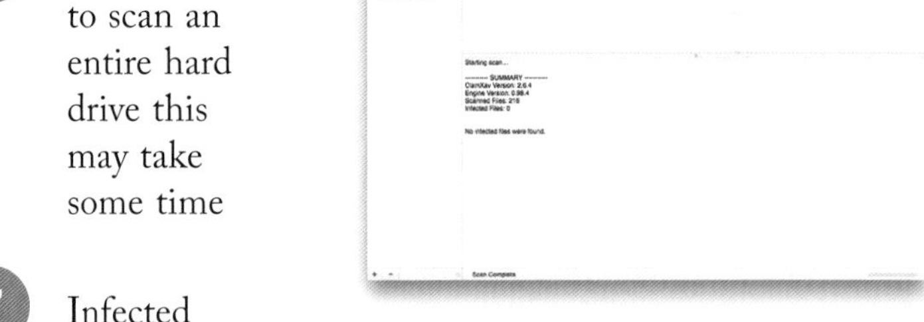

7. Infected or suspect files will be quarantined and you can delete these later if necessary

20 Troubleshooting

In this section we will look at how to solve the common problems encountered with the Mac.

My Mac Won't Start!

Empty Blue or Gray Screen

This is commonly due to incorrect disk permission problems, third-party software problems, or occasionally hardware issues.

1. **Unplug all peripheral devices** and try starting again

Try holding down the X key during startup to force the Mac to start up.

Start in Safe Mode (Safe Boot)

1. **Hold down Shift** while you turn on the Mac
2. Release Shift when you see a gray Apple with a spinning gear
3. SafeBoot should appear during startup or in the login window
4. To leave Safe Mode, restart the computer, without holding any keys during startup

Other things to try if your Mac won't start

1. Hold down the Option key during startup and you will be given the choice of which volume to use for startup
2. Try using the Recovery Partition (you will see this if you hold down the Option key) to repair the system
3. Try starting up from a Time Machine drive if you have one (again, you should see this option if you hold down the Option key at startup)
4. Try zapping the PRAM (hold down **Cmd + Option + P + R** at startup)
5. Try clearing the NV RAM (hold down **Cmd + Option + N + V** at startup)

Yosemite includes a Recovery Partition. To use this, start your Mac whilst holding down the Option key. Choose the Recovery Partition option to boot up and repair from that.

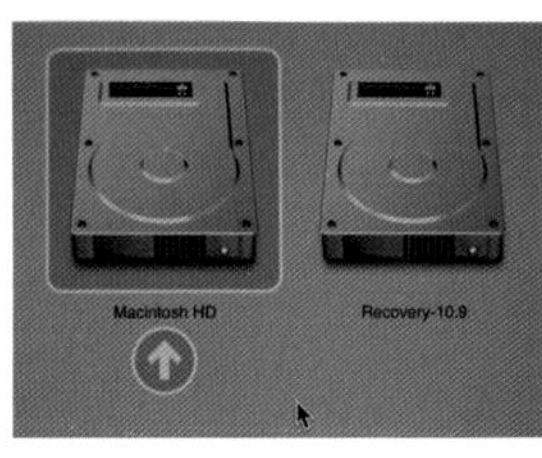

This Disk is Unreadable

This can be seen when using both USB drives and also CDs and DVDs. You will generally be told "*The disk you inserted was not readable by this computer*".

- This is caused by not unmounting USB drives properly (unplugging without dragging to Trash icon first)
- It can also be caused by corruption of data structures, faulty libraries, or invalid file systems

The disk you inserted was not readable by this computer.
Initialize...
Ignore
Eject

Beware

Never pull out a USB stick or drive without dragging it to the Trash! You may damage the disk irreversibly. Odd as it sounds, drives are unmounted on the Mac by dragging to the Trash.

Do not initialize!

1. You will lose your files on the disk. **Try plugging your USB drive into another Mac** if possible. It may mount on a second Mac and if it does, copy the files immediately to a safe place

2. Try using **Disk Utility** first to see if you can repair the USB drive

3. You can also use TechTool Pro 5 or Disk Warrior to analyze the drive, identify errors, and repair

4. If you have a backup of the files then you can reformat the faulty drive

App Crashes

Apps can crash while you are using them. For example, they unexpectedly quit, or they may fail to launch at all – simply bouncing on the dock before disappearing.

Solution

1. **Restart** the Mac
2. **Repair Permissions**

Remove the system preference .plist file for that app then try launching the app again

1. Go to **user/library/preferences**
2. Scroll through the list until you **find the .plist** file for your app
3. **Drag the .plist file to the Trash**
4. **Empty** Trash
5. **Restart** app

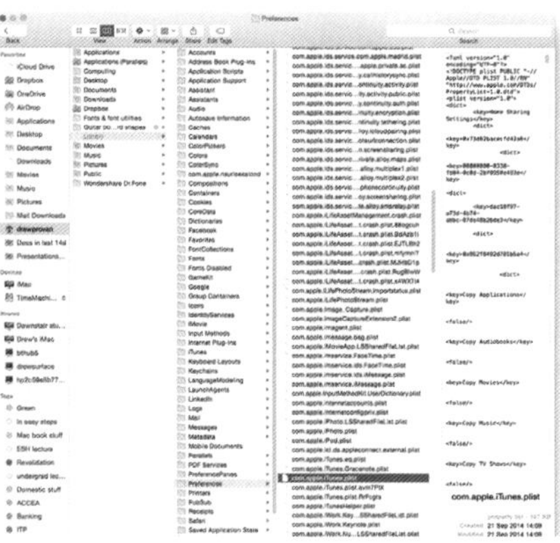

If all else fails

1. **Reinstall** the app

Duplicate Fonts

Many programs install their own fonts, e.g. Microsoft Office, Adobe Creative Suite, and many others. If they copy fonts you already have on your Mac you will end up with duplicates. These duplicated fonts can cause your Mac to misbehave, or programs to crash.

Deactivate duplicate fonts

1. **Open Font Book**
2. Look for a **yellow triangle** to the right of the font name (indicates multiple copies of font are installed)
3. **Select all fonts** (⌘ + A)
4. Go to **Edit > Look For Enabled Duplicates...**
5. When prompted, click **Resolve Automatically**
6. This should solve your problem

Duplicate fonts may cause apps to crash. Check Font Book from time to time to see if you have any duplicate fonts.

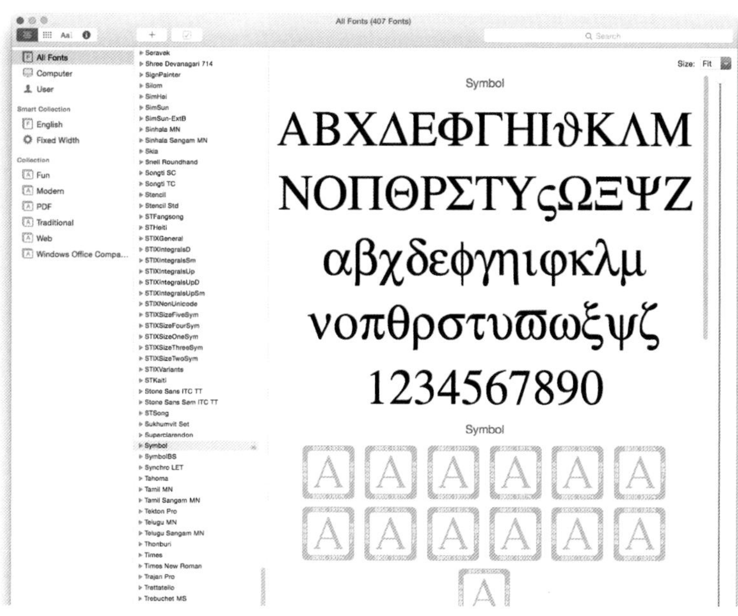

Spinning Beachball

The *spinning beachball of death* has been present since the introduction of OS X. The spinning beachball is similar to the hourglass icon in Microsoft Windows.

When you see the beachball on the Mac it often hangs and there is little you can do while it spins.

Possible causes

1. Program is **busy**
2. You have **insufficient RAM**
3. The app is **frozen** or **hung**
4. You have **hardware problems**

Solution

1. Try being patient and **wait** to see if the beachball stops
2. Quit or **Force-Quit** the offending app (**Apple Menu > Force Quit** – look to see which app is not responding)

Force Quit Applications
If an app doesn't respond for a while, select its name and click Force Quit.
Messages
Numbers
Pages
Preview
Safari
Finder
You can open this window by pressing Command-Option-Escape.
Force Quit

3. **Restart Mac**
4. **Buy more RAM**
5. **Remove .plist file** from your user library

If all else fails...

If the Mac hangs and you cannot get it to do anything, hold down the power button until the Mac switches off. Wait one minute then restart the Mac.

Folder Moved to Wrong Place

Sometimes we drag files or folders to the wrong place. If you know where you dropped it, you can find it and drag it back out.

If you don't know where it went

1. Immediately after you dropped the file or folder into another location, type ⌘ + Z (**Undo**)
2. This will undo your last action
3. However, if you perform other actions *before* you try this manoeuvre then you won't be able to find the file other than by using **Spotlight** to search for the file by name

⌘ + Z is the universal Undo command. Try it whenever you want to reverse your last action.

Undo Last Action

The ⌘ + Z command shortcut will get you out of all sorts of trouble, for example:

- You deleted text from a document in error
- You trashed a file or folder by mistake
- You made changes to text or a photo incorrectly

How to undo the last action

1. Click ⌘ + Z and your work will be restored
2. Many apps will let you undo several times allowing you to take several steps back rather than just one

Can't Find Network Printer

Adding a printer in OS X is easy but sometimes the Mac can have trouble finding a printer, especially printers on a network.

If your documents fail to print or the Mac appears to be looking for the printer for a long time

1. Go to **Apple Menu > System Preferences > Print & Scan**

2. Select and **delete the printer** that has failed (click the – button)

3. Then **click the + button** and browse through the list of available printers

4. Click **Add**

5. The printer should now show in your list in the left pane

6. Try printing your document again

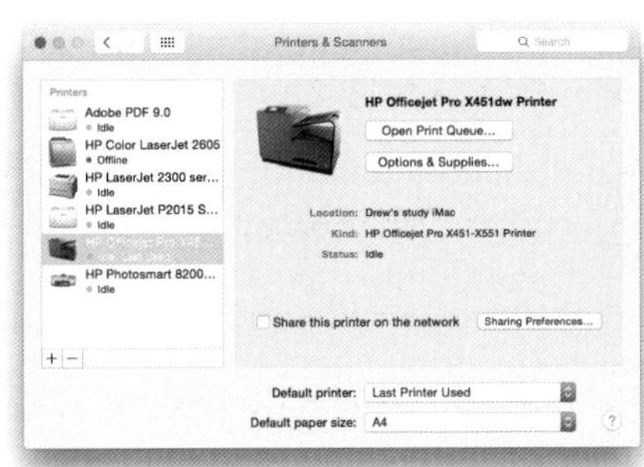

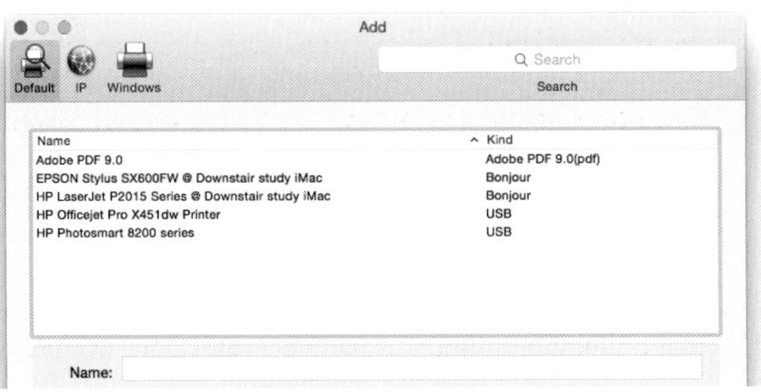

Safe Boot

If your Mac misbehaves, or fails to boot up normally, it could be due to hardware or software problems. System extensions added by third-party apps can cause problems. To determine whether this is the case you can do Safe Boot.

Safe Boot (Safe Mode)

- This forces the Mac to carry out a directory check
- The Mac loads only essential extensions
- The Mac disables fonts apart from the main fonts in /system/library/fonts
- It moves font caches to the Trash
- The Mac disables any start-up items

To start in Safe Mode

1. **Switch off the Mac**
2. Restart but **hold down the Shift key** as the Mac starts up
3. If the Mac starts you can then look for extension or font conflicts

Try logging in as another user

Programs may fail to work normally because of hardware (e.g. a USB device attached to the Mac) or because you have installed something which has created a conflict. To see if it's the Mac or just your account which has caused problems:

1. **Create a new account**, e.g. Guest, or named account and log in to the new account
2. Try running the program again
3. If the program still fails you know it's a Mac problem
4. If it *does* work then something in your account is stopping the program from working properly

Deleted File or Folder in Error

It happens to everyone – a crucial file or folder somehow gets deleted in error.

Don't empty the trash!

If the file or folder is still in the trash, drag it out

The trash has been emptied

1. **Launch Time Machine**
2. **Locate the file** from an earlier time
3. **Restore** the file to the desktop or any folder

Time Machine cannot find the file

1. You may need to buy a recovery program such as Phoenix Mac Data Recovery (**stellarinfo.com**) or MacKeeper (**mackeeperapp.mackeeper.com**)

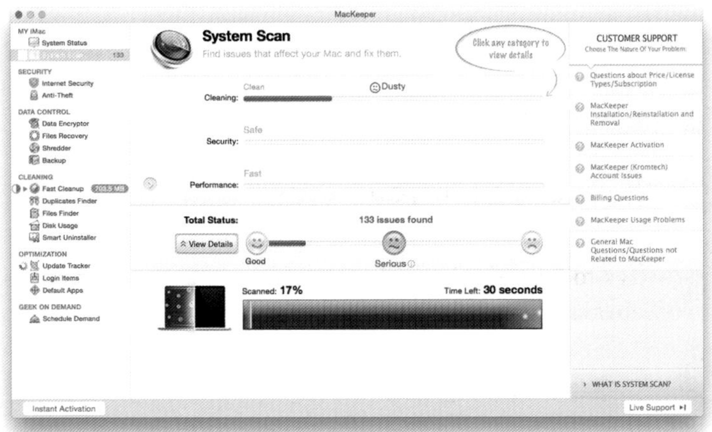

Can't Eject a Disk

Sometimes when you want to remove a USB drive or CD by dragging to the trash you are notified that the drive is in use. You probably have a file open in Word or some other application and have not closed the file.

The fact that you are prevented from ejecting the disk safeguards you against failing to save the file.

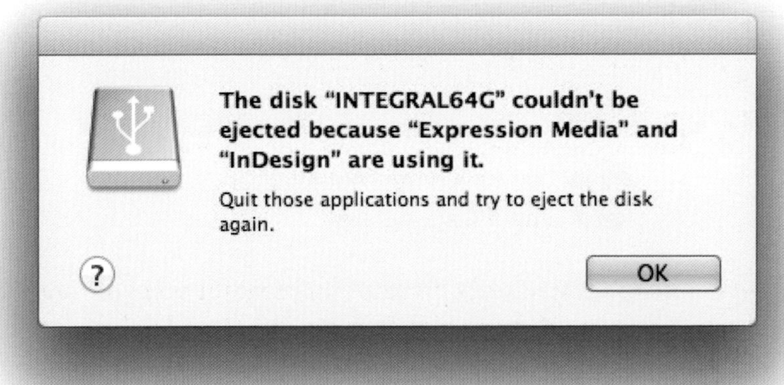
The disk "INTEGRAL64G" couldn't be ejected because "Expression Media" and "InDesign" are using it.
Quit those applications and try to eject the disk again.
?
OK

Solution

1. **Close any open documents** you're working on
2. If this fails, **close your apps** one at a time
3. Try to drag the USB drive to the trash to see if you can now safely eject it
4. If the notification tells you which app is in use quit that specific app
5. If all else fails – **restart the Mac** and that should solve the problem

Yosemite Recovery Disk

You can boot into the Recovery Partition on the Mac as outlined on page 226, or you can build a bootable USB drive which you can use to start up your Mac.

Create bootable recovery disk

1. **Download Recovery Disk Assistant (http://support.apple.com/kb/DL1433)**

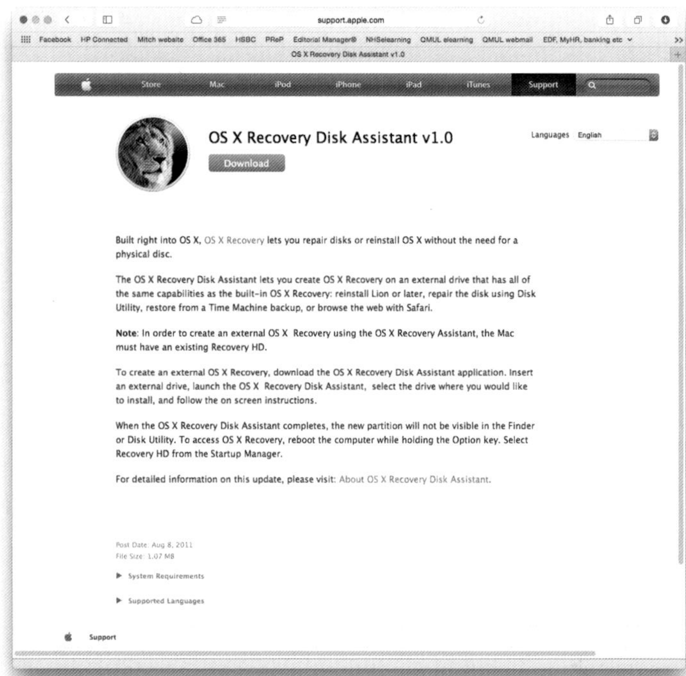

2. Install and launch the app which will then look for a Yosemite installer on your hard drive

3. You will be prompted to create a DVD but you can use a USB drive (must be 8GB minimum)

4. Although the app mentions "Lion" the Recovery Disk Assistant should work fine with Yosemite according to the Apple Support documentation

Index

A

Acrobat Reader 51
Address Book 84
Adobe Acrobat Pro 45
Adobe Acrobat Reader 45
AirDrop 119
AirPort Utility 113
Alert sounds 146
App crashes 228
Application Switcher 206
Apps
Background update 172
Uninstalling 152
App Store 172

B

Backups
Scheduled 195
Base Station 113
Beachball 230
Bluetooth 20
Boot Camp 164
Browser
Setting default 207

C

Calendar 76
Event 78-80
Invites 82
Multiple 81
Searching 83
Views 77
CD
Burning music to CD 166
Change the desktop 13
ClamXav 224
Clock display 136
Compare documents 202
Computer hangs
Possible causes 230
Connecting to other Macs 116
Contacts
Syncing 186
Contacts & Calendars 19
Create a folder 11

D

Dark Mode 10
Date & Time 22
Defragmenting drives 220
Desktop
Extending the Mac desktop 21
Dictation 40
Disk Utility 170, 214
DiskWarrior 215
Dock 139, 157
Documents
How to tell if unsaved 37
Opening 38
Drop Box 209
Dropbox 191
DuckDuckGo 67

E

Email
Add an email account 55
Adding flag 62
Attachments 57
Change fonts and colors 63
Create an email message 56
Keeping in sync 182
Markup 61

Reading 59
Searching 62
Setting default email program 207
Signature 63
Energy Saver 24
Ethernet 20, 113
Exchange or Exchange IMAP 55

F

Facebook 27
Facebook video 130
FaceTime 122
FAT32 42
Files
Cloud storage 191
Copy 34
Copy onto CD or DVD 169
Deleting 35
Finding using labels 37
Moving into folders 34
File sharing 21, 116
Finder 30
Column view 31
List view 31
Tabbed windows 31
Views 31
Folders 32
Alias 32
Creating 32
Duplicate 32
Move 32
Rename 32
Fonts
Duplicate 229
Frozen Mac 230

G

Gatekeeper 15
Genius 109
Gestures 10
Google Calendar 185
Google Voice & Video Chat 128

H

Handoff 52
Hard drive
Changing name 132
Cloning 196
How much space left? 203

I

iBooks 179
iCloud 182, 191
iCloud Keychain 188
Icon sizes 138
Image Capture 88
IMAP 55, 60, 182
Installing apps 148
iPhoto 89
iTunes 94, 100
Buying music 104
Importing audio CDs 101
Playlists 106
Preferences 102
Sharing your music 110
Smart playlists 107

K

Keyboard 17-18
Shortcuts 145, 158

L

Launchpad 11

M

Mac and PC compatibility 42
Magic Mouse 10
Mail 19
  Rebuild Mail's database 219
Mailbox
  Folders 60
  Rules 61
Maps
  Sharing map locations 208
Markup 61
Memory slots 28
Menus
  Dropdown 10
Messages 124
  Android 124
  Do Not Disturb 125
  Voice message 124
Microsoft Exchange server 19
Migrate PC files to Mac 163
Mission Control 14
Mountain Lion Recovery Disk 236
Mouse 16
  Configure right-click 155
Movies
  Editing your own 96
  Sharing your movie 98
My Mac won't start! 226

N

Network
  Printer 232
  Settings 160
  Sharing Internet connection 114
Networking 20, 112
Notes
  Syncing 187
Notes app 41
Notifications 26
  Reply directly from Notification 26

P

Parallels Desktop 164
PDF 39, 44
  Annotating 47
  Creating 48
  Emailing 50
  Open using Preview 46
  Password-protect 49
Photos
  Burning onto CD or DVD 168
Photo Stream 92
POP3 182
Power Management 24
Power Nap 135
Preference files 151
Preview 45, 88
Printing 120
Print & Scan 161
Privacy 15

Q

Quick Look 39
QuickTime Player 94

R

RAM 28
Region codes 95
Reminders 26
Remove unneeded login items 221
Repair Permissions 214
Run Windows on the Mac 164

S

Safari 66, 88, 217
- Bookmarks 70
- Browsing using tabs 73
- Change search engine 69
- Full screen browsing 67
- Importing bookmarks 72
- Making browsing secure 74
- Reading list 68
- Remove cookies 217
- Reset 74, 217
- Search the Internet 69
- Set Homepage 66
- Switch between pages 67
- Sync bookmarks 188

Safe Boot 233
Screen
- Corners 141
- Saver 13
- Savers 134
- Sharing 118

Screen sleep 24
Scroll Bars 205
Share screen 117
Sidebar 140
Skype 126-127
Smart Mailboxes 61
Software Updates 222
Special charactèrs 200
Spotlight 25, 231
- Rebuild Spotlight Index 218

System Preferences 13, 159
- Organizing 201

T

Tags 37
Tech ToolPro 5 215
TextEdit 33, 88
Time Machine 23, 192-194, 234
Time Zone 137
Trackpad 16
Trash 143
Troubleshoot
- Log in as another User 233

Twitter 27

U

Updates 176
USB disk
- Can't eject 235
- Unreadable 227

User Account 12, 162
- Removing 223

User Library 36

V

Versions 38, 211
VIP list 64
Viruses 224
VMWare Fusion 164

W

Waking from sleep 24
Wake and Sleep Options 135
Wallpapers 133
Wi-Fi 20, 113
Windows 144
Windows Explorer 156

Y

Yosemite 28
- Recovery Disk 236